Cruising
The Northwest
A Practical Guide for
the Pacific Coast Boater

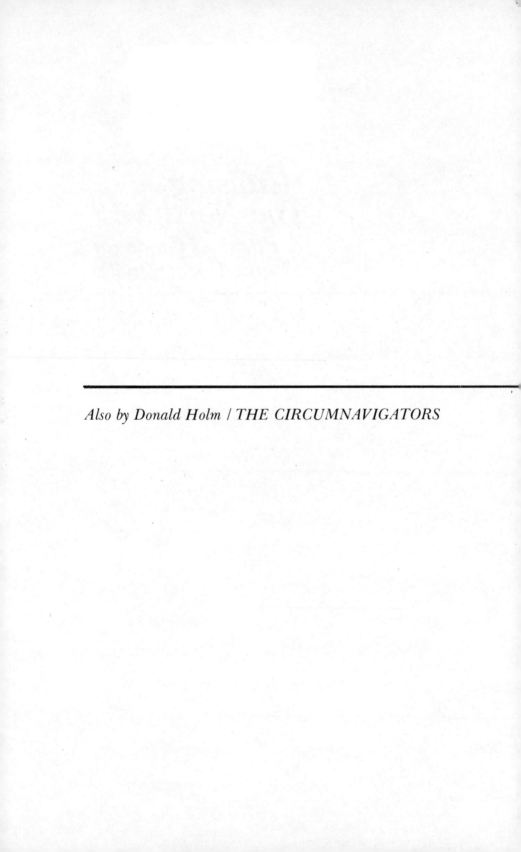

Also by Donald Holm / *THE CIRCUMNAVIGATORS*

Cruising
The Northwest
A Practical Guide for
the Pacific Coast Boater

by Donald Holm

PRENTICE-HALL, INC. / Englewood Cliffs, New Jersey

For My Bride
_____

*Cruising the Northwest: A Practical Guide for
the Pacific Coast Boater*
by Donald Holm
Copyright © 1977 by Donald Holm
All rights reserved. No part of this book may be
reproduced in any form or by any means, except
for the inclusion of brief quotations in a review,
without permission in writing from the publisher.
Printed in the United States of America
Prentice-Hall International, Inc., London
Prentice-Hall of Australia, Pty. Ltd., Sydney
Prentice-Hall of Canada, Ltd., Toronto
Prentice-Hall of India Private Ltd., New Delhi
Prentice Hall of Japan, Inc., Tokyo
Prentice-Hall of Southeast Asia Pte. Ltd., Singapore
Whitehall Books Limited, Wellington, New Zealand

10 9 8 7 6 5 4 3 2 1

Library of Congress Cataloging in Publication Data
Holm, Don.
    Cruising the Northwest.
    Bibliography: p.
    1. Yachts and yachting—Northwest, Pacific.
2. Northwest, Pacific—Description and travel—
1951-   I. Title.
GV815.H57   797.1'09795   76-44213
ISBN 0-13-194944-6

Contents

There's a time for some things,
and a time for all things;
a time for great things,
and a time for small things.

Cervantes, *Don Quixote*

Prologue
A Moveable Condominium

So here it is 4 A.M. in the crowded boat harbor at Ilwaco, Washington, behind Cape Disappointment. On this overcast dark May morning, I am waiting to join the "dawn patrol" of sport and commercial salmon boats going out across the Columbia River bar to the open Pacific.

While waiting restlessly and nervously, I sip coffee in the saloon and go through an accumulation of late mail that I stuffed into my briefcase in a hurry before leaving home. I cannot get out of the habit, after all these office years.

Two promotional brochures catch my eye. One is for a new retirement condominium on a beautiful secluded site overlooking Puget Sound, far from the madding crowd—but not so far that one can't enjoy urban conveniences. The other is a fetching full-color pitch offering the lease or rental of a sailing yacht in the mystical San

Juans, for a less alluring twelve hundred dollars a week—not including the babe standing at the mast in the sunset.

If only, I think, one could put the two together (even without
the babe) he would have the ultimate in retirement: the Moveable
Condominium.

Well, why not? Is it necessary to circumnavigate the world or
double Cape Horn just to run away to sea? You may get the same
self-fulfillment without leaving the marina.

On the other hand David, a retired insurance company execu-
tive I know, buys himself a conventional condominium on Lake
Washington in Seattle for ninety thousand dollars. He and his wife
have two nice rooms overlooking the lake and are presumably
happy and contented in their twilight years. But, ninety thousand
clams over their life expectancy adds up to about fifty dollars a day,
plus taxes, interest, utilities, security guards, insurance and other
services—just for a place to eat and sleep and look at Lake Washington. If you've got it and can spend it, okay. But I'd rather spend
what time I've got left differently.

I recall an acquaintance from a period of my life I spent in the
oil business. Division manager for a major firm, one day at a regional sales meeting he dropped to the carpet with a cardiac. This
was followed by months of hospitalization and recuperation, in-
voluntary retirement, a messy divorce, and loss of most of his
worldly goods and ability to return to his former standard of living.
He ended up with his Timex and just enough cash to buy an ancient
Columbia River gillnetter and fix her up for a retirement home.

Too old and sick to continue the corporate rat race, and too
young for Social Security and Medicare, he nevertheless refused to
roll over and die peaceably. He found himself a new life amid the
flotsam and jetsam of the old, learning to live off the land, so to
speak—and he tells me he has never had so much freedom and
security.

Well, we have learned that when you pass fifty, only then do
you understand just how temporary life is. People think of *every*
period in their lives as the prime, but it all doesn't come together
really until it's too late for many to do something about it. I felt no
older at thirty than I did at twenty; nor at forty than I did at thirty;
and now at fifty, I have never felt younger inside and in spirit, even
if the old carcass isn't all that springy. The idea that adventure is
only for the young is obviously absurd. Time is relative. I have
recently discovered that a moment of ecstasy is worth a half century
of boredom and quiet desperation.

A scientist whom I have encountered off and on, head of a
Sea Grant project at Oregon State University, has spent years build-

ing a superbly crafted version of an Atkins' *Ingrid*. Upon retirement at sixty-five, he tells me, he plans to launch her into the Willamette River at Corvallis, float her down seventy-five miles to the Columbia, and then ninety-four miles to the Pacific Ocean.

"After I cross the bar," he says, "*then* I'll decide whether to turn right or left."

Irving Johnson, who skippered his *Yankees* around the world seven times, once wrote that you should go to sea before you are twenty to really understand it; and if you're over forty, forget it. Yet I personally know of eleven people in their forties and fifties and older who are building, buying, and searching for a condominium in the form of a dream ship to carry them down to the sea and escape from the rat race or the rigor mortis of conventional retirement.

For crusty old Joshua Slocum, "cast up from old ocean" in the 1890s when the age of steam had reduced the tall ships he had commanded on the seven seas to cut-down coal barges being towed ignominiously by the nose from one coastal port to another, the old *Spray* was his condominium. He preferred resurrecting the century-old oysterman from its boneyard on the beach at Fairhaven to living with his family and relatives in Boston.

He was fifty-one when, on April 24, 1895, he weighed anchor at noon, set sail, and filled away from Boston just as the twelve o'clock factory whistles were blowing. The *Spray* leaped ahead. He made a short board up the harbor on the port tack, then came about and stood to seaward, swinging past the ferries with lively heels.

When, more than three years later, he dropped anchor in Newport, Rhode Island, he had sailed forty-six thousand miles without an engine, radios, insurance, Medicare, Social Security, sponsors, or even money, to become the first man to sail alone around the world in a small boat, and to gain immortality. But his circumnavigation was only incidental to his motivation in rebuilding the *Spray*. In resurrecting the old *Spray*, perhaps Slocum felt he had resurrected his faith in himself.

So here I am at 4 A.M. on a May morning, waiting to run down the channel to the flashing green light on Black Buoy 11 and tackle the Columbia River bar. I have crossed this bar several hundred times on fishing boats over the years as a newspaper outdoor columnist. I am not really slamming the door shut, nor yet retired from my job—nothing that romantic and spectacular. I am merely about to ferry our new 42-foot sloop *Wild Rose* to a northern base, the prelude to a voyage that comes thirty years too late.

Wild Rose is the end result of a lifetime of searching. She is a dream ship and retirement home in one. She represents more than fifty thousand dollars of hard-to-get money and months of single-minded purpose. But now here she is, ready to go, fully capable of sailing anywhere in the world in relative comfort and safety. She is ready—but are we?

As my bride, for whom our *Wild Rose* is named, always reminds me in times of stress and frustration:

"Take a deep breath, honey."

Part One
THE END OF A
BEGINNING

*If rightly made, a boat would be a sort of
amphibious animal, a creature of two elements,
related by one half its structure to some
swift and shapely fish, and by the other to
some strong-winged and graceful bird.*

The Concord and the Merrimack
Henry David Thoreau

1.
The Search

I think that over the years since my boyhood on the landlocked prairies of North Dakota, my subconscious must have stayed tuned to what would have seemed, to a midwestern farm boy, the ultimate indulgence—a dream boat capable of making long passages on all oceans, in comfort and safety (but not so much safety as to preclude an element of adventure), with a smart turn of speed, and of course within practical means.

The search for such a vessel became a secret hobby to indulge in, a vicarious escape, whenever life's pressures became too much; and then turned into serious research in the preparation of a couple of books on the sea which happily paid me in hard cash for the time spent.

In this research I discovered that every imaginable size and type of floating device has at one time or another circumnavigated the globe. These have ranged from rafts to canoes and to amphibious Jeeps; from lovely little 20-foot yawls to 200-ton brigantines. I found that motorless sailboats and sailless motorboats, plus the auxiliary-rigged craft of the in-between, had all done the job. Cutters, sloops, ketches, yawls, wishbone ketches, square-riggers, morphodite brigs—all have been used. So have open dories, North Sea pilot boats, and Newfoundland fishing boats. They have been deep-displacement, light-displacement, planing, and semiplaning in hull form. They have had long keels, short keels, fin keels, and centerboard keels (to say nothing of no keels). They have been built of wood, fiberglass, steel, aluminum, and even concrete. At least one was hollowed out of a huge Northwest Coast cedar tree. They have been, when the ultimate voyage began, either just launched or as old as a century. They have been manned by one person, or by as many as twenty-five or thirty. Their cost has ranged from as little as five hundred dollars to more than a quarter of a million.

I count it reasonable to assume that, when it comes to dream boats, no man's answer is final, and anyone who claims to have the ultimate in bluewater yachts is sailing more treacherous seas than Slocum's Milky Way. When it comes down to hard strokes, however, the practical person will make his own judgments, based on his own instincts interwoven with experience, advice from experts, and other considerations. The first consideration, of course, is seaworthiness. In *American Small Sailing Craft*, Howard I. Chapelle summed it up in cold doses of unimpeachable logic:

No known boat [of less than 40 feet on deck], can be considered wholly safe in heavy weather, for there are conditions of sea and wind that will overwhelm even the best surfboats and lifeboats. Fortunately, such conditions are relatively rare and, with forethought, can usually be avoided by small-boat sailors. [Also] a good boat is no more seaworthy than her crew—in other words, skill of handling is a part of seaworthiness in small craft. . . . For the beginner, or relatively inexperienced sailor, to venture out into a heavy sea and wind in any small boat is folly that invites disaster.

When it comes to the question of seaworthiness, I would advise a thorough study of the English yacht. In my own research, extending from the days of the *America* schooner in the 1850s, with its starched crew and great clouds of canvas, and the Cowes races, up through the Vertues and the sleek 72-footers, I have almost grudgingly concluded that these people know what a seagoing yacht looks like. From hundreds of years' experience in small boats in the treacherous waters around the British Isles and the North Sea, they should know something. From time to time, as the pendulum of popularity swings back and forth, we have been subjected to the most convincing and articulate arguments over the relative merits of beamy, shallow-draft yachts versus the traditional, old-fashioned narrow beam and deep keel. These arguments have been further enlivened by the dramatic successes of such famous sailers as *Finisterre, Stormvogel, Windward Passage,* and *Bolero.* The cruising man should not be bedazzled by yachts that are designed mainly as racing rule beaters, built at great cost and heavily manned with eager winch-apes —unless, of course, the cruising man is a millionaire and gets his jolts from the wild competition of ocean races.

Among the inescapable facts is the one that permits sailing vessels to reach a certain speed under ocean conditions, regardless of how well manned or how well designed—and for the bluewater voyager this means an average of five to six knots. Among all the dazzling claims for fast vessels, such as the multihulls, I cannot suppress the urge to point out that old Josh Slocum in his lumbering *Spray,* a yacht which almost every professional designer since Cipriano Andrade (including the great Herreshoff) has condemned as a floating coffin, made much better time on the first leg of his circumnavigation, across the North Atlantic, than did the famed Arthur Piver in one of his trimarans more than half a century later.

When it comes to traditional designs, however, the British must be recognized as being probably the best small-boat sailors in the world. From this to the late L. Francis Herreshoff, is but a short tack, and anyone planning to buy or build his dream boat has not covered all the bases until he has read Herreshoff's *Sensible Cruising Designs, The Compleat Cruiser,* and especially *The Common Sense of Yacht Design.* While some of the old master's comments seem slightly baroque and even parochial today in the light of new techniques and new materials available, his understanding of the seagoing vessel and his knowledge of what it should be is unsurpassed.

The puckish Irish martinet Conor O'Brien wrote that his ideal would be 48 feet on the waterline and 12 feet of beam, with proportions for beam to length decreasing to about 33 percent for a 38-foot-waterline vessel. Below that size, he said, he would keep to short passages of not more than a week or so.

Patrick Elam and Colin Mudie, who sailed *Sopranino,* which was only 17 feet 6 inches on the waterline, on some astonishing ocean passages, considered her an extremely efficient sea boat in every way—in fact, in their estimate, "one of the safest vessels of any kind that has ever floated on the ocean."

Elam added, however, in his book *Two Against the Western Ocean:* "I would not pretend that *Sopranino* is the optimum size. At sea she is near perfect, but could with advantage be a few inches longer to give a slightly bigger cockpit and a separate stowage for wet oils below. In harbor, she is too small [for comfort] . . . too delicate and vulnerable."

He recommended a larger Sopranino, about four feet longer. It will be remembered that when John Guzzwell asked Jack Giles for the smallest practical yacht to sail around the world, Giles came up with *Trekka*, which was about two feet longer. *Trekka* has circumnavigated twice, and at this writing is on its third trip around. Colin Mudie, incidentally, a Giles associate, went on to become a famed yacht designer and innovator in his own name.

In *Ocean Racing & Offshore Yachts*—an underestimated book, if there ever was one—the experienced sailor Peter Johnson had this to say about boat size versus seaworthiness:

"The 18 foot 6 inch yawl *Trekka*, a Laurent Giles design, was a development of *Sopranino*, and was sailed round the world single-handed by John Guzzwell in 1958–59. But this was a trans-ocean cruiser and not a racing boat. *Trekka* was the smallest boat ever to sail around the world and the feat has never achieved the acclaim that it deserved."

He also noted that such cockleshells as Robert Manry's 13-foot 6-inch *Tinkerbelle*, and John Riding's *Sea Egg*, which was only 12 feet in overall length, managed long ocean crossings. *Sea Egg*, however, was subsequently lost with all hands in the Tasman Sea; and, as Johnson pointed out, *Tinkerbelle* was frequently rolled over, and often driven backwards by adverse winds.

Errol Bruce, perhaps the most experienced and articulate of present-day English yachtsmen, with whom I had the pleasure of corresponding during the writing of *The Circumnavigators*, summed up the requirements of any yacht sailing in deep water, whatever the purpose of her cruise, in three essential factors: *Safety*, so that she remains afloat and intact whatever weather she meets; *Control*, so that she may reach her destination; and *Space*, so that she may carry her crew with sufficient stores and comfort to maintain them and the ship.

In *Deep Sea Sailing*—published first in 1953 and still the bible of the bluewater sailor—Bruce wrote that "the best type of vessel for deep sea sailing depends on the object and purpose of the voyage. . . . The type of fast cruiser that has developed on each side of the Atlantic through the incentive of off-shore racing is a thoroughly sound seaboat. She is far more easy to manage, and more fun to sail, than the yachts that developed from work boats."

It was Bernard Moitessier, more a sea creature than an alien man who sailed over the seas, who in his first book recommended a 30-footer as ideal, but when it came to building his own dream ship, the preferred length had stretched to 38 feet. He noted later that even the most salty bluewater sailors seldom make passages of more than a few weeks. The rest of the time is spent in harbor or anchored. In a world cruise of even four or five years, seldom more than ten to twelve months are spent at sea.

"The majority of long-cruise sailors will agree that at sea a boat can never be too big," wrote Moitessier of his *Joshua*.

The idea that size has handling limits has been disproved many times. Bernicot sailed alone in his 42-foot *Anahita*. The Van de Wieles circumnavigated in *Omoo*, which could easily be handled by one person and was unattended much of the time. Chay Blyth raced around the world alone the "wrong way" in *British Steel*, a sleek, modern 59-footer. Bob and Chris Hanelt managed the 53-foot Sparkman & Stevens yawl *Skylark*, most of the time alone on a near-perfect circumnavigation recently.

Even the Hiscocks, who preferred small ships and twice circumnavigated in the 30-foot *Wanderer III*, in the end grew tired of cramped conditions and the vicious roll of a narrow hull, and settled upon the 48-foot *Wanderer IV*, a steel ketch built in Holland to their specifications as a permanent home. When I corresponded with Eric and Susan in connection with *The Circumnavigators*, they were halfway around on their third circumnavigation, and I gathered that *Wanderer IV* would be their last—if not their most cherished—dream ship.

Among modern bluewater voyagers, the peripatetic Hal Roth and his wife, Margaret, summed up their grand design nicely in a 35-foot John Brandlmayr, Canadian-built, *Spencer*-class fiberglass sloop. Although they reported many difficulties as a result of the construction, they found that the basic design suited them ideally and they covered many thousands of rough miles around the Pacific Ocean before going aground on a deserted island in the vicinity of Cape Horn. At this writing they had got the yacht off and back to a Chilean port for repairs.

Cost, of course, is often the most vital factor in making a reality of your dream ship. Most voyagers are maddeningly vague about how they financed their dreams. Many of them claim to have been forced into dropping out of organized society and embracing the nomadic life because of some financial disaster. Yet somehow out of this major disaster—the details of which they neglect to reveal for the benefit of their readers—they would have us believe that because they were so good and true, a genie appeared out of a bottle found on the beach, waved her sparkling little wand, and suddenly there was the bread needed. As any frustrated yacht builder or buyer today knows, all those tantalizing ads in the boating magazines take hard-earned cash, not magic. At this writing, they won't even let you look at the kind of a dream boat needed to take you around the world for less than twenty thousand dollars. And if you are buying new and not building, my advice is to think in terms of sixty thousand, and maybe on up to a hundred thousand dollars.

That's the kind of think-talk that can kill even the most persistent dream boat.

Slocum was probably responsible for the image of the cheap boat and the glorious carefree feeling that you don't need money —just a sincere desire. When he was "cast up from old ocean," he was given a ship by his sometime friend Captain Eben Pierce. It turned out that erstwhile voyagers should look a gift boat in the hawsers before accepting such a contribution, for the old oysterman, *Spray*, lay forlornly in a pasture at Fairhaven and required a complete rebuilding, which took thirteen months and required $553.62 of hard cash in a period when cash was hard to get. Slocum got it by withholding it from the legitimate support of his family, who were reduced to sponging off relatives.

Harry Pidgeon perpetuated this myth with his *Islander*, which took eighteen months of labor and a thousand dollars cash in the World War I period. One could ask why he wasn't in the army or navy, fighting for his country and making the world safe for future circumnavigators, instead of spending his time building a dream boat on the beaches of Los Angeles harbor. I could add parenthetically that, in the 1970s, the world is a far less safe place for either democracy or circumnavigation in small boats than it was when Pidgeon began his project. But most aficionados of the sea and bluewater voyagers overlook the fact that Pidgeon was almost an "old man" when he began building *Islander*, and had lived a full and complete life already, involving various adventures from the Mississippi to the Arctic, even to having taken part in the Klondike gold rush. It was a lifetime of doing whatever he felt like, whenever he felt like it. What misleads us lesser men is the fact that his *Islander* period, which included *two* circumnavigations and the start of a *third*, all came after the age when most of us are thinking about retiring to a sedentary life of ease and comfort.

William A. Robinson's *Svaap*, a beautiful little Alden ketch, cost Robbie about two thousand dollars in the booming 1920s. His contemporary, Dwight Long, acquired *Idle Hour*—a yacht strikingly similar to *Svaap*—on the opposite coast for about the same amount during the Depression. A yacht of similar capacity, *Suhaili*, the 32-foot ketch in which Robin Knox-Johnston became the first solo circumnavigator, cost about twelve thousand dollars to build with native labor in the India of the 1950s. Jack London's *Snark* cost thirty thousand dollars in 1906. Ray Kauffman's *Hurricane*, in which he and another Iowa lad, Gerry Mefferd, sailed around the world in the 1930s, was built in the depths of the Depression by a Gulf Coast character named Sidoine Krebs for two thousand dollars and all the corn likker he could drink.

In spite of Errol Bruce's ideal, very few yachts have been built expressly for sailing around the world—or even for living aboard or for long voyages. In most cases the owners have taken what they could get, or the best they could afford, and went on from there, learning to live with whatever beast or beauty that resulted, with all the pride of ownership they could muster. This usually turned out a compromise at best, and at worst a suicidal situation—although no one could tell the owners that. Frank Wightman, who built the sister ship to Pidgeon's *Islander* from *Rudder Magazine* plans (the enlarged *Sea Bird*, also made famous by Thomas Fleming Day and John Voss in ocean passages), spent a thousand dollars building *Wylo* in South Africa, and regarded it as a no-compromise ideal ocean cruiser. Wightman, a no-compromise man who dropped out of the Establishment to preserve this principle, wrote: "You do not compromise with the sea in small yachts. You triumph or you are extinguished. The verities of the sea are few, simple, and austere. *Wylo's* characteristics were buoyancy, and speed before the wind."

There has been much nonsense written about "comfort" at sea, Wightman also noted. Any small yacht is acutely *uncomfortable* in heavy weather, in fact almost a case of survival conditions, as Errol Bruce and others have frequently pointed out. Even in mild or calm weather there is no such thing as "ease of motion" on the sea. Only Robinson, on his return to Tahiti on the beautiful *Varua*, ever wrote of a truly flat and motionless sea out of sight of land, and this for only a few brief hours. Even John London's *Snark*, which was built especially for comfort, never achieved it, under any conditions.

In all such research leading up to making a major lifetime decision like buying or building a dream ship, one must keep in mind that no single source, no one authority, no matter how prestigious, should be regarded as ultimate. I think Don Street was the first to point out in print what most experienced voyagers must know: "Seamanship is seldom really well-learned unless a person has sailed on various boats with various people. Many singlehanders have done all their sailing on their own boats, with no one to point out their errors, and with no exposure to other people's methods. As a result, they have often been doing the same thing wrong—or the hard way—for many years. They drift, as it were, around the world. They think they know how to sail, but often they really do not."

The same can be said for the whole spectrum of yacht designing, yacht designers, yacht builders, yacht brokers, and yachting writers.

When it comes to beating one's own drum, there are no more vigorous wielders of drumsticks than yacht designers themselves. After centuries of mankind's experience with boat building and water transportation, yacht design remains mostly an art, and an empirical technology at best. Certain rules have been isolated and defined (and often broken in successful boats), guidelines for scantling have been established by such special interests as Lloyd's, to whom they mean profit or loss, and the basic principles of mechanical and structural engineering have been applied to yacht designing—to say nothing of the results of sophisticated and complicated model-testing facilities.

But even Herreshoff, in *The Common Sense of Yacht Design*, denounced slavish attention to such pseudosciences. "My advice to the young yacht designer," he wrote, "is to throw the scantling rules out the window, then develop a sense of proportion—consider each part of the construction separately and its function. If you do this for a while, you will acquire a confidence in your judgment which is far better than being some sort of human slide rule or bookkeeper using formulas made by others which may not apply to the case in hand."

Yacht designers, particularly the aggressive and competitive ones, frequently become so convoluted by their own creative enthusiasm that their opinions are unreliable and often dangerous. It is a natural thing, of course, for a man to praise best his own creations and his own acquisitions, whether these consist of a yacht design, a piece of creative writing, a newly acquired wife or automobile. How much of this is justifiable pride, and how much of it is rationalization and justification of argument is difficult to assess.

For example, a more controversial boat has never existed than Slocum's *Spray*. For three-quarters of a century sailors and designers have been arguing over its merits. The controversy started on the day Slocum disappeared, and burst into flame with the well-known classic analysis of *Spray*'s lines by Cipriano Andrade, Jr., in *Rudder*, which was first praised and then condemned by none other than John Hanna, who himself had designed a modified Spray.

Although most thoughtful students today consider Andrade's analysis a little too pat, it is true that most contemporary *Spray* detractors have never even read Slocum's book—nor Cipriano's analysis, which appears in some of the more recent editions—and therefore are immediately suspected of not knowing exactly what they are talking about.

On the other hand, few persons would be inclined to doubt Howard Chapelle. As a young draftsman, he worked with Charles Mower, the great yacht designer who first put *Spray's* lines on paper for *Rudder*. In a letter to me, Chapelle wrote:

Slocum's letters are like those of a 4th grader—rather backward at that. He was 60 per cent fine seaman, 10 per cent liar, and 30 per cent showman, I would say. Had a lot of guts. He was going nowhere in no hurry so I supposed he sailed as the boat wanted to go.

As I said, no lines were actually taken off Spray, *so that poor Andrade was victimized by the old fraud, Tom Day, with Charley Mower the fall guy. Had Mower taken off the lines we would have had something to work on—now we have no reliable plans as a basis for analysis. But the whole story of the wonder abilities of* Spray *is now highly questionable.*

The legendary John Hanna, who in 1923 created perhaps the most famous dream ship of all time—the 30-foot *Tahiti* ketch—called it a vessel suitable for "all oceans and all conditions of sea . . . one that will take you anywhere you want to go" in comfort and safety. The choice of a name for his creation was part showmanship, part inspiration—for Tahiti was every man's inspiration and Valhalla in those days.[1] In fact, Hanna's construction notes accompanying the first publication of the lines in the old *Modern Mechanics* were prefaced with:

> *Poke her nose to the mornin' sun,*
> *On a tide that's ebbin' speedy—*
> *Start her sheets to the breeze fresh run*
> *On a slant for old Tahiti.*

What incurable dream-boat romantic could resist an appeal like that?

Actually, the Hanna *Tahiti* originated with a client who wanted a seaworthy small sailboat and thought the lifeboat model was the answer. Hanna adapted this, with some features borrowed from the Norwegian double-enders, the Portuguese shore boats, and who knows what else, and the happy result was *Tahiti*, which combined some age-old design features with the heady elixir of escape.

As Stephen Doherty wrote of the thirty-year-old siren in the March 1967 issue of *Modern Mechanics'* successor, *Mechanix Illustrated*, "In the history of small-boat ocean voyages, no single design ever logged more miles at sea."

Hundreds of Tahitis were built or started, and dozens of them made world cruises—some making multiple circumnavigations. Yet Tahiti is not for amateur builders. Skill and patience are needed. And time: figure three to five years, depending upon talent and resources. In Hanna's day the cost of home building was estimated at about a thousand dollars. Today, fifteen thousand would be an absolute minimum, and thirty thousand for a custom job. In early 1974, a twenty-year-old Tahiti was advertised in a Seattle newspaper for twenty-five thousand dollars.

At twenty thousand pounds' displacement, she is no ocean gazelle. It takes half a gale to drive her, as some owners noted. Yet she was not designed for speed, but for long ocean passages in the Slocum tradition. This was my impression the first time I set foot on the deck of one in San Pedro harbor in 1937. It was like stepping on the deck of a real ship. Even the heavy wake of passing ferries scarcely ruffled her skirts. One sensed instantly that if any ship could take you to the South Seas, Tahiti was the one.

Perhaps when all is said and done, and the current generation of "Tupperware yachts" has passed on, Tahiti will still remain the one and only authentic dream ship.

In the same year that Jack Hanna created *Tahiti*, the Irish rebel Conor O'Brien was scouring the secondhand bookshops in seaport towns for cruising books and the logs of old sailing vessels used for passage to the American Colonies and in the wool and grain trades. As he noted, the cult of the sailing ship had been reborn again then, just as it has every decade or so before and since. The result of his research and personal inclinations was *Saoirse*, which is Gaelic for "freedom," a small ship with a waterline length of 37.5 feet, modeled after an Arklow fishing boat but designed by O'Brien himself. It had a speed of about seven knots maximum, and an average passage-making rate of five knots. In her, O'Brien became the first to circumnavigate east-about-south of the three capes—Good Hope, Leeuwin, and Horn. And he did it with such ease and, in the telling, with such understatement of narrative, that many who later undertook the same route in small boats were misled, and failed.

Most world cruisers, of course, are designed for trade-wind running or broad reaching most of the time. O'Brien's reason for going the "wrong way," he said, was that he did not have an engine and was too impatient to wallow in calms frequently found in the middle latitudes.

Besides, he said, "Every passage is in a sense a race, a race against the consumption of stores; and even if one has unlimited time, it would still be a race against boredom." On the whole, he added, "It was worthwhile; there are not so many adventures offered nowadays, that one can afford to miss even a modest one."

That was written in 1923. And it will please dream-ship aficionados to know that at this writing *Saoirse* is alive and well and still sailing.

Summed up, one has to return to basics: What is the yacht going to be used for? What is the biggest one can afford? Where will it be taken? How much time will be spent at sea and how much in port or in sheltered waters (where perhaps an engine is more reliable than sails)? Will it be a retirement boat, a weekend cruiser, a racer, or a drinking barge? How many people do you really want to "sleep?" Why have eight bunks when only two of you will be aboard?

Today prospective buyers have it laid out for them, in spite of high costs and shortages. Largely because of the unprecedented boom in world cruising during the past twenty years, and the even greater boom in ocean racing, there have been more advances in boat design than in the previous two thousand years. Up until, say, a decade ago, the average speed of an auxiliary yacht—as Conor O'Brien had pointed out long before—was only four or five knots on an ocean passage. Today, with a modern hull, you can count on six to eight if you want to push it, and some of the fast ocean racers are now approaching the speed of the old clipper ships that could reel off twenty knots day in and day out. Modern materials such as fiberglass, steel, and aluminum, along with greatly improved paints, have all but eliminated the nagging problem that voyagers used to have in remote places where regular bottom maintenance could not be done.

I do not believe, however, that modern synthetics, nor modern alloys of iron and aluminum, are the ultimate, nor that they have even reached the epitome of yacht construction. All of these, I am convinced, are a passing phase. In the long-range view these materials are definitely limited. If one does not believe this, one has only to recall the Arab oil embargo of 1974. Oil or petroleum, from which almost all synthetics are derived, is not only definitely limited as a resource, but the cost of it will continue to rise steadily until it no longer is competitive for boat-building purposes.

Iron and aluminum, being metals, are also limited as the resource is limited. In a world increasing in population geometrically, food supplies and materials can at best only be increased arithmetically to meet the demand. There will come a point where both iron and aluminum will also not be competitive for yacht building.

What does this leave?

Why, wood, of course—and this will no doubt cause the old-timers who deplored the passing of good wood construction and craftsmanship to revolve with joy in their tombs.

Wood not only has been a proved boat-building material since the first dugout was launched by primitive man, but is aesthetically pleasing, buoyant, and vibrant with life. Most of all, wood is something no other material is: a *renewable* resource, which is being grown nowadays as a crop.

The old problems of preserving and maintenance are being licked as these lines are written. New methods of impregnating wood are being developed, so that it will be as maintenance-free as fiberglass at least. In the strength-weight category, at this writing a new method, developed in Germany, which eliminates the need for "peeler" logs of first quality in the making of veneer, is being installed by a nearby plywood mill. Any kind of wood, including bark, is chopped up, organically separated, and put back together again in a flawless veneer ten times as strong as ordinary plywood.

As long as there are boats and boat builders, count on it, there will be wooden boats.

Boat builders today also have an astonishing choice of modern yacht equipment and rigging, accessories and power plants, dependable, efficient solid-state electronics, strong rot-proof running rigging and sails, compact refrigeration units, and even small, highly dependable diesel engines that take up no more space than a generator used to. Today, with an inexpensive transistor radio, you can tune in the time ticks from dozens of stations, eliminating the need for expensive and sensitive chronometers. If you are gadget-minded, you can buy a relatively inexpensive electronic computer small enough to put in your pocket, which will almost automatically work out a navigational triangle and give you a LOP in less time than it takes to write this sentence.

As Robinson wrote in *To The Great Southern Sea*, in spite of the few diehards left over from the nineteenth century, "Sentimentality about sailing without an engine [may be discarded], the question today is what form the auxiliary power should take." Today a light-weight diesel engine costs little more than a gasoline engine and, if properly maintained, is much more dependable and economical to run.

Assuming, then, that one has the means, out of all these confusing arguments and theories what kind of a dream ship am I looking for?

CHAPTER NOTES

[1]*The original* Tahiti *was built in 1925, under the personal supervision of Hanna, as the* Neptune. *It is still afloat at this writing, having been restored by newspaperman and freelance writer Alan Hopkins of Tarpon Springs, Florida, who found her*

while on an assignment in 1953. For the full story of how the fire-gutted relic was discovered and rebuilt by Hopkins, who lived aboard her with his family for five years, see the February, March, and April issues of National Fisherman, *Camden, Maine. Hopkins renamed her* Caribbee.

In a 1975 letter to me, veteran naval architect Weston Farmer, who is also a writer, editor, and original discoverer of Hanna and the Tahiti ketch, explained how it came about for the first time.

"As a practicing naval architect, I had long known John G. Hanna and his work when, in April of 1928, I became the founding editor of Modern Mechanics and Inventions Magazine, the title of which was eventually shortened to Mechanix Illustrated.

"In gathering some editing scoops for home-built boats, I wrote Hanna for some designs to be published in a how-to-build form. He submitted first, Dorothy, named after his wife. Next, I asked him to submit a design and story based on his Neptune, designed for Anton Schneider of Lakeland, Florida, sometime in 1923. This date is pegged because the then editor of Rudder, Gerald Taylor White, in whose magazine Neptune's profile had been published, took a literary sideswipe at Hanna by referring to him in belittling terms, referring to Hanna as a 'sometime real estate operator in the kumquat belt,' or words to that effect.

"Hanna was infuriated with White, and rightly so. He agreed to work up Neptune. The agreed price was $250 for the yarn, which by today's standards would be about $1,000 or more.

"During the preparation of the story, one of our editors, Don Cooley, took a sabbatical of a few months to vacation in Tahiti. The name Tahiti struck me as being a fine one for Hanna's new double-ender, based on Neptune. Jack labeled the tracings, which I still have, as Tahiti. That's how she got her name.

"A generous royalty arrangement was set up between me, acting for the publisher, Fawcett Publications, and John G. Hanna, under which arrangement Mrs. Hanna still collects. [Author's note: The plans are still available from Fawcett Publications and Mrs. Dorothy Hanna of Dunedin, Florida, at this writing.]

"I have over 40 letters from Hanna written to me in that period. I have lost the Worden Wood drawing I commissioned Wood to do for the Frontispiece on the original story, published first in Modern Mechanics and later in How To Build Twenty Boats. I knew Jack personally and corresponded for years, calling on him at his Dunedin home, and latterly, calling again on Dorothy·Hanna.

"If anyone knows the true story of Neptune, nee Tahiti, and her genesis and midwifery, it should be the midwife who brought her into the world. That fellow was I. [Farmer also authored·the famous verse that headed up the Tahiti series.]

"Hanna had obviously sent Neptune to Rudder by his own volition. Tahiti was ordered to my needs. She was paid for, most happily so. I hope this clears up the speculation about Tahiti and her origins."

A 32-foot version of Tahiti, incidentally, appeared in the 1972 issue of Mechanix Illustrated.

2.
Some Practical Considerations

In the December 1973 issues of *Sail* and *Yachting World*, the latest study made by the Ocean Cruising Club was released. Membership in OCC is worldwide, but is restricted to amateurs who have made long passages of a thousand miles or more in vessels of less than 75 feet overall length. The study was based on a comprehensive questionnaire returned by three hundred members, who were asked to give their opinion on what they would consider the ideal ocean cruiser if they had the opportunity and the resources to build their own dream ship for a typical world voyage which would take them into northern and tropical seas (excluding the high southern latitudes and Arctic waters).

When the results were analyzed and a composite yacht drawn up by Colin Mudie, a dramatic departure from previous concepts, gathered during the decade from 1964 to 1974, appeared. This coincided with the period during which ocean voyaging in small craft had shown the most growth.

The survey showed a swing away from the ketch and yawl and toward the sloop and cutter—a trend that is directly opposed to such authorities as Herreshoff. A decade ago OCC members dreamed of a 35-foot vessel; in this survey they considered the 40-foot range as the ideal (58 percent chose a length of from 29 to 40 feet LOA). A surprising number—41 percent—chose 40 feet and over as the ideal.

Another surprise was in the fuel to be used for cooking. Unlike the old days, modern bluewater yachters chose propane or butane, 52 percent over 31 percent for kerosene (paraffin), and 11 percent for the highly touted alcohol (spirit) fuel.

Ninety-five percent wanted a single-hull vessel over the catamaran or trimaran. Eighty percent said the draft should be between 5 and 7 feet. Twenty-four percent chose wood for hull construction (this is bound to change in coming years); 15 percent, welded steel; 10 percent, welded aluminum; 15 percent, fiberglass (G.R.P.); and only 4 percent, ferro-cement.

Ninety-eight percent wanted Terylene (Dacron) sails. Sixty-three percent chose the wheel steering over the tiller. About 76 percent wanted some kind of vane self-steering. Seventy-two percent chose the aft cockpit arrangement. Ninety-four percent wanted a single auxiliary engine on the centerline (not offset); and 93 percent wanted it to be diesel. None wanted a motorless sailboat. Most, or 70 percent, wanted an auxiliary with a range of from two hundred to eight hundred miles. The greatest percentage wanted electric starting, 12-volt d.c. ship's electrical system, electric refrigeration, electric running lights, navigation systems, and their preference for batteries jumped from a single 12-volt unit to a bank of four.

The British CQR plow anchor won hands down over the Danforth (the choice of anchors seems to be more nationalistic, political, and emotional than practical, for some strange reason). The 360-degree compass card was chosen over all other types. The choice of a dinghy changed from the rigid to the inflatable type. Sixty percent chose the dry chemical fire extinguisher over the more dangerous CO_2.

Ninety-five percent wanted an inflatable dinghy; 91 percent, an RDF; 96 percent, a depth sounder; 49 percent, a high-frequency radiophone; 72 percent, a spinner log; 49 percent, taped stereo music; 26 percent, a pressure water system; 67 percent, sleeping bags over bedding; and 68 percent, a diaphragm-type bilge pump over all other kinds.

For an earlier definitive study of trends in auxiliary cruisers see the article by Pete Smyth in the October 1972 issue of *Motor Boating & Sailing*.

A study of several years of back issues of the Seven Seas Cruising Association's *Commodores' Bulletin*, 1969 through 1975, confirmed the above trends, and added some new ones. SSCA is an esoteric group of yachties—mostly man-wife teams—scattered all over the world, who live aboard or are cruising with small boats. To be a member, or "Commodore," one *must* be living aboard permanently, and even then is elected to membership only after recommendation and thorough investigation as to character and integrity.

It will probably pain the more romantic to learn this, but power yachts sans sails are gaining popularity among live-aboard yachtsmen and retired couples. I first became aware of this when interviewing Ray Kauffman of *Hurricane* fame, who chose as his late-in-life dream boat one of the sturdy Alaskan powerboats. Nothing is more thrilling and spirit-moving than the sight of a tall sailship beating to windward in a bit of a breeze—but the powerboat also has much to recommend it for the needs of many water-oriented people. There is more room, ease of maneuverability, and much more speed. For inland waters and coastwise cruising, such as Puget Sound, the Inland Passage to Alaska, the Sacramento, Columbia, and other large river systems, the Mississippi and Gulf Coast waterways, the island network along the New England coast and Maritime Provinces, and of course the Atlantic seaboard inland waterways and Great Lakes, a powerboat may be the most practical for many people.

During my youth I spent some time in Alaska as a partner in a 30-foot double-ender commercial salmon troller, the *Helen M.* Some of the best months of my life were passed aboard this vessel in a carefree existence that was ended for good by the coming of World War II. Over the years I have often daydreamed that someday, when the kids were gone, I would buy a modern 50-foot combination salmon and tuna troller and crabber, and live aboard for six months of the year, ranging from California to Kodiak. The present fleet of perhaps two or three thousand such craft is made up of at least two thirds live-aboard couples. The only thing about this that did not appeal to me was the damn hard work, and the long hours, and the hazards I imagined for middle-aged and older couples.

Of such materials are dreams built—and a dream ship may have tall trolling poles instead of tall sailing masts and still be real.

Real also is the cost in money, time, energy, peace of mind, and disposition. I was to learn, after I had taken a deep breath and plunged in, that I would be spending an average of a hundred dollars a day for more than eighteen months, every day, seven days

a week. In addition, for the same period and maybe longer, I would
have to spend from six to eight hours a day on work connected with
this project, every day, seven days a week, *after* I had first put in the
necessary ten hours a day required by the exigencies of my regular
employment.

Traveling (and my job required about twenty thousand miles
of auto travel a year), I used the long lonely stretches for thinking
out problems and dictating into a tape recorder. Lunch periods were
spent rushing around the city on errands of personal business, and
on looking for and purchasing parts and supplies in a period when
shortages of everything were beginning to be felt, especially in those
goods using critical materials such as bronze and stainless. Along
with my penknife, I carried a small magnet for testing parts and
fittings for ferro reaction (and detected frequent instances of
manufacturer's cunning). I got to be quite an expert on pricing,
discounts, sources of supply, and the relative value of things.

Evenings, at home, rare periods of relaxation were spent in
front of the television, listening to the news or an occasional pro-
gram while at the same time thumbing through marine discount
catalogues, or making lists of work to be done or parts needed, or
studying a celestial navigation course, or writing letters, or researching for books and articles.

But, in the end, I think the most satisfaction came from the
realization that I had at last, after thirty years or so, brought my
dream ship to life without investing a penny of the regular family
budget—she was financed entirely by extra work, some lucky in-
vestments, and an attentive response to any possible sources of
legitimate extra income.

Move over, Joshua, old boy! You may have created your
dream ship near the resting place of John Cook, the revered Pilgrim
father, at a cost of $553.62 and thirteen months of hard labor—but
you would not have been less proud had you done it the way I did!

3.

How Wild Rose Was Conceived

The story of *Wild Rose* really began in the middle 1930s on the drought-ridden prairies of North Dakota, as far from an ocean as you can get. And it began, as it did for thousands of the restless kids of that period, with Hanna's *Tahiti*, the lines of which were published in the 1935 edition of *How To Build 20 Boats*, the old Fawcett publication. I still have the original publication, which in the intervening years was carried everywhere I went, hitchhiking and riding freight trains all over the country looking for work, traveling to foreign lands, to boom-town construction jobs and lumber camps, to Alaska when it was still a frontier territory, through World War II, and into the postwar period. Faded and brittle now with age, with little pieces torn from them and faded pencil notes here and there, the old plans are in a safe place—a nostalgic remembrance.

Along with these plans, there is a crumbling old catalogue

from Bay City Boats of Bay City, Michigan, which sold prefabricated dream boats, one of which was *Tahiti*. In those days you could buy the frame and planking kit for about a thousand dollars, all ready for assembly, with pre-fit and drilled components. In the late 1930s, in Juneau, Alaska, I had saved enough from gold mining and commercial fishing to buy the kit when World War II interrupted my plans.

After the war came readjustments, college, family, career. Not until I was middle-aged did the chance come again to fulfill an old dream. Over the years I had acquired building plans and specifications for a number of possible dream ships. These included, as a matter of interest to others so inclined, Slocum's *Spray* model, the *Rudder*'s enlarged *Sea Bird* or *Islander*, Hanna's *Tahiti* and his larger *Carol* ketch, a design or two from the prestigious Sparkman & Stevens, a Tom Colvin junk-rigged cruiser, and L. Francis Herreshoff's classic *Marco Polo*. The latter I consider the finest world cruiser ever designed. Unfortunately, most of the yachts built from these plans were altered by the builders for aesthetic reasons, thereby destroying the original concept. In conversations with the old master himself at The Castle prior to his death, I gathered that *Marco Polo* was one of his favorites, and that he was disappointed that it had not achieved more acceptance.

Appearing in a *Rudder* series in 1945, *Marco Polo* embodied almost everything that a war-weary and disillusioned generation longed for in a world cruiser. Fifty-five feet in overall length, with a lean ten-foot beam and a modest five-foot draft, she was based on the whaleboat model. Rigged as a three-masted tern schooner, she had a low profile, an infinite combination of sail arrangements, including a square sail for trade-wind running, and could be handled by one man on watch with all lines and sheets running back to the cockpit. For the doldrums and for running up wilderness and exotic rivers, and exploring lonely channels such as the one around the southern tip of South America, she was diesel-powered and capable of making up to twelve knots, with a fuel capacity for four thousand miles under power alone. The extra fuel capacity also provided for convenient oil-burning cooking and heating facilities, to say nothing of the possibility of purchasing fuel in bulk quantities for as little as ten cents a gallon in those days.

Marco Polo was cut away forward and aft in just the right proportions for heaving to, running before a gale, or fetching up to a sea anchor or drogue. She also incorporated the spade rudder with a 150-degree range for maneuverability and for lashing down to take the strain off the blade when making leeway. Everything about *Marco Polo* showed the genius of Herreshoff in distinct relief. She was far ahead of her time in many ways.

She was then, and still is, the one bluewater displacement yacht that can consistently make two-hundred-mile noon-to-noon runs in all but the worst weather. Considering that most voyagers seldom average more than five knots, this is indeed remarkable.

A lumberman friend who built the Marco Polo in his backyard lengthened her by one foot and added two feet to her beam. He used composition construction, with steel frames and fir planking, and turned her into a two-masted conventional schooner. This version has been sailing North Pacific waters for about fifteen years with outstanding performance. The owner tells me that she is still capable of twelve knots but that she is a "roller," due perhaps to his alteration of the basic model.

Unfortunately, the Marco Polo was a little too radical for the fickle consumer market. Average blokes reacted nervously to the three masts, even though this simplified the overall rig. They did not like the narrow 10-foot beam, although the length provided adequate roominess. They were leery of the spade rudder, although this is now almost standard on racing craft. And perhaps the double-ended whaleboat model was not as aesthetically pleasing as the modern yacht-club-type reverse-canted transoms, even though the vessel was designed to be incapable of capsizing or being overwhelmed by a pooping sea. I think, also, that many prospective builders were turned off by the extensive use of handmade metal castings and fittings. Herreshoff, of course, delighted in making everything, up to and including stern tubes, rudder pintles, boom goosenecks, mast tangs, and chainplates. Most people do not have the skill and equipment for this, and custom fabrication is totally out of sight today.

One should remember, however, that when the Marco Polo was designed, custom fabrication was a common practice. Also, in the postwar period, there were shortages of everything—both materials and stock parts for yachts. Today, of course, you can buy almost every kind of a fitting off the shelf, including aluminum masts complete right down to the cleats and winches and halyards.

Marco Polo was my first choice, and still is; however, I had neither the time nor the space for such a building project, and with wood becoming more expensive and difficult to get in that period, it did not fit the circumstances. For reasons of financing, convenience, and ultimate maintenance, I finally selected fiberglass or G.R.P. as the basic material, after long consideration of sandblasted and zinced steel, aluminum, and even ferro-cement. Once this was decided, I began a search for a hull I could live with, in kit form, which I could complete myself in a convenient place, at my leisure, either in or near water.

During this period a fascinating correspondence with veteran designer Weston Farmer, who entertained ambitions of building John Hanna's version of Slocum's Spray out of aluminum, led me to buy a set of *Foam II* plans from Mrs. Dorothy Hanna. I also had some interesting telephone conversations with Tom Colvin, whose steel junk-rigged 42-footer I much admired and almost went for (until a local builder quoted me twenty thousand dollars for the bare hull). Joe Koelbel, consulting designer for *Rudder Magazine*, also offered some valuable comments during this period of Herreshoff's *Marco Polo*. At one point I even considered having a friend, veteran Portland boat builder Jim Staley, a wizard with plywood, build me a copy of *Rudder's Seagoer*, the 34-foot version of *Sea Bird*, designed by Frederick W. Goeller, Jr., which became Harry Pidgeon's *Islander*.

All this sketches out the complex mental gymnastics and the sweet sensual pleasures (and agonizing conception) that one goes through in becoming wedded to a dream boat. At one point it led me far afield, to buy an armload of offset tables from Howard Chapelle's collection at the Smithsonian Institution, in a short-lived impulse to find my dream in the traditional old Atlantic fishing boats. I even made a trip to Nova Scotia and prowled around the utterly fascinating boat-building centers such as Yarmouth, Lunenburg, Mahone Bay, and Shelburne, whence had come such famed yachts as Robinson's *Svaap* and Maury's *Cimba*. And I paid tribute to Slocum's birthplace, Brier Island, and to Cape Sable Island, whence he had taken his departure.

In the end, I often longed for the simplicity of Erskine Childer's *Dulcibella* in the *Riddle of the Sands*.

It did not occur to me until later that much of the fun is in the search, the anticipation, the acquisition expectations—not in the finding. It is like being on a prowl for a mate, on the stalk for prey. Everything that comes later is anticlimactic.

Ultimately, I was to choose a Cascade 42 sloop, designed by Robert A. Smith and built within thirty miles of my home. This had been one of the first possibilities I had looked into, so now I had come full circle, arriving back where I had started.

Here, then, are the vital statistics of our dream ship, which by happy (and sometimes unhappy) coincidence closely compared with the results of the OCC survey:

Yacht *Wild Rose*. Documented, No. 546703, 11 net tons.
Length overall: 42 feet
Load waterline: 34 feet
Beam: 11 feet 2 inches
Draft: 5 feet 6 inches
Displacement: 19,000 pounds

LINES–*The clean, conventional, modern displacement lines of* Wild Rose *are evident in this full profile with underbody configuration. Although basically a fin keel design, she has excellent directional stability in all but the worst kind of following seas. This is probably due to the placement of rudder and large-size skeg. When lying a-hull, she drifts broadside to the swells or seas with an easy, stable motion.*

WILD ROSE–*Profile of* Wild Rose *shows sloop rig with various sail combinations possible. The twin jibs, which were designed by author, are not shown. The profile in general is a typical Cascade 42 as designed by Robert A. Smith of Portland. Note the Cascade logo on sail. The number 56 is the hull number, not the racing number, of course.*

The hull is of the modern, moderate semidisplacement type, with large ballasted fin keel, large skeg and rudder, modified counter, sloop-rigged without bowsprit, center cockpit, and aft trunk cabin. The hull construction is of hand-laid-up fiberglass cloth and woven roving (no mat), with marine plywood bulkheads. The deck is also built up of two layers of half-inch plywood covered with fiberglass cloth.

The engine is a 4-107 Westerbeke diesel of 37 horsepower at full-rated rpm, with a Paragon hydraulic reverse gear, 2 to 1 reduction. The shaft is Monel, 1¼-inch diameter, with a fixed two-bladed prop plus a spare three-bladed prop stowed aboard. Fuel capacity is 184 gallons, giving a theoretical range of from one to two thousand miles under power. Cooking is done on a gimballed propane marine stove with range, with deck storage for tanks, and flexible high-pressure lines. A Sea Swing stove is used for making quick snacks or heating cocoa, with Sterno canned heat.

The engine is equipped with two alternators, one for engine-battery use only, with its special bank of two high-capacity marine types; plus an auxiliary 85-amp alternator feeding a bank of three batteries for ship's service. Separate shore-power converters take over the battery load automatically when moored. In addition, there is an alternator-run 115-volt AC unit that can provide 3,600 watts either moored or at sea.

Electronics include a VHF/FM twelve-channel transceiver, a spare portable six-channel Drake transceiver with emergency ship-to-ship marine telephone and harbor frequencies, and a couple of portable battery-operated receivers, including the Zenith Trans-Oceanic, for weather, news, and UTC time signals. Since I have been an amateur radio ham since high school days, naturally I have the ship well-equipped with solid-state SSB and FM transceivers, which gives me the potential of a worldwide communications system apart from the regular marine system—and a far better one, I might add. The use of ham radio has become increasingly popular with small-boat voyagers in recent years, and will become even more important and universally used in years to come. By patching in with other hams I can reach almost any country in the world, including some behind the Iron Curtain, almost instantly, from any place in the world.

In addition to this capability, anyone with a marine VHF/FM transceiver aboard who is within reach of a shore telephone operator can place a long-distance telephone call to any place in the world, and also to any other yacht so equipped.

Truly, one of the wonders of modern yachting is the possibility of instant communications, whether or not this is desirable by everyone who goes to sea in a dream ship.

Other details about *Wild Rose,* upon which I will probably enlarge later, include electric refrigeration and a small portable freezer; stainless rigging, fiberglass water tanks with filtered supply lines, pressure water system with hot water by dual electric and exhaust-transfer means; electric anchor windlass; a solution to the Great Toilet Debate in the form of an electric macerator-chlorinator head with provision for a holding tank later; dual freshwater and seawater galley supplies; shower bath; hydraulic center cockpit wheel steering; compact vented hard-fuel fireplaces in main and aft cabins; teak trim; and a vinyl enclosed winter cockpit shelter. The dinghy is an Avon inflatable with a *British Seagull* outboard.

As can be seen, the essence of my own independent accumulation of experience, research, analysis, personal preferences, expediency, and advice from those who are better qualified pretty much followed the general trend—a coincidence that might interest the perceptive market analysts. I departed from the general trend in some things, however, for example in the choice of a hollow wooden mast instead of the popular aluminum spars; and in going back to the old-fashioned slab or jiffy-reefing system in preference to modern roller reefing. The main reason was financial. The aluminum job would have cost two thousand dollars or more. For less than five hundred I built my own laminated hollow wood stick, which is just as light and has the advantage of being tapered for better weight distribution aloft. Moreover, it has a little give in the way of stress, and simplifies the attachment of cleats, winches, tangs, and other accessories. It requires more maintenance, but on the other hand modern synthetic glues, wood preservatives and new-type paints reduce this to a minimum.

I was to learn quickly that I could not haul my (then) 230 pounds of fat and bones to the top of the mast in a bosun's chair. I just did not have the strength. Also it terrified me. Instead, I made mast stirrups out of aluminum tubing and screwed these to the mast at alternate three-foot spacings. This gives easy access to the top of the mast or anywhere in between, and is much safer than the bosun's chair in a seaway. Climbing the mast still terrifies me, however. It is a personal challenge that taunts me from time to time.

With a little thought and planning I was able to reduce the need for so many hand winches, which are these days the most costly part of a boat. Why these should be so expensive I cannot understand. On some racers the cost of the winches comes to more than the cost of the bare hull itself. The use of carefully selected block and fall tackle in strategic places can eliminate many winches. After all, old Slocum and his contemporaries handled the much heavier gaff-sail gear alone without these chrome-plated goodies.

Among the last purchases I made with bankruptcy staring

balefully at me was the Don Allen *Wind Wand* self-steering apparatus for use under sail alone; and the Calmec *Mark X* automatic pilot. These cost a lot of money but were the least expensive of all the fifty or sixty types and brands of self-steering gadgets I investigated. They were also among the least complicated, which appealed to me almost as much as the price.

I really do not have much empathy with those tortured souls who must go primitive for reasons of aesthetics or ego, and eschew the use of engines or electronic aids. As far as I am concerned, such people belong back in the eighteenth century and have no place in modern small-boat voyaging. Philosophically, when you start to go primitive, where do you draw the line? Any line you draw has got to be arbitrary, unless you want to go out into the woods and with stone tools hew down a cedar tree and carve out your dream ship that way.

My ancestors were Vikings and sea captains, yet my instincts are to make the best use of the best tools we have at hand, providing I can afford them and they are practical. I would even have installed a small radar unit in the beginning, had I had the money and the time for such extras.* The Northwest Coast and Alaska, with some of the worst weather in the world and frequent fogs, to say nothing of rampaging tides and unexpected storm fronts, is a place where you want as much help as you can get—especially when your life and your entire fortune is tied up in one small and vulnerable dream ship.

In the case of the *Wind Wand* and the Calmec *Mark X*, I cannot resist noting that these were among the few appendages, accessories, and basic ship's equipment which I installed, which went together perfectly without extensive modification. Perhaps that in itself was a happy omen.

---

*I actually did install a radar later.

4.

The Cascade Story

At breakfast on the morning after the completion of the 1965 Trans-Pac race, the crew of the *Hasty*, a Portland, Oregon, entry, and her owner, Duane Vergeer, engaged in a critique of the event and of changes in ocean racing in general, brought about by new designs, techniques, and materials. One of the crew was Bill Nickerson, a member of the Portland Yacht Club, and a TransPac enthusiast, who commented later:

"The Cal-40s had dominated the race for ten years, and we began to speculate on a new type that would be competitive—and maybe even win in one of the world's greatest ocean races. We, of course, wanted it to be a boat created by those of us who would sail in her—a hometown project, in other words."

Back home, at the Portland and Rose City yacht clubs, the talk went on and enthusiasm became spontaneous. The *Hasty* challenge was accepted by a group of members from both clubs and a syndicate was formed to create the Columbia River's own TransPac entry. Original members included Duane Vergeer, Bud Beggs, Robert A. Smith, Howard Cunningham, Bill Nickerson, Vern Whitcomb, Hank Schwager, Wayne Bagley, Don Doerrie, Dave Cannard, Bill Webber, Merle Starr, Chester Benson, Al McCready, Jim Carlson, Bill Cole, Wade Cornwell, and Tom Green.

Each invested twenty-five hundred dollars in the project, plus hundreds of hours of personal labor. Some of the shares were owned by more than one person, and some members had more than one share. The final model chosen, however, was not a new design, but an off-the-shelf yacht, the *Cascade 42*, which had been designed by syndicate member Bob Smith, a naval architect employed by the Albina Engine & Machine Works, Inc. (a firm well known among yachtsmen for its anchor-handling gear and power takeoffs). Smith had originally designed the *Cascade 42* for Dr. Don Laird, a Portland surgeon, and it had been built by Yacht Constructors, Inc., a small firm owned by three members of the syndicate: Tom Green, Wade Cornwell, and Merle Starr.

The *Cascade 42* at that time was the top of the line of the second generation of fiberglass hand-laid-up yachts produced by this firm, which pioneered in such construction on the West Coast. The company had begun back in the 1950s when five yacht club members had pooled their resources and commissioned a young and unknown designer, Bob Smith, to draw them a 34-foot auxiliary out of the new fiberglass materials. The result was the *Chinook*, a traditional sailboat, of which all five are still afloat. The group incorporated, built a temporary shop and a mold, and pitched in, learning as they went along. After all five hulls were completed, they drew lots to see who would get which hulls. It had been a successful venture, and it seemed a shame to discard the facilities and the winning team, so three of the five bought out the others and embarked on an enterprise to build more Chinook hulls for the sailing public. Several hundred Chinooks were turned out before the design was replaced by the more modern concept, the Cascades, also designed by Smith, the first being a 29-footer.

Of the three partners, Merle Starr was a college professor of mathematics, Wade Cornwell a businessman, and Tom Green a production specialist for the Hyster Company, a Portland-based manufacturer of materials handling and logging equipment. Tom and Merle kept their outside jobs, working in their spare time and during vacations at the plant. Wade became the full-time manager. The plant facilities were enlarged several times, and a fine crew trained.

The original 29-foot *Cascade* was an immediate success, and the partners began thinking of adding a larger model, perhaps with a 40-foot maximum length overall. Dr. Laird, one of the first purchasers of the Chinooks (Hull No. 6, in fact), heard about this and offered to advance the money for the first hull and mold if they would build it to his specifications. But Laird wanted a larger boat, and being a skilled mechanic as well as a surgeon, he brought in a scale model complete to the bunks and galley equipment. The minimum length he needed was 42 feet overall.

So Bob Smith was commissioned again, and the result was the *Cascade 42*, which was born on July 1, 1964. Laird's Chinook had been named the *Falcon*, but he chose *Nova* for his *42*, the first one out of the new mold.

Thus, when the *Hasty* syndicate turned to an off-the-shelf yacht to enter in the TransPac, the best thing available at the lowest cost was the new Cascade 42. The result was the *Nimble*, the eleventh hull out of the mold.

As the syndicate rushed to complete the hull, Bob Smith was heard to exclaim, "Tell Bob Johnson to move over, we're comin' through!" The Bob Johnson referred to was Robert Johnson, Portland millionaire-lumberman, member of the Portland and New York and Lahaina yacht clubs, who then owned L. Francis Herreshoff's famed *Ticonderoga*. In *Big Ti*, Johnson had just set the new record for elapsed time in the TransPac. After a serious lightning strike in the Caribbean, Johnson sold her and commissioned Alan Gurney to design the sensational all-plywood *Windward Passage*, which, under Johnson's son, Mark, became the fastest yacht in the world during her peak career in ocean racing.

Construction on *Nimble* began in 1966 in the shop of Yacht Constructors, near the Portland International Airport, with the men of the syndicate working nights and weekends alongside the shop crew. Ready for racing, *Nimble* was valued at thirty thousand dollars. Her debut in the 1969 TransPac was auspicious. She was the seventeenth boat to finish and placed fourteenth overall and third in Class B. Her posted time was 11 days 15 hours 34 minutes and 14 seconds—not bad for the run from Los Angeles to Honolulu, in any kind of sailboat.

The Cascade 42 found a ready market among buyers who wanted a larger boat for various purposes and were short on funds. The original price of the 42 hull out of the molds, with main bulkheads and chainplates, was only $4,950.

When I first became interested in the Cascade 42, at least four of them were on world cruises from the Portland area. Many others were making long cruises, among them the *Makai*, completed by a

retired airline ferry pilot, Bud Addison, and his wife, Bunny, members of the Willamette Yacht Club. They spent three years outfitting
Makai, doing most of their work in their Vancouver, Washington,
backyard. They had chosen this model after crewing on another
Cascade 42, the *Born Free*, completed by Clarence Perrault, a retired
airline pilot. The *Makai*'s first cruise was made to Central America
and the Caribbean, the Galapagos Islands, South Seas, and New
Zealand.

One Cascade 42 that caught my attention was the *Blanquita*,
completed by Robert Amos, a San Francisco Bay area contractor,
engineer, and real estate speculator, who named her after his wife,
Blanca, a svelte and gracious lady from El Salvador.

As crew member Michael Dolbrin told it in *American Boating*,
Amos had parlayed a lifetime of hard work and some quick profits
into a dream ship capable of racing or cruising around the world.

Dolbrin, who had answered an ad for a crew member to sail
to the South Pacific, describes his first view of the boat:

Blanquita *was $30,000 worth of glistening new white fiberglass, gleaming
aluminum and burnished mahogany. She was sloop rigged, he having
bought the bare hull from a Portland, Oregon, firm and finished her off
himself.*

*She was built to go long distances and make good time. Four bunks
amidships in the main cabin, all deeply recessed. Plenty of headroom. Huge
working chart table on starboard. An ingenious dining table, made from El
Salvadorian mahogany pods, folding down like a giant clam when not in
use. Head and sail stowage forward. Ninety gallons of water in two tanks; a
healthy, well-proven 13-horsepower Lister diesel engine and 65-gallon fuel
capacity (enough to motor 800 miles). There's a large galley area with
gimbaled primus stove, sink and stowage area, and room below floor planks
for endless rows of soup, vegetable, fruit, and juice cans.*

*There's a full complement of sails: big genoa lappers, small working
jibs, spinnakers, two main sails. A Hassler wind vane perches like some
Rube Goldberg trapeze out over the stern (complex as it is, this proved
almost totally reliable and helped cut down on many man-hours of tiller
work).*

*She was equipped with fathometer, two-way radio, every conceivable
replacement part and tool, a dinghy and a life raft. No leaky ship this, but a
solidly-built, well-prepared working sailboat outfitted by a sailing man
who'd won a shelf full of racing cups.*

On a shakedown race from San Francisco to Half Moon Bay,
Blanquita got her first real test, as did her skipper. "Sailing abreast of
the ocean beach, about three miles offshore, we ran into the biggest

waves I have ever seen before or since—massive, glutted, blue rolling tunnels 25 feet high and spitting white foam from their curling crests. Bob cooly angled *Blanquita* into the first comber, she crested, made the long slide into the silent trough, and angled up the next slope. Each wave drew the collective breath from six experienced hands aboard."

The new Cascade 42, had already earned a respectable reputation for seaworthiness, ease of handling, and comfort when I first became acquainted with her. She was a homegrown product, which meant (all patriotism notwithstanding) that I would be able to buy a kit and complete her myself, or at least under my personal supervision, without the expense of freight from other sections. But more than that, she was the best dream boat I could find for the money, on a pound-for-pound and foot-by-foot basis.

But, best of all, I could get started with an initial down payment or deposit of only five hundred dollars, paying for her as the work progressed.

5.

The Agony
and the Ecstasy

After an extended period of negotiations, deliberations, consultations, and cross-examination of the three partners in Yacht Constructors, Inc., I wrote a hundred-dollar check for a set of study plans for the 42-foot model—the first positive step toward an actual decision, and one that, puzzlingly, turned out to be a reluctant one. Maybe I didn't want to end the sweet anticipation that had kept me going for years on end.

Anyway, at that time I was still undecided between the 36-footer and the 42-footer. The 36 was a more popular model, and would have had a more immediate resale value, but somehow I could not picture cramming myself and all my books and belongings into its more confined spaces.

Finally I made up my mind to go for the Cascade 42, and so I made a $500 deposit and put myself on the list for the first available hull out of the mold, which I anticipated would be ready sometime in January of the coming year. The full price for the bare hull, with chainplates molded in, shaft log, and deck stringers, was $4,950. For what seemed like nominal amounts I could also order the floors, keelson, main bulkheads, deck beams, molded freshwater tank, and molded shower and head installed. Altogether I estimated that the hull could be completed, ready for engine and equipment, for about $12,000, a figure which I could afford.

One would assume that with all my previous experience and research I would not mislead myself so badly. It was at this point, after I had committed myself too far to back out, that the trap was sprung.

Recently I reread Jack London's *Cruise of the Snark*, which describes his experiences with boat-building sharpies. He estimated his probable cost at seven thousand dollars in 1906; the *Snark* cost more than thirty thousand and was uncompleted when London departed San Francisco for the South Pacific. I estimated twelve thousand in 1972; the project came closer to fifty thousand. Afterwards I realized that it would have been cheaper to purchase a stock boat from a production builder, or at least to save half the cost by shopping for a used vessel.

But I didn't.

London laid the keel for *Snark* on the morning of the San Francisco earthquake. The genesis of *Wild Rose* was not quite so earthshaking. As I learned later, another customer had backed out of his deal for a Cascade 42 sloop, leaving the firm with the hull still in the mold. I had originally wanted a ketch, but was talked out of it in favor of a sloop. Undoubtedly this friendly persuasion had its bias in builder expediency. This was the first of a number of compromises that developed primarily for the convenience of the builders rather than through the judgment of the owner. I am told that this is not uncommon in the trade.

Thus, I was informed to my surprise in October, that "my" hull was ready some four months ahead of schedule—which also is uncommon in the trade. This moved up my financial schedule and began crowding me, but with a payment of thirty-five hundred dollars around Christmas I was back in business again, keeping up with progress on the hull.

I was in good shape then and determined to keep it that way. In general, it was a pleasure doing business with and working with the partners and crew in the little shop on the Columbia flood plain that winter. Everyone seemed personally interested in my boat and went out of his way to be helpful. Because of this, I suppose, I became lax in supervising the progress and especially the accounting. When I received the next statement, in March, with a "partial accounting," I was stunned by a twelve-thousand-dollar bill —having not even $100 in the bank.

The situation was entirely my own fault. My only excuse is that I was near exhaustion, physically, spiritually, and mentally from months of trying to carry on three exacting jobs seven days a week. One should not start this kind of project until he knows he has the finances available. He should contract for only those parts and subassemblies which are standard production items. He should not permit any cost-plus work to be done on his hull in the builder's shop. Builders charge for this by the hour, which is usually two or three times the hourly rate they pay their workers. Get the hull completed only up to the point where custom labor is required, then move it immediately off the builder's premises, set it up in a convenient place, and then hire *your own* craftsman. Often you can hire the same employees to work for you part-time at nights and on weekends, for a fraction of what the same labor would cost in the builder's shop.

Another practice, common to both boat building and private airplane maintenance, is the old tradition that the workers keep record of the time spent on your craft in a special book. If there are several craft in the shop, with workers jumping from one job to another, they almost certainly will record full time for their work on each craft they hop to. This is especially true if the workers are getting paid by piecework. All shops do this, so even though it is dishonest, it is accepted. However, you do not have to accept it if you are careful and keep a taut line on costs.

Obviously, the sooner I got my boat out of the shop, the more I would save on costs. I tried to hurry things along, but the work went agonizingly slow, interrupted by other jobs that came in, and delayed by growing material and parts shortages. Instead of a March launching, it began to look like late May.

Meanwhile, in my feverish state I suspected that the delay was caused mainly to keep my boat in the shop as a floor demonstration to sell other prospects. For weeks my hull was subjected to a daily procession of dreamers, curiosity seekers, cigar-chomping dudes, dentists and doctors, bearded hippies, and erstwhile yachties, crawling under, climbing through, poking into every compartment, getting in the way, distracting the crew with questions and me with insipid remarks—all this sales promotion being subsidized by me. I began to feel like a drowning man, gasping my last, reaching out for rescue, which could be realized only when I got the boat out of the shop and away from the vultures and harpies.

After I had got a handle on costs and progress, there were

many advantages to being in the shop. At hand and convenient was a complete stock of hard-to-get screws, bolts, small parts, and tools, only a few steps away, and at a reasonable price. Moreover, the management and crew were unfailingly ready to show me an easier way to do something, based on their long experience. I was not charged shop rent, and the plant was open nights and weekends. Not the least advantageous factor was the availability of equipment and gear at reduced prices, sometimes even at wholesale prices, and of a quality British equipment imported in large quantities at competitive prices.

At times I had to battle for my own choice in equipment, and to get my own way. Sometimes the shop went ahead and installed things their own way, presenting me with a *fait accompli* which I would have to tear out and redo at my expense. I have definite and unswerving opinions on many things, and among these is that I will not permit copper tubing to be used for fuel and butane lines. These were installed over my protests, and I promptly ripped them out and reinstalled flexible high-pressure hoses at extra cost.

The shop's idea of a 12-volt electrical system was truly that of a pre-World War II sailing man. I redesigned and installed all the wiring myself. No provision was made for removing the engine shaft in case of a break. I had a small battle over this one, and another over my insistence on a flexible shaft coupling. Another controversy arose over my insistence on an automatic bilge pump before launching. I was told I would only need a vacuum cleaner for the bilges. I ordered bronze through-hull seacocks on all hull penetrations, but brass gate valves were in some, and in the case of exhaust fittings, no valves were installed "because they are above the waterline."

And so it went, week after week, month after month.

Much of the frustration was due to shortages, inflation, and poor quality of much marine equipment and parts. Often I would wait weeks for delivery of an order, only to find some vital part missing, requiring more delays and telephone calls and correspondence. Pride and dependability seemed to have been two qualities abandoned by manufacturers. I found much marine equipment of poor design, worse quality, and incredibly overpriced. For example, a six-hundred-dollar marine head arrived without a single piece of instruction for installation of its complex mechanism, without a parts list, and without a special high-amp solenoid switch. The navigation sidelights, designed for recessing into the side of the trunk cabin, did not have enough overlapping lip to cover the hole necessary for recessing them. The horn turned out to be made of pot metal. A cabin light fixture, of popular brand, costing fifteen dollars, disintegrated into pieces as I unpacked it. The Plexiglas cabin windows were covered by protective paper with a glue so tenacious that the paper could not be removed without scratching the surface of the windows. I tried every known solvent without success. Some of the glue remains on the windows to this day, impervious to the worst weather and sea conditions.

The fuel and water pumps, without exception, burned out impellors immediately during initial tests. I paid eighty dollars for a stainless sink that I later saw advertised for thirty dollars in a Montgomery Ward catalogue. Many standard items of rigging called for had been discontinued, and substitutes could not be found. Other standard parts, such as bronze turnbuckles, were priced at forty dollars apiece, plus toggles at twelve dollars each—quite a markup for an item that costs about two dollars to manufacture. It was impossible to find the proper size sheaves for running rigging: not manufactured any longer. The expensive gimballed stove was built with the hose attachments in the rear, so that it was impossible to check for propane leaks once installed. Marine-type cabin light fixtures were costly beyond belief, but I solved this by shopping in trailer parts stores where the same ones can be bought for half the price. The marine diesel engine came without the proper filter and hoses, and with a parts and operating manual I'm sure was put together by a backward grade school pupil, with most of the instructions applicable to models other than the one I bought.

Like Eric Hiscock, the famous voyager, I found that nothing ever fit the first time, nothing ever worked the first time, and nothing ordered ever arrived complete or on time.

On launching day I again checked to see if the bilge pump was working, and also rigged up an anchor and line in case of engine failure, much to the amusement of the shop crew and hangers-on. The crane lowered *Wild Rose* gently to the water. As the skies emptied in a late-spring deluge, I toasted the occasion with a few friends and a couple bottles of champagne. Then, light-headed and gay, I started the engine and maneuvered out into the channel.

The engine quit cold. Air in the fuel line. We tied up again and bled the lines. The second departure got us a little further into the channel. The engine quit again. Air in the lines. Fortunately, I had the anchor ready, which saved us from drifting aground. We bled the lines once more, started up, and headed out again. After a few preliminary maneuvers to check the steering, I put into the dock to let off some guests. At the dockside, the shaft pulled out of the engine coupling. Someone had forgotten the set screws and safety wiring. The shaft slipped back until the prop rested against the skeg. Water gushed into the engine compartment.

That's when my foresight in demanding an automatic bilge pump saved *Wild Rose* from sinking on her initial launching.

Getting a tow back to the crane, we hauled *Wild Rose* out and reinstalled the shaft. Then we had a second launching, this time without champagne. I was thankful for one thing: My bride had to work on launch day and could not be there to witness all our misadventures.

Half an hour later we ran aground on a mud bank on the way to the marina. I was able to back off. At the marina, we no sooner docked than the engine quit again. Air in the fuel line.

For the next three months I fought that "Red Devil" in the engine room, bleeding lines repeatedly and reinstalling fuel filters, lines, and fittings. Nothing worked. The engine would run for about an hour, then quit. I changed filters. This did not help. I appealed to the factory and received an asinine form letter instead of usable advice. Obviously I was going to have to fight for my warranty rights.

At last, after a frustrating summer during which most of my spare time was spent trying to get the engine to work, I accidentally discovered the source of the problem: The machine screws holding down the top of the fuel pump had never been tightened at the factory. The engine had gone through final assembly and inspection and testing this way, and had then been covered with a heavy coat of paint which hid the defect.

Lost were three months of time, a couple of hundred dollars in spare parts and hired help, and all the good weather for the season.

Meanwhile dozens of other defects showed up. The pressure water pump was defective and had to be replaced; the main line from the combination hot water heater came off and flooded the engine room; the rudder tube leaked and filled an aft compartment; the hinges pulled out of the cockpit hatch covers; the propane storage proved inadequate and inaccessible, and I had to redesign and reinstall new tanks on deck; the main engine shaft developed a wobble at certain speeds; the bow pulpit, which was to have been installed by the shop, wasn't, and it didn't fit; the custom-made drawers did not fit—if closed, they could not be opened, and if opened, could not be closed; the fiberglass water tank had not been steamed out and I was stuck with a resin-flavored water supply.

One of the few bright spots in this endless tale of frustration was the discovery of the mobile-home and trailer-parts industry. Unlike some marine suppliers, this industry offers a wide variety of parts and equipment that can be substituted easily for many marine items, at a fraction of the cost. I made a few fortuitous purchases. I found an anchor windlass and capstan in a surplus equipment catalogue for a hundred and ninety dollars that works just as well as a nine-hundred-dollar marine model of the same capacity.

Once the decision is made and you are hooked, and it's too late to turn back, you have no choice but to sail on and make the best of the bad weather. Sooner or later you learn to be philosophical about the whole thing, and even take pride in the result, as did Slocum, Pidgeon, O'Brien, and even Gerbault, none of whom could say they sailed in a finer ship than *Wild Rose*.

We have since come to believe that she is a basically good yacht, and her performance has been all we had expected. What more can you ask? Out of all the misery, the agony and the ecstasy, has come a more intimate knowledge of her parts and peculiarities than we could have got otherwise.

As with any expensive mistress, you either have to live with her or kick her out. We plan to live with her for some time to come.

Part Two
WILD ROSE GOES ON TRIAL

Of morning, pierce the Barcan wilderness,
Or lose thyself in the continuous woods
Where rolls the Oregon, and hears no sound
Save her own dashings . . .

Thanatopsis
William Cullen Bryant

6.
Shaking Her Down

It is now late September, a damp, foggy Saturday morning. We should have come aboard last night to get settled and organized, but there had been too many chores to do at home. With both of us working in town, as we have been for so many years, Friday night comes as the whiplash from a week of tension and exhaustion and ragged loose ends. Only an established routine makes this bearable. To break the routine creates a sense of something being wrong, out of place. So, for now, we don't fight it. This is only to be a trial run or a shakedown cruise—and under power only, as we do not yet have the mast and rigging on.

So after a routine evening at home, and a good night's sleep, we have got up early, packed some things, and driven the thirty miles from our home in Beaverton, over the Tualatin Mountains and Cornelius Pass, down to Multnomah Channel, one of the

Columbia-Willamette waterways, to Greg's Moorage, where *Wild Rose* awaits our pleasure.

We are a little self-conscious about all this. It seems a little unreal, even this routine shakedown cruise. Such an event has been for so many years just some vague dreamy goal. Now here we are, about to depart downriver to the ocean aboard the real thing. It is not a letdown, exactly; just difficult to adjust to, this idea of actually taking a dream ship, on which so much time and money has been spent, and so many years of yearning, on her very first cruise.

More like a trial run than a shakedown cruise. As a lad I had been an outfitting foreman in one of Henry Kaiser's shipyards and had gone out on dozens of trial runs on Liberty ships and C-4's. It seems to me that this is what we are now doing—making sure the systems all work and turning up the defects.

When you make a shakedown cruise, you are going somewhere and are reasonably certain everything does work. And shakedown cruises have a way of shaking down the cruisers more than the ship. We have no glorious voyages and exotic landfalls in mind for the time being, but to us this trial run is one of the most important things we will do this year. It will tell us something about our ship, and something about the concept of living aboard, cruising aboard, and perhaps of someday a retirement afloat. And something about ourselves and our intentions.

We have talked about it for years, this getting away from it all, not just in terms of boating but as some vague notion of a "better way of life." A person's age seems to have little to do with it. When I first arrived in the Pacific Northwest, riding the rods at nineteen, I was looking for the same thing; and it manifested itself in efforts to ship out on a freighter to the Orient, the South Pacific, Alaska, anyplace, to say nothing of an attempt at a homestead on Indian Island in the Puget Sound area.

These things come back to us again as we complete our stowing of food and gear, and all the little preparations of departure. Finally, at 10 A.M., I start the little Westerbeke which had given me so much spiteful trouble at first, the lines are loosed, and we back out into the channel now crowded with weekend boaters, loose at last from the umbilical cord of shoreside power to which *Wild Rose* had been tied all these months she was being born.

Multnomah Channel splits off from the main Willamette River about three miles above the confluence with the Columbia, and it winds some twenty miles down between the mainland Oregon side and the west side of Sauvie Island, to rejoin the Columbia at St. Helens. It is a low period now, with our draft of five and a half feet or more, something to keep in mind. That is the main

UPPER MAST—The construction and rigging arrangement of the mast are shown in this detail. Note that with a hollow wooden mast I was able to taper the upper section for more efficiency and lighter weight. The spreaders are shown in detail with inner attachment to the combination shroud tangs, which are attached with screws and a heavy through bolt. The spreaders were designed for easy standing or sitting by a lookout. Note the handholds bolted above the spreaders. Provision was also made for four signal halyards, and two spreader lights which are controlled by separate switches. Not shown are the aluminum mast steps, which I later designed and installed for ease of climbing the mast alone.

reason we do not run right down the channel to St. Helens. I have already been aground with *Wild Rose* once—on the way over from the launching crane to the moorage. I do not like the feeling.

So I come around and head up past the lines of floats and moored boats toward the Willamette, round the dolphin, and set a course down the Big Bend ship channel toward the big river, going the long way around.

The little auxiliary runs sweetly at an easy 1,300 rpm, which is translated to about 650 rpm at the prop through the reduction gear. It is a joy to run, now that my little Red Devil and I have got acquainted and understand each other. She pushes *Wild Rose* along effortlessly, without the hammering that so many auxiliaries so annoyingly provide.

Outwardly our 42-foot dream ship shows little of her sleek, efficient, and functional beauty. She looks something like a demimonde awakened too early on a dull morning and before the cosmetics go on, for *Wild Rose* is barren of mast, rigging, and sails, and festooned with temporary fenders made from discarded auto tires; with much disconnected electrical wire deadened temporarily, equipment lashed down for the trip and not yet permanently installed. Her cabins are jammed with loose parts, spools of ropes and plastic tubing, anchor lines, cooking utensils, paint cans, clothing, food, and stereo cassettes.

I have purposely not stowed everything away. I want all compartments accessible quickly for any emergency that might appear. We have put our sleeping bags and personal toiletries in the aft cabin, leaving the rest of the vessel pretty much as she has been all during the outfitting period. Even much of the electrical system is only temporarily installed, so we can see if it all works and is all installed in the most logical and convenient places before securing it permanently. Many of the fixtures we wish to live with awhile to make sure they earn a permanent place in the shipboard scheme. I recall, for example, that back in the 1930s, before they began their life afloat, Bill and Phyllis Crowe lived aboard their *Lang Syne* even while the planking and timbers were being installed on the beach at Waikiki.

I stay well out from the stubble of broken piling, exposed by the low water in ominous clusters, pick up the range markers on the Post Office Bar, then change course to the Kelley Point marker where the Willamette enters the Columbia.

The low, dirty-looking scud and mist is breaking up, with some sky showing. The air is still crisp. There is a fresh northwest breeze coming up against the current, which has increased now that the tide has turned. Debris from upstream sawmills swirls along in

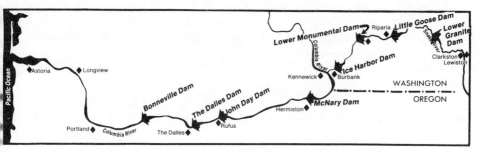

INLAND CRUISING—The Columbia-Snake River system is one of the most extensive and least-known inland cruising areas in the United States. Through a system of dams and locks, ocean vessels can now penetrate more than 400 miles to Lewiston, Idaho, from the mouth of the Columbia.

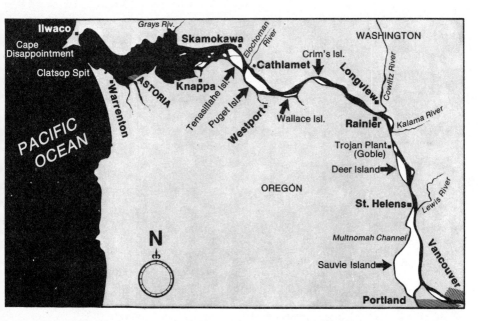

LOWER COLUMBIA—The waterways of the Lower Columbia from Portland to the sea are shown here in more detail. The distance from the mouth of the Willamette River to the Columbia bar is about 96 nautical miles. The lower estuary is about 20 miles long and in places about 9 miles wide. The effects of tides are felt as far up as Portland harbor. The main ship channel is well marked and charted, but the lower 50 miles remains a little-known maze of islands, sloughs, secluded coves and creek entrances, sand bars, auxiliary channels, inaccessible shoreline, log-storage booms, isolated salmon gillnet camps, and the crumbling remains of the salad days of the salmon-packing industry in the late 1800s.

patches. The pungent odor of sulphides from paper mills on the Washington side comes to us on the breeze. There is a vague, tantalizing intermingling of marine scents from the Columbia, although we are more than ninety miles from the ocean. We pass two or three skiffs carrying salmon anglers, who salute us. A large Corps of Engineers tug throws a solid four-foot bow wave against us.

Then we pass the mouth of Columbia Slough on the starboard side, and the new marine park at Kelley Point. The current accelerates. We come abreast of the Kelley Point marker and Belle Vue Point on the northeast hip of Sauvie Island; the ominous swirling of the Columbia passing over the entrance reef at the mouth of the Willamette grabs *Wild Rose*, and she fends off easily, as we move out into the great river with its traffic of ships, barge tows, tugs, weekend yachts, and fishermen.

We are underway at last. It is time to set a course on the range, relax and savor the moment of the start of our voyage down the Columbia to the ocean.

7.

Kelley Point
to Westport Slough

Although the Willamette, on which the city of Portland is mostly situated some nine nautical miles above the mouth, is a great navigable river, when you first enter the Columbia all else diminishes by comparison. You feel not only its power and strength, but the subtle impact of a pulsing artery that extends all the way from the continental divide of the Rocky Mountains and dominates a region of three hundred thousand square miles—steeped in commerce, fisheries, industry, history, and tradition. It never fails to awe me.

From the mouth of the Willamette at Kelley Point, about four and a half miles below the interstate bridge at Vancouver, Washington, the Columbia bears northward and slightly west until it passes the cities of Rainier, Oregon, and Longview, Washington; and from there on it flows westward to the ocean, penetrating the low, heavily forested coastal mountains, the last twenty miles being brackish estuary with scattered, shifting sandbars and low wooded islands.

It is 51.3 nautical miles from Kelley Point to Westport Slough; 77.5 miles to Astoria's West Basin; and 94.2 miles to the lightship *Columbia* off the river entrance. The Columbia is also navigable, through the lockage of four dams, to the Pasco-Kennewick complex and the Hanford atomic works, 285 miles above the mouth; plus another hundred miles through four more dams on the Snake River, to Lewiston, Idaho. Small vessels can continue on up the Snake for another 50 miles or so to the lower end of Hells Canyon. So a yacht of reasonable size, if its masts are not over fifty feet tall, can navigate approximately 500 miles inland from the ocean, almost to the continental divide; not counting the Willamette, which is navigable for the lower 50 miles, nor any of the Columbia above Pasco-Kennewick.

Detailed charts cover all of this river waterway, although a comprehensive, up-to-date cruising guide has not yet been prepared as of this writing. The new system designation for charts covering the lower river are NO 18521, NO 18523, and NO 18524.

The Willamette River light at Kelley Point, mile 88 on the Columbia, is located at 45° 29.2′ North and 122° 45.7′ West, and is about twenty-five miles closer to the ocean proper than is Seattle, Washington, which perhaps explains why the ports of Portland and Vancouver actually handle more tonnage than any others on the West Coast.

Right now, because of a shipping strike, half a dozen ships are riding high at anchor in North Portland Harbor, a couple of miles above Kelley Point, as we turn downstream and pick up the Willow Range markers, with Sauvie's east shore to port and Washington on the starboard. Sauvie today is a low, diked island about twenty miles long and ten miles wide, half of it consisting of truck and dairy farms, and half of marshy, channel-entwined wildlife refuge. It was the ancestral home of the now-extinct Multnomah Indians, and was first seen by Captains Meriwether Lewis and William Clark in 1805, who called it Wappato Island after the aquatic root the Indians harvested and traded in, and camped there. It later became a Hudson's Bay Company pasturage and the site of some early colonies and trading posts.

It is perhaps best-known today for its sandy shoreline, called "Social Security Beach," because it is inhabited year round by retired senior citizens in little clusters of beach tents, chairs, campfires, and long rods spouting out of holders stuck in the sand, as the owners smoke, pass the time, reminisce, and wait for the sometime strike of a salmon or steelhead, to be announced by the tinkle of the little bell on the end of the rod.

The pulsing river holds our keel and hurries us on toward the ocean. I turn the wheel over to my timid bride, who clutches it warily and then, discovering that it takes only the pressure of a little finger to control all 11 tons and 42 feet of *Wild Rose*, quickly finds confidence. For the rest of the run, in fact, I am pleasantly surprised that she would rather steer than do anything.

Indeed, *Wild Rose* handles beautifully under power. Although of moderate displacement, and a fin-keeler, she has excellent lateral and longitudinal stability. I attribute this to the basically conventional underbody, and also to the large skeg and rudder.

We are making good time, seven or eight knots plus the current, as we line up on the Henrici Range and soon pass the entrance to Bachelor Island Slough. Then Warrior Rock Light comes up to port, and the mouth of the Lewis River on the starboard side, with its "hogline" of anchored fishing boats on the bar.

We pass Columbia City, a small sawmill settlement on the Oregon side, take up the Martin Island Range, turn onto the Kalama Upper Range at Martin's Bluff, bucking the usual windy chop, and bend around to the north of Sandy Island. The enormous cooling tower of the Trojan Nuclear Power Plant looms up, its fat hourglass shape dominating even the hills behind. We follow the channel close to the Kalama side, through a scattering of private boats. Coming downstream fast behind us is a large ship, filled with grain, rolling up an ominous bow wave. As the river bends around to the Oregon side, opposite the mouth of the Kalama River, a half-mile-long log raft towed by a tug appears in center channel. Then, to my consternation, I see coming upriver another large steamship, riding high on her Plimsoll and boring on. By some awful coincidence, it looks as if we will all converge off the Trojan tower. There could not be a worse place to meet on the whole lower river.

At this low stage, the sandbars lie exposed, along with old pilings and scattered large boulders. I do not know which way to turn and I do not have much time to make a decision. Poor judgment leads me to run inside the dolphins off the Kalama, and run through the scattered anchored fishing skiffs. The inevitable happens. With a sickening, slithering stop, *Wild Rose* goes aground on the bar, under the worst conditions—an ebbing tide and current from the upstream side.

As she stops, her wake catches up and boosts her further onto the soft sand and mud bottom. Meanwhile the two ships and the tug are maneuvering past each other. How they're going to do it I cannot imagine. They loom up so large they seem to fill the entire gorge between the wooded bluffs. Yet perhaps it's the perspective, foreshortened as it is, that deceives me into thinking that in a moment they are all going to pile up into a monumental heap of logs, superstructures, and iron plates.

But they pass without incident, the ships going up and down, and the little tug chugging along with its log raft in tow and half submerged. *Wild Rose*, meanwhile, is still stuck in the mud and sand. I throw up my hands, with all the release of weeks of frustration and impatience.

"Now what, for God's sake!"

"Don't excite yourself," quoth my bride. "Just cool it. We'll get off."

She is right, of course, and help is coming at us about fifteen miles an hour via the huge bow wakes of the passing ships. The first one hits us and lifts *Wild Rose* four feet up on its crest. That is all I need. I gun the engine, and the little Westerbeke jumps to full power. *Wild Rose* lifts out of the mud and sand and starts forward. I swing the bow around toward the middle of the channel and get out of there fast, porpoising violently through the successive waves and rebounds.

It is no sweat. There is no damage, except to my pride and confidence. The ignominy of making a stupid ass of myself in front of all those fishermen and, no doubt, the amused people on the bridge of the passing ships! Worse yet, it is the second time I have run *Wild Rose* aground, before she even has a dozen hours on her log. I am still not used to that sailboat draft.

Free once more, we roll on down, passing the log raft, then we pick up the Longview Range and hurry by the complex at the mouth of the Cowlitz River, running under the soaring bridge and by the ships anchored off the wharves.

Below Longview the river is streaked with ugly foaming pulp waste, but the beaches are crowded with weekend plunkers. We pick up the Cottonwood Range, pass Lord Island and Walker Island on the left, and Fisher Island on the right. Next comes the mouth of Coal Creek Slough at historic Stella on the Washington side, and the upper end of Crim's Island, site of a number of old Indian villages where in the past we have dug up doughnut-shaped net sinkers in the same places the ancients once camped and fished.

Few people know that as a young man none other than Captain Joshua Slocum himself built gillnet boats and fished for salmon here on the lower Columbia, back in the salad days of the packing and canning business. He claimed to have been the original designer of the traditional 25-foot Columbia River gillnet boat, but there is plenty of documentation that says otherwise. In any case, it was a fascinating period of his life, which Slocum fans would have liked to know more about.

Much later, with a family aboard, he arrived in the Columbia from the Okhotsk Sea with a load of salt cod bound for the Portland market. His vessel then was the beautiful schooner *Pato*, meaning "duck," which he had acquired in the Philippines. The *Pato* had been built on the model of the famous American racing sloop *Sappho*, which defeated the British *Livonia* in the America's Cup races. The *Sappho* was one of the fastest sailing vessels ever built, and the original owner had copied the lines for *Pato*.

Slocum, his four children, wife, Virginia, and crew left Hong Kong with two nests of dories, sailed through the Sea of Japan to the Kuriles and Petropavlovsk, the Russian port of entry for Kamchatka, a run of 2,900 miles. Off Cape Lopatka they found the cod banks and put over the dories with long lines. In a short time they took aboard 25,000 fish and salted them down. Here, after his wife gave birth to twins, who were stillborn, they ran the Great Circle by the Aleutians for Victoria, British Columbia, and down the coast to the mouth of the Columbia, obtaining a tow upriver by a sternwheeler.

At the lower tip of Crim's Island, which hides the mouth of Bradbury Slough, we pass the site of one of the least-known and strangest episodes of early Oregon history. The site had been named Fanny's Bottom by William Clark, in a puckish mood, after his favorite sister. Five years later, on May 26, 1810, Captain Jonathan Winship of Boston sailed the *Albatross* into the Columbia and with his brother attempted to found a town and seaport on Fanny's Bottom, including a blockhouse armed with a cannon. They planted gardens and attempted to open trade with the Indians. The Chinookian tribes along the river, who controlled the centuries-old aborigine trade, did not like someone muscling in, and let the Winships know this. A fatal confrontation was avoided when the spring freshets swept over Fanny's Bottom and wiped out the fort, post, and gardens. The Winships returned to Boston, leaving the field open for John Jacob Astor a year later.

Coming up on Cape Horn (one of the three Cape Horns on the Columbia) my bride calls me to decide which channel to take —down the north side or Cathlamet Channel, or around the south side of Puget Island. Cape Horn, a long, heavily wooded promontory that drops steeply into the water, will probably be the only Cape Horn I ever double. But *quien sabe*? We would like to stop at the quaint little river town of Cathlamet, as we have in the past on smaller vessels, but the depths are questionable and I have had enough of this business of running aground. I decide to go down the Westport Channel, and this we do in the twilight with a dark roily overcast coming in from the ocean.

At the entrance to Westport Slough we meet the ferry

Wahkiakum coming out. I cannot tell from the old chart I have if there is enough depth or not, but surely we do not draw more than the *Wahkiakum*, and we must stop somewhere, even if it is necessary to anchor off Puget Island or Wauna. The light at the entrance already gleams brightly through the descending mist.

We ease into the narrow channel warily, keeping close to the boomed logs to starboard, and running up the placid waterway between almost overhanging trees. I continue past the ferry landing, hoping for enough depth. Our battery-operated sailboat depth sounder had failed us early in the day, and now that we need it, we do not have it.

I want to get above the ferry landing so we will not be in the way of the comings and goings of the *Wahkiakum*, which is scheduled every hour. As it turns out, we have plenty of water —more than thirty feet, and no problems with tide as it seldom ranges more than two feet here. I come up by the old abandoned lumber wharf, drop the Benson hook far enough off so we can swing free, and hope we have sneaked in without attracting attention in the village up behind the trees. I do not feel in the mood to be harassed by kids throwing rocks or drunks throwing bottles during the night.

I test the anchor to make sure we are secure, then shut down the engine and turn to the shipboard chores. As it is now dark, I hang a battery anchor light. Cut off from our umbilical cord of shore power, we must remember to keep a reserve for starting the engine in the morning. We find it easy to settle down for the night. It has been a long day and we are drowsy. In the quick darkness, only the pale overhead floodlight at the ferry landing casts its glow over the scene. The *Wahkiakum* comes in from a run, takes aboard two cars, and departs again. Its wake bores up the slough and rocks us gently. This will go on all night, calling me out to the cockpit frequently to check our swing.

So far on our trial run all systems seem to be in working order (except the Mickey Mouse depth sounder). We have plenty of hot water from the tank, which is heated by the engine exhaust system. The electric Crown head works perfectly, as do the anchor windlass—a homemade lash-up of mine—and the cabin lights, fridge, and freezer. What more could we ask for?

Rather than bother with the butane range, my bride makes supper with the now dependable Sterno and Sea Swing combination, fixing a prepared casserole and a pot of hot coffee.

"That Sea Swing," she says, "is the greatest invention since the rudder. In fifteen minutes I can cook a meal on it."

Just as we are settled down in the aft cabin we hear a muffled outboard motor coming down the slough, pausing slightly as it passes. I rise and peer out a port, seeing the shadowy form of a skiff with two men crouched in her. Gliding by, one of the men shines a flashlight over *Wild Rose* from stem to stern, examining her in detail. I duck my head back as the light splashes across the port, and after they have started up and gone on again I break out my little 20-gauge shotgun and place it in a handy spot.

I am awake when the skiff returns at 1 A.M., and get up to watch it pass, this time without using the flashlight on us. The men are, of course, fish pirates on their clandestine rounds. There is no other reason for anyone to be going out on the dark Columbia in these parts in the middle of the night in a small skiff.

8.

Around the Lightship

At daybreak we got up to find Westport Slough filled with a heavy
mist. The anchorage is muffled and still, the water glazed, broken
only by the wakes of a brace of mallards. I go out on the deck, now
slippery with beads of moisture, and scatter the mallards. My bride
makes coffee and toast. We prepare for leaving. The Westerbeke
starts on the first light touch. While the engine warms up, I go
forward and bring up the anchor, hitting the deck switch momentarily with a toe to start the capstan turning. The line comes in, drawing *Wild Rose* up. But the anchor seems heavier than it should. We
are snagged. I hit the switch again, and presently the anchor breaks
the surface. On it hangs a huge, thick, rusty logging cable. I secure
the anchor and by hand wrestle the bight of the old cable off the
flukes and let it drop. The exertion of this, so early in the morning,
brings on a sticky sweat and heavy panting.

The tide has turned again and is ebbing. I maneuver *Wild Rose* around and we head down slough past the *Wahkiakum*, which is tied up silent at the landing, and bend around and come out in the broad Columbia. We turn down the Wauna Range, pass the huge pulp-mill complex, and the mouth of Welcome Slough on Puget Island to starboard. This bucolic, winding waterway, aptly named for the friendliness of the local farmers and the coziness of its anchorage, is no longer available to us. Unfortunately, *Wild Rose* needs at least six feet now, and this cannot be carried up the slough during low-water periods.

We make the turn under the Bradwood cliffs, on the Oregon side, and cross the bottom end of Puget Island over to the main channel along the Washington shore. To our port is Tenashillahe Island, large, sandy, and wooded, separated from the Welch Island below it by Multnomah Slough, and from the Oregon mainland by Clifton Channel. During wild winter storms small craft and barges use the secondary channel along the Oregon shore, with Clifton Channel connecting lower down with Prairie Channel, then Knappa Slough and Calendar Slough, coming out into the main estuary again at Tongue Point.

From Puget Island to Tongue Point a stretch of almost forty miles of river, secondary channels, back sloughs, sandbars, islands, and islets remains today almost as first seen by Lewis and Clark. It is remote, little-known by outsiders, a haven for wildlife, to say nothing of poachers, market-hunters, squatters, and refugees from the law. One could spend a whole season exploring it by skiff and not really get to know it.

We pass the lower end of the Cathlamet Channel and run along Hunting Islands past the mouth of the Elochoman and Price Island, behind which lies Steamboat Slough, where we have tied up in the past. We move in close to the light at the entrance to Skamokawa Creek just for a look going by. The quaint and colorful little village of Skamokawa, sprawled in the deep side gorge of this tidal creek, is one of our favorite stops—even though the last time we saw it was during a wild storm, when we had tied up there next to a sewer outfall from the general store up on the road, and had to endure its putrid stench all night long. Now Skamokawa is a haven and anchorage that is barred to us because of *Wild Rose*'s draft. We are beginning to understand that our dream ship is a creature created for the sea, not for pastoral inland waterways.

We come up now on Three Tree Point, and from here on the Washington shore rises abruptly into almost sheer forested cliffs, with the channel up close to shore and deep. Across the way, on the Oregon side, the land falls away into low islands and marshy humps, separated by a maze of tidal channels. In the far distance, the land begins to rise again, in densely wooded steps up to the silhouette of Saddle Mountain on the southwest horizon.

It is raining lightly now, the tops of the cliffs to starboard swirling with dark clouds. We come up on Pillar Rock, a monolith rising conelike out of the water to the side of the channel. It was here that on November 7, 1805, the Lewis and Clark party stopped for the night, their canoes tied up to rocks and their camp clinging to the steep wet shore, in a downpour of frigid rain. Here, in the dawn, Captain Clark climbed to the top of Pillar Rock. With his glass he looked to the west and between rain squalls, saw what the expedition had set for its goal.

"*Ocian in view*! he wrote in his log, in his inimitable syntax and spelling. "*O! the Joy!*"

Today this section of the river is virtually unchanged, outwardly, from what it was in those times. In between had come a period when some thirty-five salmon canneries had operated full steam along the lower river here, and fleets of butterfly-winged gill-netters had plied the channels, and fish camps stood on every island. But that had been in the salad days of the middle 1800s. Now all the canneries are gone, as are most of the fish runs, and all that remains is a stubble of rotted pilings and net racks here and there, and a few poachers. Further down, on Grays Bay around Harrington Point, hidden among the Douglas fir and cedar forests, are the rotting remains of an old ghost town called Frankfort, a remnant of the town-site boom that followed the salmon-packing boom. The last time I made my way into Frankfort—by skiff, for it is cut off from any roads by the rugged terrain—I found a small colony of elderly people living in patched-up cottages, overgrown with vine maple and covered with moss; and one hippie, who had squatted in the old hotel, whose gingerbread porch was collapsing but whose old piano, which had come around the Horn, was still intact.

Pillar Rock today is about half the size it was in Clark's time, however, it having been cut off by man to make room at the top for a cement cap and a navigation light installation. The Lewis and Clark party had also camped here again on November 25, 1805. Having found the lower estuary too stormy to cross, they returned upstream to this point, then crossed over to the Oregon side through the Woody Island channel and went down Prairie Channel, spending a night with a village of Indians on a high promontory above what is now the Knappa Landing.

I have explored this site on the high knoll with the permission of the family which now owns the property and lives in the old two-story house. It was the permanent village of perhaps nine lodges of the *Calt har mars* nation of the now-extinct Chinookians, related to the Cathlamets and the Wahkiakums on the north bank.

The high knoll stretches inland on a small grassy plain, backed by the deeply ravined Coastal Range, where elk and deer were plentiful (and still are). It was easy, after a heavy rain, to pick up artifacts from the old middens, some of which go back perhaps thousands of years.

This is all Chinook country, from the Cascades to the sea. Here the natives lived in permanent villages—in planked wooden houses, not tipis—used canoes instead of horses for transportation, and had a culture and economy that subsisted on salmon fishing rather than buffalo hunting. Archeologists tell me that much of the culture is lost because of the humid climate and the biodegradable characteristics of their artifacts. Even the remains of Fort Clatsop, which the Lewis and Clark expedition built some twenty-five miles to the southwest, did not last into the pioneer-settler era, having crumbled and disappeared under the second growth.

At Harrington Point, the channel changes abruptly, crossing to the Oregon side at an angle to Tongue Point. Now, with the rain letting up and the skies clearing, we see ahead a flotilla of boats riding up on the flood tide. It is a ragged fleet of salmon charter boats, their hundred-day season of fishing off the mouth now ended, returning to their winter quarters at Portland, Vancouver, and other upriver havens from their operating bases at Astoria, Warrenton, Hammond, Chinook, and Ilwaco.

Coming up along the waterfront of Astoria, we discuss whether or not to stop at the West Basin. Since it is still early, we decide to run down to the bar and take a look. Although we are not ready for sea by any means, if conditions are right we might give *Wild Rose* her first taste of the open Pacific.

Passing under the soaring arch of the Astoria-Megler Bridge, we run on down the Tansy Point Channel, bear to starboard along the Desdemona Sands, past the entrance to Skipanon Channel, past the port of Hammond and the Coast Guard station at Point Adams, picking up the line of buoys.

The day now turns sparkling blue and clear of clouds, with a brittle autumn sun shining. The river runs silent and placid, even as we cruise by the inner buoys and feel the slight surge of ocean. We pass close to Red 14, then bear a little to port to pass Red 12 close aboard. The open bar now lies ahead of us, and there is considerable small-craft traffic coming and going. At Bell Buoy 11, we turn to port on the Sand Island Range and continue on to the bar along the red line of buoys.

Wild Rose leaps ahead like a salmon smolt returning to mother ocean. She seems to recognize and feel the need for the freedom of the sea. She takes on a new vigor. I think she is going to like the Pacific Ocean.

Red number 6 comes up, then 4, then 2, and we have passed the last one to the seaward end of the South Jetty. Now we are six miles out from the inner junction, and only three miles from the *Columbia*, which is anchored in two hundred feet of water.

In the gentle swell, with a light northwest breeze, *Wild Rose* romps along. We come up to the north side of the lightship, circle around, and take up a reciprocal course back to the outstretched arms of the jetties. An hour later we are crossing the bar again, in company with some returning fishing boats that gradually overtake and pass us. We turn up Desdemona Sands again and retrace our course upriver past Astoria to the soaring bridge.

We turn in through the narrow entrance to the West Basin and find a convenient berth, bumping up against the float with a heavy jolt. The currents are tricky in this basin, especially for large craft with single screw. I hold her against the old auto-tire fenders, while my bride jumps off and secures the lines. I leave the helm to help her, and as I jump off I hear the water pump whining, but think nothing of it. Later, when I shut down the engine, the water pump can still be heard running. Lifting the hatch, I see the engine compartment under a foot of water. A hose has come off the freshwater heater and the main freshwater tanks are now being pumped into the bilge.

Later inspection shows that the hose clamp had never been screwed up tight on the fitting. When the hose came off, the automatic water pump had come on. It is easily fixed, but worrisome.

We spend the rest of the day in Astoria, and in the morning head upsteam on a flooding tide. In the Kalama and St. Helens section, we encounter a storm front with violent rain squalls, which cuts down visibility to about one length of the vessel. This is where we decided that we need a windshield wiper. We also discover the inevitable leaks that show up in the deckhouse and ports, and I find that a small compartment around the rudder post is full of water which has come in through the stuffing tube under the hydraulic pressure created by the rise and fall of the stern.

At St. Helens we come up the channel on the Oregon side of Goat Island, and as we reach the municipal dock at the Courthouse another violent rain squall hits us. I maneuver in and tie up somehow, getting thoroughly soaked. But then, snug inside with a fire of Pres-to-Logs going in the Cole stove, we are soon cozy for the night and eating a leisurely dinner while the rain and hail pelt down outside.

It is a quiet night, spent restfully—although the bell on the old courthouse tower strikes loudly every hour on the hour, waking us up each time.

Then, in the morning, we complete the last leg of our trial

run, up around Sauvie Island to the Willamette, and up the Willamette to Multnomah Channel and our moorage at Greg's.

It has been a good trial, revealing some minor flaws and raising a fresh perspective. We feel we are now entering a new and different phase in the life and times of *Wild Rose*. There is much work yet to be done—mast, rigging, sails, deck hardware, interior finish, and the like. We are satisfied in all respects. We now also have a better feeling about the future.

Part Three
COLUMBIA RIVER
TO THE STRAIT OF
JUAN DE FUCA

I will go back to the great Sweet Mother,
Mother and lover of men, the Sea.

Triumph of Time
Algernon C. Swinburne

9.

The Dawn Parade

And now, finally, months after our initial trial run down the Columbia, across the bar, and out to the lightship and back, I am back again with *Wild Rose* and ready for sea duty.

I have been awake most of the night, unable to sleep because of the anticipation as the great moment of truth approaches, and because of the all-night hustle and bustle of this crowded charter-boat and tourist center. I finally get up, get dressed, and begin preparations with a detailed checklist:

Seacocks and hose clamps, engine and transmission oil levels, cooling-water reservoir, batteries inspected and well secured for a rough ride, list of radio channels and RDF frequencies handy, *Coast Pilot Number 7* flagged at the appropriate pages, charts from the Columbia River (NO 18159 for departure) to the Strait of Juan de Fuca, paper and pencils handy, flashlight, change of clothes, wet suit for use in cockpit if stormy, Thermos bottles filled with hot cocoa, soup, and cold milk, sandwiches made, binoculars cleaned, sunglasses and antispray goggles in place, water pumps and head checked, gear stowed securely, footboards installed in companionway hatches and taped to keep out water in case a sea is taken aboard, vane and autopilot secure but ready for use, electric fuses checked, decks cleared and emergency anchor lashed ready to use, stays and shrouds checked, running lights, radar reflector, foul weather gear . . .

And so on.

This is the second or third time I have gone over the list, and now I am convinced I am as sea-ready as I ever will be. Ahead lies the first real ocean test of *Wild Rose*, and a single-handed one at that, since two friends who, in the comfort of a dinner party weeks before, had been delighted to accept an invitation to go with me and somehow lost their enthusiasm as the day approached. Not that I blame them. Just crossing the bar in May can quickly dissipate one's enthusiasm for ocean sailing; to say nothing of the often difficult uphill run to Cape Flattery. I am committed, however, because of business demands. It is now or never. The weather pattern for the immediate future is favorable for the run north. I have a few days available. If I do not do it now, we might have to waste part of our prime summer cruising itinerary getting *Wild Rose* up north.

This was to be the first leg of our extensive cruising plans, but my bride could not get away either, because of some commitments to her favorite charity, the Foundation of Retarded Citizens, and I was privately preferring that her initiation into a totally different life of living aboard a small vessel come while cruising the inland waters of Puget Sound and British Columbia, rather than on the hard-slugging uphill climb to Cape Flattery. This time of year anything can happen—if it doesn't it just isn't a normal year.

I had brought her downriver from our moorage in Multnomah Channel below Portland, alone and riding a spring freshet and bull ebb tide in one long day, berthing at Astoria's West Basin overnight. The next morning I had run the twelve miles down past the Skipanon entrance to Warrenton, past Hammond to the bar, but the Coast Guard had closed it because of breaking seas. Already late in the morning, I had run up the channel on the north side to Ilwaco in Baker Bay to wait for a better time, rather than go all the way back to Astoria.

From the lightship *Columbia* to Flattery Light is a straight run northwest about 130 miles, thence 50 miles or so down the Strait of Juan de Fuca to Port Angeles. It is a heavily traveled route, with numerous aids to navigation, several havens of shelter for emergencies, plus the vigilant facilities of the U.S. Coast Guard within signal distance. It is no big deal.

Wild Rose is well founded for ocean travel now. Aboard is a complete set of charts from Sixty North to Sixty South, the latest pilot books and sailing directions, light lists, and tide and current tables. She has electronic communications, direction-finding equipment, and a dependable diesel auxiliary power with enough fuel to go to Alaska and back, even without sails. In the event of a sudden storm closing the bars along the way I can heave to among the offshore fishing fleets. I am familiar with this coastline, with experience going back thirty years, and I feel that I have anticipated every possible contingency.

It is still dark and a low fog bank shrouds Cape Disappointment. To the east the first pale lightening up of daybreak appears over the Coast Range, exposing the black sheen of the estuary and outlining the spidery Astoria-Megler bridge. Here in the harbor, a labyrinth of tall pilings separate the stalls and aisles but linked by pools of misty light from the reflectors above. The stalls and alleyways seem to come to life all at once. Engines roar into life and then settle down to idling throbs. Acrid streamers of diesel exhausts spread up and down the rows of boats.

This is a major fishing center on the West Coast, base for both offshore salmon and tuna fleets. From May until October, it is jammed with boats that parade out over the bar at dawn and return in early afternoon or later, bar crossings depending upon weather and sea conditions, of course. At times, when the infamous Columbia bar is up in all its fury, there is more excitement than expected; but in normal years, from late May or early June until Labor Day, it is usually safe for small craft, if a little forethought and sea logic is used.

Now I am aware of engines rumbling all around me, and my own Westerbeke 4-107 throbs busily under the cockpit sole. *Wild Rose* moves smoothly out. There is a tense moment working into the parade. I find an opening behind the 46-foot charter boat *Wind Song* and follow her out between the entrance lights, bear to starboard of flashing Red 22, and am immediately caught up in the mad race down the Ilwaco channel.

Ilwaco, at the upper end of Baker Bay, was just a tiny obscure commercial-fishing and crabbing village until the 1960s when, under pressure of the booming salmon-charter business, a boat basin was built. Since then it has been enlarged several times and can't keep up with the growth. It is popular with both sport and commercial boats because it is well protected from even the worst weather and is the closest harbor to the bar. It is about three miles down the wind-

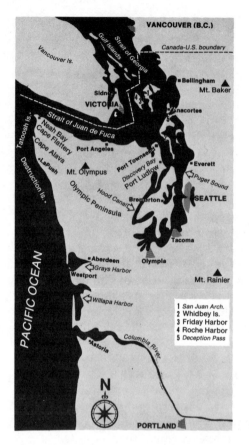

FAR CORNER—Sketch map shows principal features of the Far Northwest coast of mainland United States, from the mouth of the Columbia up around Cape Flattery and the Strait of Juan de Fuca. Wild Rose's first cruise took her down the Columbia and up the coast, around Flattery, and down the strait to Port Townsend.

NORTHWEST CORNER—Sketch map shows orientation of Cape Flattery, 50-mile-long Strait of Juan de Fuca, and the south tip of Vancouver Island. Tatoosh Island lies just off the tip of Flattery. This is the northern portion of the Olympic Peninsula in Washington State. The strait averages about 12 miles wide.

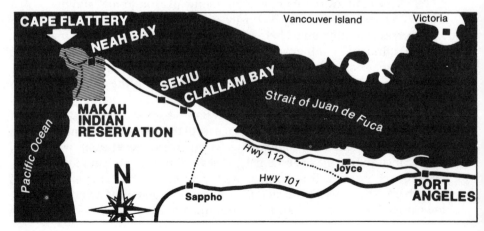

ing narrow channel behind the cape to Buoy 11 off Jetty A, the inner entrance.

This is where the Columbia meets the ocean, after draining a region of almost 300,000 square miles in five states and two provinces. Although the effects of tide are felt as far up as the Bonneville Dam, 150 miles inland, only the lower 20 miles of estuary relate to the sea. This estuary, nine miles wide in places, spanned now by a four-mile-long bridge from Astoria on the south bank, is one of shifting sands and channels, islets and bays. The main shipping channel is now on the south side, although on May 11, 1792, when Captain Robert Gray entered the river, it was on the north side.

Here the legendary Great River of the West at last meets the South Sea, as the ancient map makers of Europe designated them. It is believed that monks from Southeast Asia sailed along here in A.D. 400 on junks driven by winds and currents around the North Pacific, but the first Europeans to see this coast were survivors of wrecked Spanish galleons on the Manila–Acapulco run. Sir Francis Drake prowled up this way in 1579, looking for these rich galleons to plunder, and went on to circumnavigate the globe. This galleon traffic went on for about two centuries, westbound via the trades and eastbound in the higher latitudes to take advantage of the winds and currents.

The interest of the English and Russians in the Northwest Coast prompted the Spaniards to explore northwest along the Pacific coast, beginning with Sebastian Vizcaino in 1604. Northward exploration, mainly seeking a northwest passage through the continent to the Atlantic, was also stimulated by the tales of an old Greek mariner named Apostolos Valerianus, who sailed aboard Spanish ships as a pilot for about forty years, and who took the name of Juan de Fuca because his shipmates could not pronounce his real one. Back home and retired, he developed the story that he had in 1592, on a mission for the viceroy of Mexico, found the long-sought Northwest Passage. Before he could talk the English into financing an expedition with him at the head of it, old Apostolos Valerianus died, but not his tale. Later adventurers for a century and a half sought the Strait of Juan de Fuca and the shortcut between Europe and the glittering markets of the Far East.

In 1728 the Russians, under Peter the Great, sent out the Dane Vitus Bering to explore the eastern Pacific and found a fur empire built around the sea otter, but it is doubtful that any of them got as far south as the Columbia. In 1774 another Spanish expedition, under Juan Perez, sailed north to find the Russians and claim all the territory in between for the king. It was Perez who established the first post on Nootka Sound, on the west coast of Vancouver Island.

On August 17, 1775, when the first shots of the American Revolution were echoing around the world, Lieutenant Bruno Heceta, commanding the *Santiago*, hove to off the entrance of the Columbia, realizing by the outflowing of fresh water and debris that the bay must have a river flowing into it, and made a crude chart of the area, which had a great east–west distortion. He named the headland on the north Cape San Roque (now Cape Disappointment), and the low cape to the south Cape Frondoso, or Leafy Cape. This later became Point Adams and is now the low grass and sand Clatsop Spit. Heceta christened the indentation the Bay of Our Lady of Ascension, for the feast day on which he arrived.

Most of the crew were so ill with scurvy that they could not handle the anchor or man the ship's boat. Moreover, from seaward, even on a clear calm day, the entrance is impossible to discern for any distance. During the night, the heavy outflow carried the *Santiago* far out to sea, and Heceta set course for San Blas. For the next two decades this indentation was known as Heceta's Entrance, and some navigators suspected a large river here, but few of them wished to take a chance on trying to enter.

In the spring of 1778, the great oceanographer Captain James Cook arrived off the Oregon coast on his third Pacific voyage, making his landfall off Cape Foulweather. Continuing north along the coast, he missed the entrance of the Columbia entirely. Cook's voyage did result in opening the Northwest Coast to a polyglot fleet of free-booting English, French, and Yankee trader-adventurers, beginning with Captain James Hanna, who came in the English packet *Sea Otter* from Canton in 1783. He was followed by Captain John Meares, who built the first ship on the Northwest Coast, which he named the *North West America*; and by Nathaniel Portlock, George Dixon, James Strange, and William Barkley.

Meares almost discovered the mouth of the Columbia, but refused to believe Heceta's chart and renamed the promontory, Cape Disappointment—thus blowing a chance to claim all the vast Columbia drainage for England. The expedition of Captain George Vancouver also explored this phenomenon and dismissed it haughtily as a Spanish pipe dream, again sacrificing the chance to claim it for England.

Meanwhile back in Boston, a group of six local businessmen-adventurers put up fifty thousand dollars and outfitted two ships under the new American flag: the ninety-ton sloop *Lady Washington*, and the ship *Columbia Rediviva*. Inspired by Cook's journal accounts of vast profits in the sea otter trade between the Northwest Coast and Canton, the ships were dispatched around Cape Horn and up to the Northwest via the Sandwich (Hawaiian) Islands. After a season trading, Captain Robert Gray took over the ship and sailed her to Canton to sell furs and take on spices, silks, and tea, and then to continue on around the world in what was the first circumnavigation under the new U.S.A. flag.

Only six weeks after returning, the *Columbia* departed again for the Northwest Coast. Besides the thirty-five-year-old Gray, the crew of thirty-one included five mates ranging in ages from sixteen to twenty-six (one of whom was a rated captain sailing as second mate), and a crew of seaman and artisans ranging in age down to a nine-year-old cabin boy.

From the log of John Boit, fifth mate, age seventeen:

May 12, 1792 [ship's time] N. Lat. 46° 7'; W. Long. 122° 47'. This day at four a.m. saw an appearance of a spacious harbor abreast the ship. Hauled wind for it. Observed two sand bars with a passage between them to a fine river. Out pinnace and sent her in ahead and followed with ship under short sail. Carried in from ½, 3 to 7 fathoms. When over the bar, had 10 fathoms; water quite fresh.

This single bold venture by a tough, competent young Yankee captain-trader in an 84-foot sailing vessel would have enormous consequences, especially after being linked up to the cross-country land expedition by Messrs. Lewis and Clark under President Jefferson. [1]

It is about a mile from the Ilwaco harbor to the Coast Guard station under the lee of Cape Disappointment. Now I am in a solid wave of boats of all sizes and types, stretching the entire length of the waterway from the entrance back to the harbor, all racing for the bar to be the first out. The narrow channel churns with turbulence and rebound wakes, heaping up into angry pyramids six feet high. A stratum of diesel exhaust lies over the scene at mast height. I can barely see my steady-burning light atop my stick. I switch on the Whelen anticollision strobe, more from nervous tension than hope of its usefulness. Its snapping flicker adds to the confusion.

Smaller craft, powered by fast outdrives, crowd around the main body of traffic, leaping and porpoising through the wakes, sometimes a few feet off my rail, sometimes close to the lines of piling on the edge of the channel. I think how similar this is to the morning pileup of auto traffic going into Portland from suburban Beaverton. This is getting out of the rat race?

Suddenly, as if on signal, the parade of boats slows to no-wake speed as we turn the corner past the Coast Guard station. This is regulation, but it also symbolizes the respect and appreciation that all vessels crossing this bar have for the men of the surf and rescue vessels at the station.

Now it is another mile or so to the end of Jetty A and Buoy 11.

The eastern sky has opened up, showing a heavy overcast but clearing in patches. Another parade of boats in sight, coming down from the southeast along Desdemona Sands from Hammond, Warrenton, and Astoria on the Oregon side. Both flotillas come together at the entrance buoy, and from here on the bar crossing begins and it's every man and every boat for himself.

The infamous Columbia River bar stretches out beyond us into the ocean.

CHAPTER NOTES

[1]*For some fascinating reading see* Voyages of the Columbia, *edited by Frederick W. Howay; Bibliotheca Australiana Extra Series; N. Israel/Amsterdam; Da Capo Press, New York, first published as Volume 79, Massachusetts Historical Society Collections.*

The Columbia Redivida, *which means simply the* Columbia *"reborn," was built in 1787 at Plymouth, Massachusetts. According to the National Archives, she was broken up in 1801 and her license cancelled—"ript to pieces" is the way the record puts it.*

The Columbia *was a full-rigged ship, not a brig as she is so often described. She was 83 feet 6 inches between perpendiculars, with a beam of 24 feet 2 inches, and a documented tonnage of 212-8/95. She carried twelve guns for protection, as was common among merchant ships in those days. Her three masts were rigged with full courses of square sails, plus the boomed-out jibs and headsails, and the jigger or fore and aft steering sail on the mizzen. She was typical of the preclipper-ship era, when vessels of her type were often called a frigate when used as a privateer or warship.*

10.
Take a Deep Breath

As we come up on the flashing green light and hear the bell on Buoy 11, I see far out to westward a dense fog bank. The lights on the lines of buoys, which stretch to sea with opening arms, flash intermittently, and I can't tell if this is a signal or just a rhythmical sinking into a swell and rising. To the southwest there is a white frothy line on the horizon. I fear the bar is breaking all across, but now the current has grabbed *Wild Rose*, as if she is a small outboard skiff. There is no turning back even if I wanted to, for the eight-knot maximum hull speed would not be enough to stem this current.

Confidence returns rapidly. After all, I have been over this bar hundreds of times, and have seen a lot worse, and have never crossed it in a better ship. On the crest of the next big swell I can see ahead now and find that the surf is not breaking clean across, but only on the south side along the red line of buoys. Behind the North

Jetty, the bar is relatively easy, and there is a clear opening out to sea.

The two main jetties, thrusting out from Cape Disappointment and Clatsop Spit about three miles, mark the entrance, with the lightship *Columbia* anchored about six miles out. The inner channel is about half a mile wide and maintained at a project depth of forty-eight feet.

Jetty A extends out from the sandy skirts of Cape Disappointment and is designed to deflect the heavy ebb current toward the South Jetty. On bull ebbs this creates a vicious current of up to 10 knots, and a six- to eight-foot chop off the end, extremely hazardous for small vessels.

The North Jetty extending out from the foot of Cape Disappointment is the safest and provides shelter in all but southwest blows. The main danger here is running down the black line of buoys and turning too close to the end of the jetty across Peacock Spit. Sneaker waves at times come roaring down from the north here to sweep the superstructures off ships and overturn smaller vessels. One should never get closer to the end of the North Jetty than a line from Buoy 7 to the jetty, and then only on a flood tide.

Peacock Spit, north of the North Jetty, along with Clatsop Spit, on the inner side of the South Jetty, is a graveyard of ships and boats, and every year the list gets longer.

The tides here vary from as little as three feet to as much as nine feet or more. Where the level of the water must drop six or seven feet in about six hours, the ebb current combined with the river current may run against a 25-knot northwest wind and cause the entire estuary to develop a dangerous chop, but there is shelter of sorts behind the North Jetty. On a southwest wind there is no shelter at all, and most of the worst storms come from that direction.

The entrance all along the inside of the South Jetty is shoal water and can change from a millpond one minute to a raging mass of spillers and combers five minutes later. A boat has no chance at all if caught in this situation. Around the south side of the South Jetty there is fine shelter from all but southwest winds, and I have often fished there over a big salmon hole I know, on quiet placid water, while through breaks in the jetty I could see giant spray-laced plungers marching in across the bar.

No vessel should attempt the bar, either going or coming, on a bull ebb with an onshore swell or fresh wind. I have seen this attempted by all manner of vessels, and have myself been caught on the bar in such conditions at least three times—believe me, it is a traumatic experience.

Small vessels are also subject to a brisk northwest wind that comes up about 10 or 11 A.M. during the summer season, and creates a vicious chop. It reaches maximum velocity in midafternoon and dies down at dusk. A frequent hazard is morning fog. Usually this lifts about 9 A.M., but I have several times seen it hang on all day and through the next night. Once, on a charter boat, we circled the lightship for hours with a Mickey Mouse handheld RDF and never found it.

Every time I cross this bar I have more respect for adventurers like Gray, Meares, Heceta, Baker, Hanna, and hundreds of unknown captains who, without electronics or auxiliary engines, without charts, thousands of miles from home port on the other side of the world, and with often hostile and murderous natives waiting on shore, would even think of trying to sail through the breakers and enter an unknown inlet or river mouth. Theirs were tall ships and they were men who stood tall.

I have caught the tail end of an ebb, but the current is still strong, pulling *Wild Rose* along with it. This strong ebb meeting prevailing onshore wind and swell is the basic problem here. There is a lot of difference between a low tide and low slack, sometimes as much as an hour. The moment of zero velocity is short, but there is a period on each side of slack water during which the current is negligible, and I have not entered this period yet.

Off the mouth and away from the influence of the coast, the tidal current is completely different. Instead of setting one way for a few hours and then the opposite direction, it is a rotary current and over a diurnal period may set in every quadrant. The current at the lightship, in fact, is rotary in a clockwise direction, but is relatively weak there and overrun by the outgoing river runoff.

The Columbia pours an enormous amount of fresh water into the ocean, and often this turbid plume fans out as far as four hundred miles during spring freshets.

The bitter end of this bull ebb that we are all riding out, along with the onshore swell and the churning wakes of hundreds of boats, has created some confused seas. I am in no particular trouble and plan to run right along behind the *Wind Song*, whose skipper I have known for years and fished with often. I will go out along the black line until I am safe at sea, giving Peacock Spit a wide rounding as I have no taste for tempting this unpredictable menace. The surf can now be seen crashing against the end of the North Jetty, throwing spray a hundred feet into the air, but we are all heading for a hole between the buoy line and the main channel, which appears flatter than the rest.

Buoy 9 comes up quickly, and judging from the speed of *Wild Rose*, plus the eight knots or so of current, I expect to be well out to sea in fifteen minutes.

I hear the shrill warning buzzer on the steering console. I

glance down quickly at the engine temperature gauge and see the needle way up in the red range. The engine is overheating. Probably raw water intake has become clogged with debris from the river runoff. This has happened on at least one previous trip, and on the way out I had noticed patches of flotsam. The raw sea water is drawn in through a strainer, then circulates through a heat exchanger, cooling the closed freshwater cooling system. I figure I have only a few minutes before the freshwater reservoir boils over—longer than one could normally expect, since the fresh water is also detoured through the hot water tank used for cooking and bathing.

I have to make a decision: to carry on for a few minutes and get safely out past the end of the jetty, or take a chance on a ruined engine. I decide not to ruin this engine. I shut her down.

Drifting now, *Wild Rose* settles in the water and turns broadside to the swell and chop, rocking violently from side to side. The parade of boats ahead quickly pulls out of sight, and those coming up behind veer off. In the half-light, I cannot accurately judge the current, but a moment later Buoy 7 with its quickly flashing light and clanking bell appears out of the smoke and gloom just ahead. I am bearing down on it at incredible speed, and it is lying at a crazy angle, almost pushed under water by the force of the current, humping up a roll of waves on its upstream side.

We are on a collision course, and a collision with one of these iron obstacles would be certain disaster. I pull the fuel shutoff lever on again and prepare to start the engine as a last desperate maneuver. Then *Wild Rose*, sensing the danger, swings slightly from a hull position to the direction of the drift, and we sail past the buoy with less than three feet to spare. Judging from the speed of passing, we must be drifting at a rate of about seven knots, perhaps more.

Ahead are the last two buoys in the black line, numbers 3 and 1. By the time we come up on Buoy 1, the current has diminished some, but another current has caught us and we are now drifting southwest out beyond the lightship.

It is now safe to work below, and for the first time I am aware of the motion as we lie a-hull in the confused seas. I leave the wheel, jump below to the main cabin and open the access door to the starboard side by the navigation table, and crawl into the engine room. I snap on the overhead light, immediately seeing that the sea water strainer is clogged with mud and debris. Swallowing the sour mash that wells up in my gullet, my head buzzing, I fight off the seasickness. Shutting off the seacock, I unscrew the top of the housing on the Raritan strainer, lift out the filter unit, and instead of trying to clean it there, simply replace it with a new one. I then screw the top back on, open the seacock, and get out of that hot black hole as fast as I can.

It has taken fifteen minutes to accomplish all this, and I am thankful that somewhere back in those dark, frustrating days when I was installing the engine and cooling system I exhibited the unusual foresight to install this lash-up myself and make it easy to get at out at sea.

Topside again, I look around to find that we have drifted well past the lightship, perhaps fifteen miles to sea.

But I look back upon the crossing, doing a quick mental critique, and find I have done everything by the book and cannot fault it. Once again, I think, I have cheated the gods and crossed safely over the bones of ships and men lost here over the past two hundred years: the *Peacock*, the *Tonquin*, the *Nimbus*, *Benson*, *Cavour*, the *Vancouver*, the *Gov. Moody*, the *Rosencrans*, the *Iowa*, the *Potomac*, the *Rival*, the *Ariel*, and even one of the lightships. The list is endless. Sometimes, as with the *Tonquin* in 1811, the ship and some of her men survive but some of the crew are left behind. This does not deter many. Each year the fishing fleet grows larger. Last Labor Day the Coast Guard counted five thousand boats fishing out here on the weekend, with about twenty-five thousand anglers. Each season the bar takes its toll of a half dozen or a dozen of these.

To the southeast rises Saddle Mountain, landmark of so many mariners for hundreds of years. Cape Disappointment now appears as a low promontory, partially obscured by patches of haze and fog. North Head, on the seaward side of the cape, looms up much more prominently. A dense bank of dark fog blocks out the ocean to the west and obscures the Russian, Polish, and East German trawler fleets, well outside the twelve-mile zone as daylight opens up.

I am approximately on the meridian of 124° West Longitude. I punch the starter and the Westerbeke jumps into action with its workmanlike rumble. I turn to a northerly heading, set the speed at 1,300 rpm, lock the wheel, and sit down on the coaming to enjoy a rest and a hot cup of instant cocoa. I will worry later about getting some sails up.

This moment, I realize, is the culmination of years of effort and struggle, and of many disappointments and frustrations. It is a feeling of complete accomplishment and fulfillment that I thought I would never experience.

For the first time *Wild Rose* has broken her landlocked bonds.

11.

Northbound at Last

From the lightship *Columbia* I take my departure on a true course of 340°, intending to maintain about ten or fifteen miles off all the way to Flattery. This will place me outside the busy trolling and charter boat fleets, and inside the main ship lane, I hope. The coastline trends north-west here, this being the farthest-west bulge of the lower forty-eight states. It is subject to frequent fogs at this time of year, which makes the heavy traffic hazardous. When there is no fog, you can usually depend on a prevailing northwesterly swell chopped up by confused currents. Every time I have gone north along the West Coast, it has been an uphill climb all the way. There is no reason to expect anything different this time. My main object, in any case, is to make the approach to the Strait of Juan de Fuca in daylight and on a slack or flood tide.

Right now that seems a far-off thing. After a rather choppy

crossing of the Columbia bar with the salmon fleet, I pick up the 10-fathom line. The fog bank has moved out to the horizon and begun to dissipate. The ocean, except for the wakes of several hundred boats, flattens down and turns pewter-colored in the first light. The hills and sand dunes to the north of Cape Disappointment take form with the rich colors of morning. The sea turns blue then and stretches away to the horizon to meet an almost silvery sky. The bird and marine life become busily active. The sun, rising quickly now on its swing southward, brings warmth to soften the pungent marine scents of the night.

I slow down to about three knots and set the autopilot. Rigging up an eight-foot salmon trolling rod, I tie on a pink diving plane, and to this add a three-foot leader with the standard two-hook herring harness for trolling and mooching here. I pass one of the hooks through the mouth and gill opening of the bait fish, then pull it through and impale it under the backbone behind the dorsal fin. Working the other hook through the lips to keep the mouth closed, I pull the leader up tight through the slip knots until the bait is bent into a shallow crescent. This shape gives it a darting motion in the water which no feeding salmon can resist.

I set the rod into the holder on the aft pulpit and pull out about eighteen "arms" of line as the diving plane takes the bait down to proper depth. Then I set the drag on the reel and go back to the cockpit. For chinook salmon, the angle of line going into the water should be about 45° to 50°, and for coho about 30°. The rest is just a matter of passing in proximity to a frenzied school of feeding salmon. Schooled up here in these bountiful waters, their biological instincts triggered for the coming spawning runs, they become voracious.

Soon there is discordant vibration and I look around to see the rod bent almost double. I leap for the fantail and pull the rod out of the holder, feeling the vibrant power of the salmon come up the line and through the rod to my hands. The taut monofilament line rips through the sparkling water as the chinook makes runs to one side and the other, unable to break loose, then dives deeply as the line peels off the reel against the drag. The water here, however, is relatively shallow, and the fish has no place to go.

He comes up again, rolls and thrashes on the surface, his glistening steel-gray back reflecting the morning sun. As he flips over, I can see the little "sea lice" around his anal fin, the sign of an ocean-feeding salmon.

Later, if he had survived all the hazards of sea and man, on his spawning drive upriver, he would have to live for weeks and maybe months on the fatty energy he had stored up here feeding in the ocean. His gullet would close, as if triggered by nature, and his metabolism would change all his digestive processes into the single goal of reaching the spawning gravel and completing his destiny before dying as a battered decaying piece of blackened flesh.

Nature has provided him with one single purpose for his life, and that is perpetuation of his species. Only one percent of his brothers and sisters will survive to reach the ultimate nuptial gravels far up in the headwaters of the tributaries of the Columbia. Out of one mating pair will come perhaps five thousand eggs on the redds, to start the process over again; and out of these, perhaps only two or three pairs will reach the sea again as smolts.

As I bring him over the transom, he tries one more lunge to escape, but it is too late for him. He has been defeated by a springy fiberglass rod and the open end of a large landing net. He comes aboard, I deliver the *coup de grâce*, and his role in the scheme of things is ended.

I clean my salmon, drawing the intestines and exposing the delicate rich red flesh. I pack it carefully on ice, for thirty pounds of salmon would be far more than I would be able to consume on this trip. I would enjoy broiling steaks from the first fresh fillets, and then perhaps baking a salmon loaf with white sauce, and smoking or pickling what was left. But there is no finer treat than choice broiled steaks off a prime chinook salmon right out of the ocean.

For that I thank my recent adversary, and the sea.

12.
Cape Disappointment to Point Chehalis

Now I have begun to move out of the congested fishing activity, and my course takes me further offshore. On the depth sounder the squiggly contours on the chart are detected. It is my plan to stay inside the hundred-fathom curve and outside the ten-fathom ledge, wherever my heading may take me.

A gentle southwest zephyr appears to ruffle the ocean, and to send cat's-paws skittering here and there. Sea birds are all around me in abundance, some soaring overhead watching for schools of small fish and ball-ups being circled by their predators. I see a storm petrel or Mother Carey's chicken, which I had never observed before. They had been reported by mariners at least as far back as the 1846 Wilkes Expedition in these parts, but I had thought that was an error, associating these little swallowlike birds with Cape Horn and the high southern latitudes, although the fork-tailed petrel is common enough. Gulls, murres, skimmers, the pigeon guillemot, the owlish-looking puffins, auklets, scoters, and cormorants appear in scattered congregations.

I leave the throttle at idle and go forward to wrestle clumsily with my new twin headsails, which I had devised myself totally without any previous experience. These went up on the forestay with staggered hanks, with a five-foot pennant to hold them well off the deck and up in the air, and the clews boomed out with special spinnaker poles I made out of aluminum tubing. I have no intention of ever using a spinnaker, as I always expect to be shorthanded, but I had installed all the rigging and hardware needed for one just as a matter of preparedness or conventionality. I bring the sheets back through snatch blocks to the cockpit winch consoles. The light breeze billows the twins, which are 1.5-ounce multicolored nylon made to my specifications in Hong Kong. I shut off the engine and the silence rings in my ears momentarily. Then I am aware only of the easy snapping of sails and lines, the slithering of the hull through the lapping waves, and all sorts of little sounds, odd noises from the rigging, from below, which I cannot identify but which all seem friendly to me.

Even under light sails drawing almost imperceptibly, *Wild Rose* seems to come to life and become an integral part of the sea. The thrust of the wind surges through her and she seems vibrant and willing, rather than something to be crowded and pushed through the water.

The white and light-blue decks now reflect a blinding glare from the sun and I have to change to dark glasses, though even these do not prevent my squinting. Light decks are fine, and keep the cabin from becoming too stifling in the bright hotness of the summer or tropical sun, but they are also terribly reflective and, I believe, could permanently damage one's eyes without protection.

Wild Rose sails herself easily under the twins with some minor adjustments. From the bosun stores under the starboard cockpit hatch I break out the Allen Wind Wand vane and rudder assembly. This is as good a time as any to complete the installation. I had not installed the rudder assembly before because under power, even going in a straight line, there is some turbulence from the prop around the skeg and main rudder that sets up oscillations and stress points. The manufacturer, in fact, recommends that the servo rudder be removed when under power and moving at five knots or more.

I had chosen the Wind Wand for use on *Wild Rose* for several reasons. After spending months researching the whole concept of self-steering and the availability of various systems, I decided that the Wind Wand seemed most practical for my situation—to say nothing of being the least costly. I had considered all of the commercial models—including the famous Hasler, which was the most successful one since Marin-Marie devised his ingenious lash-up—as well as all the other well-known and highly recommended types. The Wind Wand was my choice because the configuration of *Wild Rose's* after section and transom made installation and maintenance simple, and because the under-$500 price tag was less than it would have cost me to design and build my own. For anyone who has the time and likes to putter with mechanical aggravations, there are books available to help stimulate these inclinations.

I have always felt instinctively that anything that *looks* good *is* good, which is another way of saying, of course, that functionally designed products function well. In this the Wind Wand, with its straightforward arrangement and simple linkage, seemed to measure up; although the real proof was yet to come on future offshore voyages. Anyway, the large wind vane provided an ideal place to letter my boat's name and her home port, and perhaps that was the final reason for my choice.

When not in use, the system can be easily dismantled and stowed aboard. Underway, with a proper apparent wind, you need only trim the sails to desired course, lash the wheel, and pull on the lanyard which leads back to the gear train. The vane sail then immediately catches the attitude of the apparent wind and takes over control of the rudder direction through the servo rudder.

All this, of course, is purely theoretical right now, as I have not yet had the opportunity to test the system. Now ghosting along on a mild ocean with a light southwest wind, the whole lash-up seems spongy on the controls, perhaps because of the light apparent wind and the influence of the large twins flying up there.

But *Wild Rose* is tending herself and I am free to do whatever I wish on ship's business. There is time to break out the Vectra hand-held RDF, and a set of modules for all the radio aids from the Columbia to Port Angeles. The radio beacon system along this coast uses 304 kHz for Cape Disappointment, Willapa Bay, and other stations in sequences; plus 288 kHz for Amphitrite Point, Carmanah, Cape Flattery, Umatilla Reef, and Point Grenville, which would bring up the entrance to the Strait of Juan de Fuca, and including the southwest corner of Vancouver Island. Inside the strait there are 314 kHz, 288 kHz, 296 kHz, and also 1450 kHz for the broadcast station KONP at Port Angeles, all of which can be used and which I have modules for.

This hand-held unit is marvelously simple, accurate, and easily used. It is highly effective from harbor entrances to as much as twenty-five miles out to sea. With so many of these radio beacon stations established on the North American coast, as well as on the Hawaiian and Aleutian chains, I consider it indispensable for 90 percent of the offshore cruising on the North Pacific—so indispensable, in fact, that I was persuaded to buy two of them and a complete set of modules from the Bering to Panama.

I make practice plots with bearings from the lightship, Willapa Bay, and Point Grenville, and the plot comes together so easily and neatly that I am beginning to feel like a real salty mariner.

From North Head the coastline trends northward twenty-two miles to Willapa Bay past a low sandy beach with the terrain rising into heavily wooded hills, the foreshore dotted with clusters of summer homes and resort communities. The entrance to Willapa Bay opens into a large shoaled estuary with shifting channels leading up to the lumbering towns of South Bend, Raymond, Bay Center, and others. A number of rivers empty into the bay. There is much logging and sawmill activity, and oyster farming.

In recent years the bay has been discovered by trailer-sailors who bring in their day boats from all over the Northwest to launch. From seaward, however, the approach is treacherous. Range lights do not always mark the best water and local knowledge is essential. Large lumber ships regularly call at the wharves at the head of the channels, but only with local pilots. The bar currents average three knots but often reach a velocity of six knots. There is good holding ground inside for anchoring.

From Cape Shoalwater to Point Chehalis, the coast extends as a low sandy beach backed by heavy timber to Grays Harbor, which is forty miles northward from Cape Disappointment and ninety-three miles south of Cape Flattery. This bay was first entered by Captain Robert Gray on the Columbia in May of 1811. It, too, is a large shoaled estuary with numerous shifting channels, but more accommodating than Willapa Bay. At the head of the bay are the large towns of Aberdeen and Hoquiam, important fishing and lumber ports. Just inside the entrance, on the south side, is the busy commercial and sportfishing haven of Westport—perhaps the largest salmon sports fishing center in the world. The charter fleet here operates from late April to October and anglers come from every state and province during the peak salmon season. The commercial trolling, gillnetting, and kelper fleets also base here, as do the crab boats.

Grays Harbor is the last good haven of refuge until the Strait of Juan de Fuca. Even so, when conditions are such that one must make a run for a haven of refuge, the bar here can be a real smoker and one that strangers may wish to avoid by staying well outside and heaving to.

Because as a hobby I have been developing an uncomplicated system of celestial navigation for the simpleminded navigator like myself, I had programmed a series of practice celestial sights for the run north. The sun now being at a convenient altitude, I break out the sextant and approach the business somewhat self-consciously. The ocean is so docile, however, that I have no trouble snapping several shots. I do this from the cockpit, where the height of eye would be about ten feet, from the cockpit seats which raise this a couple of feet, and from a position standing on the cabin trunk in front of the mast. I had previously recorded the dip from the Almanac at each of these positions.

Using *Ageton's H.O. 211* tables, I sit in the cockpit as we move along easily under the twins and agonize over the simple arithmetic needed for the work forms I have modified for use by numbskulls who cannot keep even their checkbook balances straight. The first result is an intercept 250 miles from my dead-reckoning position, and away from the body. The second puts me 48 miles toward the body. This would be amusing if it were not so frustrating and disappointing. As for my DR, I have had the advantage of knowing exactly where we are, so the error has to be in the computation. And believe me, I have made every possible bonehead error, and a few that even Admiral Ageton never thought of. As it turns out, I have made the usual mistake—transposed figures from the "A" column of functions in the tables to the "B" entry, and failed to observe a couple of simple rules which were printed right on the work form.

In the end, when I settle down to serious business, the line of position works out to an interception of three miles, which is acceptable in any man's navy, inasmuch as from the cabin trunk I have a radius of vision more than twice that.

From Grays Harbor the coastline trends considerably northwestward. The lightship *Columbia* is at 46° 11.1' North and 124° 11.0' West; Cape Flattery Light lies at 48° 23.5' and 124° 44.1', or 132.4 nautical miles north and 33.1 nautical miles west—about one mile west for every four miles north.

Northward from Grays Harbor there is a long stretch of sandy beach with yellow bluffs behind, but from here on the coastline becomes broken and rocky, backed by low timbered hills. On a clear day, as today, the Olympic Mountains rise up to the northeast in a high misty purple-gray line topped with snow and usually a cloud cap. Copalis Head sticks out thirteen miles northward from Point Brown, near the entrance to the Copalis River. The Moclips River enters six miles north of Copalis Head. Next comes Point Grenville and an indifferent anchorage for small boats in northwesterly blows.

The Quinault River cuts through cliffs just south of Cape Elizabeth, with Taholah, an Indian village, on the banks of the river mouth. There is some skiff and dugout canoe movement in and out of the river, but it is not accessible to larger craft.

Sonora Reef extends southwest from Cape Elizabeth and is to be avoided. Northwestward from the cape, Destruction Island lies about three miles offshore. This haven and obstacle is a flat-topped island about 90 feet high and brush-covered with a few clumps of gnarled trees. Its name was given by Spanish explorers, and for good reason. The light here is 147 feet above water on a 94-foot white conical tower and equipped with a fog signal. An indifferent anchorage from northwest weather is used by local fishermen off the southwest face of the island in twelve fathoms, sandy bottom, with the light bearing between 293° and 315°. If the wind hauls to the southward, however, it becomes a dangerous obstacle and lee shore. But it is the only offshore shelter between Grays Harbor and Cape Flattery.

To Hoh Head it is about 6.5 miles with cliffs rising fifty to one hundred feet. This section of the coast is more scenic, and U.S. 101 highway approaches the beach here, one stretch of it being within the Olympic National Park boundaries.

Quillayute Needle sticks up about 80 feet, marking the approach to James Island, about fifteen miles northwest of Destruction Island. There are many sea stacks and small wooded islets along this stretch. The James Island light is 150 feet above water on the southern side, with a marker radio beacon and fog signal. Lapush, the main Indian village, is up inside the entrance to the Quillayute, which is formed by Bogachiel, Sol Duc, and several lesser streams coming down out of the Olympics. Although I have fished out of here and once did research on sea otters in this area, I would not like to run in or out of Lapush alone.

The coastline is rugged from James Island to Cape Alava, the westernmost point of the continental United States, which projects about 13 miles south of Cape Flattery. Flattery Rocks and Umatilla Reef are located about 2.3 miles northwestward. The famed lightship *Umatilla* no longer is on this station, having been replaced by fixed aids. Mukkaw Bay circles in a shallow bright, with a low neck of land about 3 or 4 miles wide crossing over behind Cape Flattery to Neah Bay on the strait side. Cape Flattery itself is a bold, rocky headland with cliffs 130 feet high, rising to 1,500 feet elevation about 2 miles back. It is flat-topped and looks like an island from the southwest because of the narrow neck connecting to the mainland, which is actually the valley of the Waatch River.

Tatoosh Island is half a mile northwest of Cape Flattery and is 108 feet high, flat-topped and barren. The whole area around these rocks is a milky way of foam in heavy weather, and even in good weather is dangerous because of strong tide rips and reefs. Fishing boats out of Neah Bay often use the passage between Tatoosh and Flattery, but only on the calmest of days.

Off to the northwest, outside the strait, lies Swiftsure Bank on the edge of a submarine valley. It has a minimum depth of ten fathoms and during the salmon season sometimes hundreds of boats will anchor overnight here. It is the destination also of the Swiftsure yacht race from Victoria in early spring.

Small vessels approaching the strait close to Flattery should look for Duncan and Dunze rocks, which lie about a mile off Tatoosh to the north. There is a shortcut through the channel, but in heavy weather, without local knowledge, one should enter the strait north of these obstructions.

13.
Grays Harbor to Destruction Island

By about 2 P.M. I am abreast of Grays Harbor and about ten miles offshore, just outside another flotilla of sport and commercial fishing boats from Westport. The light breeze has freshened to windrows of white against a blue sea. We tool along effortlessly, the gaily colored twins flying full, the wake gurgling happily. It is time to relax and doze off on a drowsy spring afternoon.

Northwest Coast waters, inland and offshore, carry much debris as a result of the intense logging activity and the tidal currents. For a thousand miles along the coast there is always an immediate danger of coming upon loose logs, half submerged, and sometimes whole trees, with roots and branches, rafts of bark, stumps, chips. A hazard indigenous to the region at any time, they make traveling at night particularly, in small craft, at high speed, suicide on the more restricted inland waters. Offshore, where the debris is more dispersed and speed is limited by sea conditions, it poses less of a hazard. At the same time, I am convinced that 90 percent of the casualties each year among commercial fishermen and other professionals results from indifference to this problem. Often these craft are underway on automatic pilot with no lookout while the crew grabs a few minutes' shut-eye. A direct hit on a deadhead always results in severe damage, and often a sinking within minutes.

Even if these craft don't hit an obstruction, they are themselves a danger. John S. Letcher, Jr., in his *Self-Steering for Sailing Craft*, on two occasions was run down and nearly sunk, once by a commercial fisherman on autopilot, and once by a large ship.

Even when loafing along at trolling speed or mooching, I have always made it a practice to keep one eye out for logs and debris. Sometimes a floater can be spotted by the seagulls perched on it, looking as if they were standing on water. Not all deadheads or sinkers are marked by seagulls, however, and any of them can punch a hole in the toughest hull at cruising speed. This was the main reason I had equipped *Wild Rose* with a pair of survival suits designed for North Pacific waters, where one has less than five minutes in the sea before hyperthermia sets in. The suit can be put on within ten seconds over your normal clothes, even over sea boots. In it you can float indefinitely without a raft and maintain a normal body temperature. A batch of the first suits made saved the lives of the crew of a crab boat which capsized in the Bering Sea just after leaving Dutch Harbor.

So when *Wild Rose* suddenly strikes an object and shudders to a stop, my first reaction is to leap for the survival suit. Then, as the bow lifts, I see that we are rising upon the gray, barnacle-blotched back of a whale, and I can smell the foul gaseous odor of the animal. I am immediately panicked, but unable to think of a single thing to do except wait helplessly. Slowly, at last, the whale begins to submerge and I feel *Wild Rose* catch the wind again and surge forward. The surface swirls violently off the port rail, and then fifty yards astern the whale rises again, blows, and disappears. I wait tensely for the huge mammal to come up under me, but the next time it surfaces it is a quarter-mile away.

As are most of them along this coast, it is a gray whale. At one time they were extremely numerous, providing sport and food for the coastal Indians, who went far out to sea in pursuit of them. Distressed or wounded whales also washed upon shore frequently and provided villages with food and oil. One such incident was related by Captain William Clark in a journal entry during the Lewis and Clark Expedition's winter stay at Fort Clatsop. The gray whale summers in the Arctic and winters in the shallow lagoons along the central Baja coast, where the calving is done. They make the five-thousand-mile migration at an average speed of ten miles an hour. Indiscriminate killing reduced the herds to just a few hundred by the beginning of this century, but the United States and Canada, by limiting this harvest, enabled the mammals to increase until they again numbered in the thousands. The Japanese and Russians, however, who kill probably ten thousand or more a year in the Arctic and Bering, have prevented a complete rehabilitation. Even so, the exotic sight of the migrating gray whales continues to delight residents and visitors to the Oregon and Washington coasts.

RDF and sun plots show me to be fifteen miles offshore, but on my heading with the northwest trend of the coastline, land keeps drawing closer. The wind freshens and comes around to the northwest. The twins begin flapping furiously and I now face the disagreeable job of getting them down. At such moments I think of how much nicer a power yacht must be. This is when the routine of a single-hander becomes real and not just a vicarious experience sitting in a comfortable chair at home reading a book.

Getting in the big twins of four hundred square feet each, against the pressure of the wind and the rising sea, very nearly brings me to my first disaster. Even the light nylon is almost unmanageable under the circumstances. I have no choice but to release the halyard and take up the downhaul, letting the billowing cloth drape down over everything and drag over the sides into the sea. Somehow I get the poles loose, pull the cloth aboard, and haul in the trailing lines. *Wild Rose* now rolls in the trough, with the wind-driven tops of whitecaps flying across the deck, soaking me to the skin. My glasses become so drenched with salt water that I cannot see through them. Securing the mess on the foredeck, I get back to the cockpit, start the engine, and come up on course again.

Holding at about five knots, I set the autopilot and go below to change clothes, putting on a wet suit. It is a new outfit and I have not tried it before. I also break out a pair of "foggles" to wear over my glasses to keep off the spray. Then I go back to the cockpit with a sandwich and a vacuum bottle of hot cocoa. I immediately feel warm and comfortable. The wet suit works perfectly and is much more practical than bundling up in heavy clothes, and wearing rain gear over them. I wonder what old Slocum would think of this. I think he would like it, as he was a practical gent and an innovative one, who would never stand on tradition if there was a better way of doing it.

Heavy scattered clouds appear over the Olympics. Offshore on the horizon, a wall of dirty gray obscures the meeting of sky and water. The wind has now come around to 340 and freshened. It is something I expected but hoped would not happen. Further offshore and just ahead appear the topworks of a cluster of ships —the trawlers and support vessels of the Soviet distant waters fishing fleet. They are holding just beyond the 12-mile fisheries zone, I know, until cover of darkness or fog when they will move in close to the beach, drop their trawls, and haul offshore in violation of the zone and various agreements.

It is now late afternoon and I am faced with a decision, one that I should have been thinking about before. The wind has increased to twenty knots, and I am driving into long waves with foaming crests, throwing much spray. I should have gone forward and stowed the twins. They are secure for all normal conditions, but I do not like the worry of it. To continue means a sleepless night, plus an approach off Flattery in the dark, for which I have no taste at all.

Most of my plots at the navigating table below show Destruction Island coming up soon. With the wind hauling more to the northwest, this makes the anchorage off the south side of the island more interesting by the minute. I check the chart and alter course slightly. Within an hour I come up on the lee of the island in fifteen fathoms out of the heavy swells and wind. Idling forward, I open the hatch and shackle a ³⁄₈-inch chain to the working anchor. I move closer to the beach, coming into quieter water. There is a heave in here but *Wild Rose* rides it easily. The light bears about 300° which puts me in the protective cone of shelter. The sounder shows about twelve fathoms. I go forward and let go the anchor and chain, tailed with a ⅝-inch nylon rope, feeling the hook bite in and the tension as I snub the nylon around the capstan on the windlass. I leave the engine running until I am sure we are holding, then secure the deck and stow the sails.

During this activity a thirty-foot troller comes in, poles still out, and anchors close in under the shore in a spot he obviously knows well. I am reassured. After determining that the hook is holding, I shut down the Westerbeke and go below to get settled for the night.

Destruction Island is a mariner's landmark going back to the first Spanish explorers. It was on July 14, 1775, in fact, that Captain Juan Francisco de la Bodega y Quadra anchored the *Sonora* in this same place and sent ashore a boat with seven men to get wood and water near the Hoh River. Indians ambushed the men and killed them all, after which Bodega named the island Isla de Dolores, meaning "Island of Sorrows." In 1787, English Captain Charles W. Barclay anchored here with the *Imperial Eagle,* and sent a crew ashore to explore the Hoh. All six of these men were also ambushed and killed, whereupon he renamed the Hoh calling it Destruction River, a name that later was misapplied to the island itself.

There is only a reef nearby to commemorate the *Sonora*, a little 36-foot schooner on which fourteen Spanish seamen and farmhands lived for ten months during Bodega's astonishing expedition north from San Blas. Those Spaniards were sea dogs without equal.

Although these are violent waters, and the Indians were vicious and treacherous, the island itself was never an evil. It is the home of thousands of hornbilled auklets, those so-called poor man's penguins, with their dress suits of black or brown, and their hilarious antics. They arrive in the spring and dig a nest in the hillside or occupy an abandoned hole for the mating season. They are prized by the Indians, who came out here to kill them for food. The island was also used by Indians for clamming and smoking fish.

The first light on this forlorn island, which to the early light keepers seemed almost like a penal colony, was established with a $45,000 grant from Congress in 1885. Construction was not completed until 1888 because of the isolation of the site and the difficulty of getting materials and supplies unloaded. Three miles offshore, the flat-topped island is less than a mile long and three hundred yards wide. The first keepers brought their families out and supplemented their supplies with gardens and a few milk cows, with mixed success. Legend has it that one keeper brought a bull out for his herd, but the sound of a new foghorn so infuriated the animal that he battered down all the fences looking for his rival.

Nowadays a submerged cable from shore near the mouth of Steamboat Creek supplies power and communications for the automatic facilities. The light is 147 feet high and visible for eighteen miles, flashing every ten seconds. Only the south side of the island is safe for vessels, the rest being dotted with reefs and rocks. The island is the only offshore shelter between Grays Harbor and Flattery, and so it is important to small craft.

It is now time to slice off a couple of steaks from the fresh chinook and light the oven broiler. The meal elicits nothing but praise from all the guests on board.

The next morning I awake shivering in a pale, damp, cold light. I sit up, alarmed, grab a stanchion and look out a port. We are in an eerie world of filmy wet fog. The horn on the island moans loudly. The depth sounder shows we are in approximately the same position, allowing for a shift during tide changes. The same gentle swell lifts the vessel rhythmically.

Coming fully awake, I stuff the Cole stove with paper and some log chips and light it. In a few moments the little bulkhead fireplace roars and warmth spreads through the cabin. I break out the Vectra RDF and go up into the cockpit to try to take bearings on the James Island and Flattery beacons. There is no need for plotting. We are still anchored precisely where we were last night, only now everything looks different: I am in a world of billowy white, silent except for the moaning horn. I cannot even see the troller.

There is nothing to do but have breakfast and busy myself with little shipboard chores. I find a couple of leaks around hatches and ports that will have to be fixed. The electric head is jammed, so I remove the clean-out plate and inspect it. I find nothing, but after that it works perfectly. The pressure water-system pump refuses to come on while I am washing dishes. I trace this down to a loose fuse in the panel holder.

Afterwards, with the fog still hanging in, I break out the fishing gear and jig for bottom fish, meanwhile dropping over a crab pot baited with a can of dogfood in which I have punched holes. In short order I hook a lingcod of about five pounds, and as I am bringing him up, he is grabbed by a larger lingcod of about ten pounds, so I land them both on deck. I quickly kill these grotesque-looking, voracious bottom feeders, with their mouths full of needle-like teeth, and fillet them. The flesh of lingcod is truly a delicacy, despite their vicious outward appearance. I also have six Dungeness crabs in the trap, so account it a morning well spent.

Later, when we are aboard more permanently, and exploring the vast waterways and island mazes of Puget Sound, British Columbia, and Alaska, there will be plenty of time for this sort of thing. But now I would like with as little trouble as possible to double Cape Flattery, that great wrecker of ships and killer of men and marker of the entrance to the mythical Strait of Anian of ancient times.

14.

Doubling Cape Flattery

By noon the fog has lifted until I can see the shoreline of Destruction Island, but not the tower. The small troller is already gone, and it leaves me feeling deserted.

My instinct tells me I am just caught in a pocket of fog and that it is clear over the ocean offshore. At 1 P.M. I can see the mainland shore, some rocks and reefs with whitecaps breaking. There is a breeze rising and the fog should be dissipating soon. I make ready, check all systems, start the Westerbeke, which kicks over on the first turn, secure everything loose, go forward, and haul in the anchor with the windlass.

This windlass, which I made from war surplus parts, works better than some high and mighty commercial marine jobs—but when I installed it I made an error in the direction of rotation, and consequently the bow roller was located for the opposite rotation.

For a vessel of this size, however, and for a single-hander of my age, some mechanical means of hauling up an anchor is absolutely essential. I had further installed a foot switch covered with a piece of rubber about three inches in diameter, and an eighth of an inch thick, held down by a bronze ring screwed and glued to the deck. The foot switch operates a solenoid under the deck, and it is only necessary to tap the switch momentarily, as the extremely low geared windlass has a flywheel effect once momentum has been achieved. Thus, the actual drain on the battery occurs for only a couple of seconds at a time.

The anchor comes up easily. I stow the chain and rope in the forepeak and lash the anchor on deck in the chocks, as it may be needed later. Then I go back to the cockpit and take up a heading due southwest to clear the island and off-lying rocks.

In twenty minutes the fog thins out and I am startled to see, coming out into a clear bright morning, a Soviet BMRT-class trawler with its vanes down and plowing at ten knots. Obviously the trawler did not pick me up on the radar as I was screened by the island.

Under power, I quickly alter my heading, but a bearing on the BMRT shows there is no change in its heading. We are on a collision course for sure, and it is no accident. With some frantic maneuvering, I apply full power and barely avoid the oncoming ship. The BMRT sweeps by me at full bore, angrily blowing a horn. The bow wave catches me broadside and throws me over on the beam. Everything below crashes down. I am almost thrown over the winch console. We oscillate violently in the following waves. If it weren't that I have to hang on with both hands, and had I a rifle handy, I might be incited to put a shot through the pilothouse windows. Since we are within six miles of the beach, it is obvious that the Soviet trawler has sneaked in under cover of fog to drop her vanes and make a trawl run out to sea again before being intercepted by a fisheries patrol.

The Russian gone, I stand out beyond Cape Alava, running under power at an angle to the usual afternoon northwesterly breeze and swell. The sun is out bright again today, although it is not as warm. Near Flattery Rocks the small-vessel traffic increases, and coming in on the horizon are two or three large ships almost hull-down, a tanker and a couple of container ships. Now in a better mood, I go below and get my own official code flag identifiers and hoist them to the starboard spreader. My code, for which I applied when I documented the vessel, is the same as my radio call: WYZ 9304. Although nowadays this does not really mean anything, it is official, and it gives me a vain pleasure and a sense of belonging to the great maritime tradition.

Cape Flattery now stands in sharp relief against the late afternoon sun, with its white buildings and radio towers, as I leave Flattery Rocks and Umatilla Reef behind. The Flattery light, radio beacon, and horn are situated on Tatoosh Island, about half a mile off the end of the cape, and bearing 324° from Umatilla Reef. I continue northwest on a true course of 340°, until Tatoosh bears 036°, and then alter course to 021°, which will bring me outside of Duncan and Duntze rocks.

With the glasses I can see the small craft fishing in the hazardous passage between Tatoosh and the cape, so I know that the approach to the Strait of Juan de Fuca is going to be an easy one and I relax.

With the glasses I can make out Fuca's Pillar, which is rather obscure but is supposed to mark the mythical strait to which the Greek pilot Juan de Fuca gave his name. Today it is hardly known, and is overshadowed by Tatoosh and the cape itself. In olden days the Indians lived in huts on the western face of the cape, from which a magnificent view can be had of the approaches to the strait. Their high-rise condominiums, however, were used for two more useful purposes—watching for whales, and for the marauding Haida Indians from the north.

On June 28, 1792, John Boit, fifth officer on the *Columbia Rediviva*, out of Boston, logged this position as "N. Lat. 48° 42' W. Long. 124° 0'''". He wrote:

Entered the Strait of Juan de Fuca and hove to abreast the village of Nitinat [on Vancouver Island]. *Found strong tides. Vast many natives came off with sea otter and other furs which we purchased with the same articles as before* [iron chisels, nails, and pieces of copper]. *They appear to be friendly. It was evident these natives had been visited by that scourge of mankind, smallpox. The natives say the Spanish brought it among them.*

We keep beating off the entrance of the Strait until June 3rd. Off a small island called Tatoosh, we collected many otter. These natives gave preference to copper. Fine halibut and salmon were produced in abundance. Nails, beads, etc. served for this traffic. The chief at Tatoosh offered to sell us some young children they had taken in war.

In John Hoskin's log of the *Columbia* for the same period, this officer noted:

[The] *wind was light and flattering with a heavy swell on the morning of the 28th . . . A canoe with ten men came alongside. They were from Nitinat, bound awhaling. They requested us to go to their village, saying, as an inducement, that there were plenty of skins. No sooner were they informed that that was our intention, than they returned to the village with the news of our arrival. It was two in the afternoon before we were enabled to get in with the land. When we were still two or three miles distant, several canoes came off, in one of which was Cassacan, the chief, and his lady. They tarried with us until evening. We purchased several valuable skins. We then made sail, crossing what Captain Cook called the pretended Strait of Juan de Fuca, bound for Tatoosh's Island.*

Because of the favorable conditions, I elect to pass between Duncan and Duntz rocks and Tatoosh, and soon after find myself running westward into the Strait of Juan de Fuca with a following swell and a light wind. I stay outside the kelp line, along which there are dozens of fishing skiffs trolling for salmon, moving eastward under power now at seven knots. It would have been a glorious sail with the rags up, and indeed the strait is dotted with multicolored sails. A fleet race appears in progress. From here on in I will see a lot of sailing craft, as the Puget Sound country is, at this time of year, a body of water entirely covered with Dacron. But it is late in the afternoon, and I wish to get in somewhere before dark. The strait is an extremely hazardous place to be at night because of the floating logs and debris.

In good time I make the breakwater at Neah Bay, and at 6 P.M. I come around Waadah Island and enter between the bell and horn buoys. The harbor is crowded, but I find swinging room in four fathoms off the rubblework breakwater's sandy bottom. Waadah Island is about half a mile long, high and wooded, and protects the harbor from the west. In easterly weather the anchorage is a rather indifferent spot to dock in, but this time of year it is excellent.

There is a wharf on the southwestern side of the island, near the foul ground. The western shore is high and steep, with rock outcroppings. A rock that bares is marked by a lighted bell buoy. Coast Guard installations, piers, and other works, along with log booms, form the waterfront of this Indian village. On the south side is a fish wharf which supplies small craft. Neah Bay, on the Makah Indian reservation, is a customs port totally owned by the tribe, where one can get fuel, ice and some marine supplies. A paved road connects along the south shore of the strait to U.S. 101 and Port Angeles. Neah Bay is a popular sport fishing center, as well as a haven for commercial boats, and has guides, boat rentals, and bait shops operated as concessions by non-Indians.

A Spanish expedition, led by Lieutenant Salvador Fidalgo, attempted to make a settlement here early in 1792. After a nine-week voyage from San Blas on the frigate *Princesa*, he landed on May 29 at Neah Bay, sending a party ashore at Village Creek. The Spanish settlement was to be placed so that it commanded the entrance to the strait on the south side, and on the site where, two years earlier, a party from Quimper's expedition had come ashore to wash clothes and erect a cross of possession.

The Spaniards' first priority was to build an oven on shore for baking biscuits. The *Princesa* could not get into the shallow bay, so it had to anchor in the lee of Waada Island and send work parties in by longboat. A stockade was erected at the head of the cove, straddling the creek. The men felled trees, and carpenters erected two rough buildings to shelter the bakery and a blacksmith shop. The woods were cleared in all directions for the distance of a gunshot, and four cannon were mounted.

Neah Bay offered poor anchorage and no shelter most of the year, so the idea of a permanent settlement was abandoned—but not before a garden of vegetables from Mexico had been planted —mostly cabbages, turnips, carrots, and lettuce—and eight head of scrawny Mexican cattle, some hogs, and pigs were landed.

At the first opportunity, however, Indian attacks began, and in a final skirmish Fidalgo turned the ship's guns on two canoes approaching, killing eight men and women and sinking the craft. Only a small boy and a girl survived. The Spaniards hung on to the settlement for two more months and then abandoned it.

Settled down at the anchorage, I prepare for an early bed-time. Before closing up shop I work out a sun sight I had taken off the cape on the way in for practice. My calculated position turns out to be 2,750 miles from my observed position. Later it turns out that I had been using watch time from my wrist watch, which had been set to Pacific Daylight Time. When I corrected for this, the LOP turned out fairly accurate.

Just after dark, a gang of Indian kids comes out on the breakwater and throws rocks at *Wild Rose*. I think of up-anchoring and going on to places more hospitable, but then decide I am not going to be intimidated by any goddamn kids. After dark, someone fires two shots from a .22-caliber rifle in my direction, the slugs ricocheting off the water into space. Without going on deck, I make a quick check of the hull and even pull up the floors to inspect the bilge. I break out my own weapons, more for self-assurance than out of any plans for counterattack.

15.

Running Down the Strait

A heavy, musty marine odor hangs over *Wild Rose* at first light, mingled with the scents of resinous timber, mill and cannery discharges, stale waterfront, and mud flats.

It is my desire to leave Neah Bay as early as possible, so I am content with a breakfast of hot coffee and some toast, and while waiting for a break in the fog I sit at the saloon table with a small fire blazing in the fireplace and record some recent impressions in the "commonplace book" I keep in addition to the official ship's log.

Keeping a commonplace book was a practice the young officers on those adventurous voyages to the Northwest Coast indulged in. A sort of personal journal or log not the property of the ship, the commonplace book was a place in which they could work off their hostilities and vent their frustrations during those voyages of three to four years, from the Atlantic seaboard, down around the Horn, up to the Sandwich Islands, back across the North Pacific to Juan de Fuca's Strait, and thence homeward via the Sandwich Islands, Canton, and the Cape of Good Hope.

In the official log of *Wild Rose* I record this morning's departure from the moment of weighing anchor at 7:59 A.M. Pacific Daylight Time, for that is when I hear the first of the kicker fleet heading out of the fishing dock for the harbor entrance. I am ready and the Westerbeke is rumbling busily. I ease down past the channel buoy, seeing the break in the overcast outside in the strait and the sun bright in the east. Then, going between the bell buoy to starboard and the horn to port on the lower tip of Waadah Island, I am clear of the entrance and feeling the swell of the open sea.

To the west, the Pacific is curtained on the horizon by a gray bank of crud. To the east, the rising sun blazes brilliantly, casting a burnished copper sheen on the snow-rimmed Olympics. About twelve miles to the north, the Canadian shore of Vancouver Island closes in on the strait, with Port San Juan immediately opposite me. The south shore is dotted with kicker boats slowly trolling or mooching for salmon. Large commercial seiners are at work along the Canadian shore.

Through this narrow strait, penetrating into the continent of the northwestern coast of America, come the anadromous fish runs for a hundred spawning streams, concentrated into vulnerable schools. Nuclear subs from the base at Bangor also appear, sometimes submerged, other times with their large towers slicing along the surface like the fins of some enormous killer whale. It is a waterway of commerce and fisheries and recreational boating of all kinds, and it strikes me as almost identical with the great St. Lawrence, which is on the same latitude, also penetrates deep into the continent, and like Juan de Fuca, was at first thought to be the entrance to a northwest passage.

Up and down the strait plied the old fleets of tall clippers headed for the Orient, and the lumber schooners of four, five, and six masts, each ship carrying a couple of million board feet of fresh-cut Douglas fir, cedar, and spruce for the markets of Asia, Australia, and the California coast. It often took ships a week or more to make a board westward to the open Pacific and then, likely as not, they would encounter a wild southwester driving them onto the dangerous lee shore on the coast of Vancouver Island—from October through May, to double Cape Flattery in a sailing ship was an achievement equal to rounding Cape Horn from east to west. On the rocky, surf-lashed shores of Cape Flattery and Vancouver Island, opposite, lie the bones of hundreds of sailing ships and powered vessels, too, the ghosts of which stalk you up and down the Strait of Juan de Fuca to this day.

Through this strait in 1901 went those two pint-sized adventurers with the big egos and the enormous capacity for showmanship and hyperbole, John Claus Voss and Norman Kenny Luxton. Starting from Victoria on the converted cedar war canoe *Tilikum*, they set out to go around the world and outdo old Slocum himself. One of them a superb seaman and inarticulate but consummate liar, the other a young, impulsive, imaginative, and articulate newspaperman—also a consummate if glorious liar—these two would sail their three-masted Indian canoe into fate and legend and immortality, even if they never did make it all around the world, and even if no one today can determine exactly what happened to them, and between them, before or after they had parted company in Fiji.

Down this strait in 1934 had also gone the ebullient young Dwight Long, University of Washington student, son of conventional, middle-class Seattle people, who got the notion from reading the stories of another colorful exaggerator, the French circumnavigator Alain Gerbault, and set out on his 32-foot *Idle Hour* to become the youngest person to circumnavigate the oceans of the world up to that time.

Through here, too, had passed the competent young Britisher John Guzzwell, who had built his 20-foot *Trekka* behind a fish and chips shop in Victoria, where he worked, and one day sailed her out past Race Rocks and made his boards back and forth until he gained the open sea and immortality as the first to sail around alone in the smallest vessel.

Guzzwell also was with Brigadier Miles and Beryl Smeeton when, as a crew member on the famous west-to-east passage around Cape Horn in the Roaring Forties, they were pitch-poled and dismasted. Then, through his skill and calm competence, he was able to patch up *Tzu Hang* and they were able to limp into a Chilean port for rebuilding.

The Smeetons themselves passed through here many times, the last time on their red-hulled *Tzu Hang* with Bob Nance from England, this time around the Horn east to west, to sail into the strait to its old mooring at a private dock on one of the islands near Sidney. As Miles Smeeton wrote:

When I left Tzu Hang, *I noticed that an otter had left its droppings on the edge of the float to which she is tied. While I waited at the dock by the motor boat that was to take us to the shore, a kingfisher was scolding from the top of one of the piles and a number of Canada geese flew, talking low, over the breakwater, close past* Tzu Hang, *to the lake behind the house. These and the loons, murrelets and grebes will be her companions. . . .*

111

The matter-of-fact prose of the United States Coast Pilot Number 7, *Pacific Coast*, says:

The Strait of Juan de Fuca separates the southern shore of Vancouver Island, Canada, from the north coast of the State of Washington. The entrance to the strait lies between parallels 48 36' N., on the meridian of 124 45' W. This important body of water is the connecting channel between the ocean and the inter-island passages extending southward to Puget Sound and northward to the inland waters of British Columbia and southeastern Alaska.

At its entrance and for 50 miles eastward to Race Rocks, the strait has a width of about 12 miles, and thence it has a width of about 16 miles for 30 miles eastward to Whidbey Island, its eastern boundary. The waters as a rule are deep until near the shore with few outlying dangers, most of which are in the eastern part. The shores on both sides are heavily wooded, rising rapidly to elevations of considerable height, and except for a few places, are bold and rugged. The north shore should be avoided as it is the lee shore for most gales, and with the exception of Esquimalt Harbor, there are no anchorages for strangers that afford shelter from all winds.

In addition to the winds, which can get violent at times, the dangers include the extensive kelp beds close to shore and around rocks, the tide rips, which can be hazardous to small craft, the floating logs and debris, and the heavy ship traffic. This traffic is now controlled by designated east–west zones and by remote radar installations connected to a traffic control center in Seattle. All craft must conform to these regulations, and crossing these east–west lanes, such as in sailing from Port Angeles or Port Towsend, must be done under prescribed procedures under penalty of heavy fine.

Now, with a fair wind blowing home, *Wild Rose* skips eastward down the strait toward Port Angeles. Kydaka Point comes up, followed by Slip Point, Clallam Bay, Pillar Point, the mouth of the Pysht River, and Crescent Rock, for a change of course to 110° True. Then, proceeding up the long narrow sliver of Ediz Hook, with its Coast Guard station and airstrip, we move around the hook and up into the bay at Port Angeles, sailing 2.5 nautical miles to anchorage off the municipal moorage.

Later I would leave Port Angeles to make a short but symbolic voyage out of the harbor, around the sands of Dungeness Point, circling Dallas Bank and heading toward Admiralty Inlet, the entrance to Puget Sound proper. I would, however, bear off around Protection Island and head south along the Quimper Peninsula to an anchorage under the lee of Cape George, in almost the exact spot where in 1792 Captain George Vancouver anchored the sloop

Discovery for the winter, while mapping the adjacent waters. The U.S. expedition under Wilkes also anchored here, in 1841, for the same purpose. Wilkes had called the peninsula the Dickerson Peninsula, after the Secretary of the Navy at the time, but later this was changed to honor the Spanish explorer Manuel Quimper, who had been the first to anchor here in 1790.

This quiet, protected anchorage also has a more personal meaning for my wife and myself, because from here we can look up to the steep brown and green partly wooded hillside of the cape, directly above us, and see the property which we had purchased many years before as a possible site for a retirement home.

From this property you can look out over Protection Island below and raise your eyes to see Victoria in the far, hazy distance to the northwest. To the north are the mystical islands of San Juan; to the southwest, the high, snow-crested ridges of the Olympic Mountains and Mount Olympus; and then straight west, out the Strait of Juan de Fuca, is the Pacific Ocean, Alaska, the Orient, the whole world.

From here, where we will be based, it seems we will have the best of two worlds, afloat and ashore.

Part Four
PETER PUGET'S
COUNTRY

By understanding the tidal phenomenon and by making intelligent use of tide tables, the mariner can set his course and schedule his passage to make the tide serve him, or at least avoid its dangers.

The American Practical Navigator
Nathaniel Bowditch

16.
Return to the North

Up to now it was all prelude. Job and family considerations and on *Wild Rose* a long list of necessary repairs and modifications meant that it would be late spring or early summer before we would really be able to take her out for a long cruise. Best to bring her home, where she would be close and convenient—although I hated to think of another long period of eighteen-hour days. So we sailed her down the Strait of Juan de Fuca, turned the corner at Cape Flattery, ran downhill to the mouth of the Columbia, then motored to Portland and a berth in Multnomah Channel.

The construction and maintenance log had accumulated 150 jobs for me to do, from fixing a defective bulkhead reading light to rebuilding the freshwater system. During the winter I crossed off 200 of these, and then wound up with 100 more. Work lists are fine for jogging one's memory and keeping one's priorities in line; but they also are self-generating, multiplying like amoebas, and the presence of one tends to give the impression that the ship will never be ready to sail.

Since we intended to operate for several years along the Northwest Coast and Inside Passage, after much thought I finally bought a Seascan radar. Justifying the cost was awkward. What it came down to, my bride suggested, was buying a new set of store teeth or a new toy that might keep us off some fog-shrouded reef.

The long winter and spring passed, and then came a day in July when it was time to take *Wild Rose* north again. Some friends —Jim and Mary Bigelow of Portland—joined us for the cruise down-river, got off at Warrenton, and returned home with my bride. From Warrenton another friend and fishing buddy, Art Lacey, came aboard to accompany me to Port Townsend. We intended to make a fast weekend trip by motoring most of the way. It turned out to be a trip of five days.

As we passed the Point Adams light (see Chapter 8, "Around the Lightship") we could see those we had left behind watching us go by. They had driven down as far as they could for a last glimpse. At 8 A.M., we passed Buoy 14, a key point to judge bar conditions, and found the tide slack and the buoy standing straight. It was an easy crossing, until we came out from behind the shelter of the North Jetty and began plunging into a fresh northwesterly that whipped eight-foot swells into galloping white sea horses.

Rounding Peacock Spit, it is a shock to see the depth sounder rise to twenty feet. This is why the Spit has been the graveyard of ships for 150 years. It was named for Lieutenant Charles Wilkes's flagship, which went aground and broke up here in 1841. Art was steering and it took some firm commands to keep him from giving in to the common tendency to cut too short around the North Jetty. I did let him cut inside Buoy 1, where we were getting into thirty-foot depths, providing he angled offshore. We held on to the ten-fathom line as soon as we reached it, and as the morning wore on we found ourselves plunging head on into increasing winds and an adverse tidal current. *Wild Rose* held steady, seemingly happy to be in her element again. A river of seawater ran down along the port deck and splashed out through breaks in the teak toe rail. Spray at times came over the top of the canopy, but everything in the cockpit remained dry.

An hour more brought us into the middle of a big charter fleet from Westport. A Coast Guard cutter stood by, its crew also fishing off the fantail. I thought to myself, I am glad to see those lads just in case we have trouble on the Grays Harbor bar. Nets were flying all over the fleet. They were over a school and the bite was on. We got carried away with all this excitement, ignoring the strong southerly current setting alongshore. We had estimated reaching Westport about noon, but with the headwind and adverse currents, we kept revising this ETA all day long.

Gales are rare on the Northwest Coast during June, July, and August; the really bad storms come in winter from the southeast or south. But winds of gale force caused by gradients from the land mass colliding with marine air are not so uncommon. The headwind we were bucking strengthened by noon, with frequent gusts, but we were not uncomfortable and nothing below in the cabin was falling. The offshore current is normally moving south reaching out to three or four hundred miles, depending on the season and the winds. There is supposed to be a northward current inshore from the Columbia to Cape Flattery, but I have never found it. The new editions of the *Pilot Books* and *Coast Pilots* are somewhat ambiguous about this. You have to go into the old editions, with their information for sailing vessels, to get a better understanding. That's why the old editions are valuable to the small-boat sailor.

Sailing vessels approaching the Columbia were advised to stand off and wait for a favorable tide and wind before crossing the bar; this meant standing well outside the lightship, or about ten miles off. Often such vessels would find themselves drifting all the way to Grays Harbor during the night, on a north-flowing current. On the other hand, the same current we bucked close in off Willapa would have sent them onto the shoals of Peacock Spit. Boats mooching for salmon off Long Beach often drift five or six miles toward the North Jetty in less than two hours.

The conclusion is for small craft and sailing vessels between the Columbia and Cape Flattery to stay well offshore, but within ten miles, to take advantage of northward currents while avoiding inshore tides, and to take advantage of westerly or northwesterly winds by keeping them on a slant.

But if it's the salmon season, chances are you will tend to hug the coastline where the boats are, and this will be your undoing, although the fishing will take your mind off it. At one point I took running bearings of a radar station high atop a mountain. For more than an hour the bearing did not change, although we were making seven knots through the water.

Lacey, who could never sit still or be just a passenger, grabbed the wheel when we were crossing the bar and did not relinquish it for the rest of the trip for more than a few minutes. This was all right by me, as I would rather have an automatic pilot I can talk to than a mechanical one. The idleness, however, made me lax in my navigation and I failed to note that the land mass to starboard had an irresistible attraction for Art. We kept edging closer until we suddenly found ourselves trapped in a vast crab-pot field in twenty feet of water off the Willapa bar. It took two hours to claw our way off this and get offshore again. We never got into the cone of visibility of the Point Chehalis Light, and several times mistook the reflection of the sun on parked cars for beacons.

The speedy charter fleet's passing us up finally convinced us that we had horribly misjudged our speed and position. That's what salmon fever will do to you. Making a true approach to Grays Harbor, we encountered roughening seas and a wind shifting to westerly, bringing in vicious cross seas. The wakes of five hundred fishing boats returning all at once also helped create rough, confused waters. Looking astern, I saw a wide line of boats plunging for home, throwing great white Vees. I thought we would easily beat them to the entrance buoy, but a few minutes later I looked back to see them overtaking us. In a moment they had overhauled us and forged on ahead, their diesels rumbling and their wakes throwing us about.

Below, chaos took over. The doors began slamming, books fell out of shelves and cabinets, glasses and pots leaped out of the galley sink, charts and navigation tools ended up among the books and wreckage on the floor.

About two miles from the red buoy 2, I went below to straighten up. That's when I saw the red automatic bilge-pump light glowing. I peeked into the engine room and, to my horror, saw water up to the engine and sloshing from one side to the other as we rolled, each time splashing over the banks of batteries. I yelled to Lacey, who took note, but there was not much he could do but hold on to the wheel and keep steering. Opening the cockpit hatch, I could see it was an old problem—the hot-water hose had come loose and the automatic freshwater pump had come on, and now we had about fifty gallons of water in the engine room bilges. I rushed below and shut off the water pump, which stopped the additional flow. Then I called the Coast Guard on Channel 16.

During a break in the static and traffic, a calm voice zeroed in on *Wild Rose*. I was asked if I was declaring an emergency. I said not yet, but that I had an engine room full of water and thought I could cope with it if the engine didn't blow up. He stood by while I made another check, and then I asked to have him monitor our progress. He said a cutter was on the way (it turned out to be the one we had passed off Long Beach), and to switch to Channel 22.

The seas were now violent. I had to man the emergency pump because the automatic pump was not fast enough. I opened the aft cockpit hatch to get access to the emergency Guzzler, while

Lacey hung on to the helm. The pump intake hose was stiff and unruly. It was hard to keep the end of it submerged and, at the same time, man the pump handle and hold the short outlet hose over the rail. Each time the boat rolled to starboard, the hatch cover came down on my head. Each time this happened, a shower of wood shavings and sawdust left over from construction days flew out of the crevices and settled on my hair. Lacey said later that he had thought it was coming out of my head, which confirmed his suspicions. In any event, when I finally turned the outlet hose into the cockpit so I could let go of it and use that hand to keep the hatch from beaning me, he thought I had lost my senses. I yelled at him that the cockpit drains would handle it. He hadn't noticed that.

The engine throbbed steadily, not missing a beat. The engine temperature gauge was inoperative as usual. I got most of the water out of the bilge to protect the batteries, and secured this operation. By the time we turned the corner and started across the bar, led by the Coast Guard cutter and followed by hundreds of returning boats, we were getting a handle on the situation and I so informed the Coast Guard. Long swells now heaped up into monstrous following seas, but as each one towered up behind us, *Wild Rose* lifted easily and let them pass under. Lacey exclaimed in amazement how easily she handled before them.

We followed the cutter into the narrow harbor entrance, and it led us to the fuel dock, where we took on twenty-five gallons of diesel while the petty officer filled out his report. Then he directed us to a stall he knew was vacant, and we were at last secure for the night and sipping double tequilas on the rocks.

17.
Westport to Port Angeles

Next morning we walked around to Del Fender's "Golden Fleet" charter office, where he was now busy with sleepy salmon anglers and preparations for the departure of his fleet. Del turned on his VHF (I didn't have WX 2 channel) and we heard forecasts of thirty-five and forty-knot northerly winds and small-craft advisories.

"All your boats going out?" I asked.

"Certainly," replied Del.

These charter ops don't pay much attention to the weather until the light poles on the strand are bent over. They have only a hundred-day season and it takes a lot of weather to cancel a trip, especially for boats that have a full load of sports worth five hundred dollars.

We weren't pros and we did not have the type of vessel and equipment the charter ops had, yet chickening out did not appeal to either of us.

After breakfast it was light enough to work below on the *Wild Rose* with the hatches open, so we pumped out the remaining water and cleaned the engine room bilge. The hot-water hoses were all loose, so we tightened these and double-clamped the one on the water tank that had blown off several times. We checked the engine and transmission oil, and made a flashlight inspection over everything.

That done, we went up on deck to witness the "dawn parade" of boats out of Westport Harbor—hundreds of them, mostly salmon charters but also a lot of commercial trollers, and here and there a private yacht, all oozing out of slips and squeezing into the outgoing lines to maneuver through the narrow entrance and then swing around to the left to face the bar and open sea.

Westport cuddles just inside the hook of Point Chehalis at the entrance to Grays Harbor. It is a major port for Washington coast commercial and sport fishing boats. Since the 1960s it has been the leading salmon and tuna port on the West Coast, with sharp competition between charter operators.

In the next slip, a man-and-wife team maneuvered nervously out into the stream of traffic with their Cascade 29—the smaller version of *Wild Rose*. Its name was the *Malia*, Hawaiian for "Mary."

Art looked at me. "Are we gonna get chickened by a little thing like that?"

"Well, why don't we just go out and take a look. We can always come back," I said.

By 6 A.M. we were backing out of the slip and intimidating our way into the parade. We eased out the entrance, keeping away from the rip, and turned toward the bar. Fanned out before us was the fleet, some heading south, some north, and some straight west. The bar proved to be flat except for the confused seas left by the wakes of the boats, through which we bounced and rolled. A light westerly caressed our faces when we peeked out from behind the shelter. Behind us the sky had turned red, and then the color dissipated as daylight brought over a layer of clouds. We angled out to the northwest, keeping well off the surf at the end of the North Jetty. Only when we reached the twenty-fathom line did we turn north on a course of 340 degrees true. The wind had backed around to northwest and actually was giving a little assist. We left the bulk of the salmon fleet behind, and saw ahead the single stick of the Cascade 29.

A half hour later we caught up to the *Malia*, which seemed to be making some weather of the fifteen-knot wind and the six-foot swells. She would rise up on a quartering sea, then fall off and yaw. We thought they were having steering problems, but were later told that this was normal behavior for the 29, and how much they admired the performance of *Wild Rose* as we bored on by them without even throwing spray.

The fog bank receded seaward and the blue haze rose off the Olympic Mountains to the northeast. The coastline here was still low, with stretches of sandy beach. Each year on May 12, local booster-types gather at midnight on the beach, after suitable preparations, and in unison roar, "Hey, George!" to the winds and seas. This, they say, is in honor of Captain George Vancouver, who sailed up this coast on May 12, 1792, and failed to find either the Columbia River or Grays Harbor.

It is easy to see why old George missed. The coastline is nondescript here, although it becomes mountainous further north. Although we needed no aids to navigation, if I had to, I would certainly choose Loran. The charter skippers tell me that radar is of little use to them because of the lack of targets within range. With Loran, however, they simply set the coordinates before they leave the harbor, after which they know their position within a few yards all day long without touching the dials. They even navigate across the bar by Loran. With radar, they can't tell whether the targets on the bar are buoys or kicker boats.

As the morning wore on, the wind and seas softened. *Wild Rose* held her course steady. The sun, coming out bright in a clear sky, sparkled on a blue ocean. The snow-capped Olympics loomed up on the starboard quarter. We held to the twenty-fathom line, avoiding the inshore currents. Even without the sails, the mast, boom, and deck hamper provided enough windage to benefit from the westerly breeze.

The shoreline became more rugged. We saw two new forest fires billowing reddish-gray smoke along the Olympics. We passed occasional schools of bait with seabirds working around the ball-ups in frenzy. We saw a sea lion or a whale now and then. There were scatterings of terns, murres with black backs and white bellies, many species of gulls, as well as a brown albatross and a shearwater perhaps on its long clockwise migration of the Pacific rim.

The weather seemed to get even better. Coming abeam of Destruction Island, the light and buildings showed up clearly in detail. Then we left it behind and picked up, far ahead, James Island at the mouth of the Quillayute River. This lonely coastline is strewn with offshore rocks, islets, and sea stacks, most of which are now wildlife refuges administered by the Fish & Wildlife Service. A whale appeared close by to starboard. We encountered a number of the odd-looking, red-beaked, parrotlike puffins, some pigeon guillemots, auklets, and skuas.

Aside from a badly wrenched knee, which later proved to be dislocated, a nasty crack on the other one from colliding with the hatch coaming during the Grays Harbor episode, plus various cuts, contusions, and a knob on top of my head from the hatch cover—the day became one of the most relaxing and soul-filling I had experienced since the *Wild Rose* project began. It takes awhile to gear oneself to a six- or seven-knot speed, but once you do, your perspective undergoes a reformation.

At 3:30 P.M., I called the Quillayute Coast Guard station. Not expecting an answer, I was surprised when a voice came back: "What can we do for you, Skipper?"

I asked for a rundown on bar conditions, channel depth, fuel, and moorage, getting back the information that there was no bar problem, the channel was plenty deep for a six-foot draft, and to report to the port captain for moorage. Whitecaps furrowed the afternoon sea now. We approached the entrance cautiously to pick up the buoys. The tide was low, exposing rotted pilings and rocks. We turned in and "threaded the Quillayute needle" with a number of returning fishing boats, keeping to the center of the channel while the depth sounder held onto a nervous twelve to fifteen feet.

Then we found ourselves coming up along a rickety waterfront of fish buyers, ice houses, and commercial chandleries at the bend of the river, just outside the Lapush harbor—all of it on the Quillayute Indian Reservation. Quillayute means "river of no head," probably because it is only six miles long, coming out of a pool formed by the Bogachiel and Soleduc, which are major rivers heading up in the rugged Olympics. The river forms a bow near the ocean with a spit on the west side and the harbor breakwater on the left bank. We followed the traffic right through the narrow harbor entrance, seeing ten boats waiting to get at the fuel dock and the rest of the harbor jammed as badly, the traffic ranging from Indian dugout canoes hot-rodding around with brand-new 25-horsepower outboards, to 65-foot seiners and draggers. We extricated ourselves from this situation, backed out, and coasted along the fish wharves talking to long-haired, rubber-booted youths who assured us the anchorage was deep enough. The overflow traffic was anchored in the river channel just above the harbor entrance, and some of these vessels were large commercials. We moved up among them and dropped the hook in twelve feet, mud and weed bottom. I put down the big Benson, and also the smaller Danforth, which held our position without slippage but without much scope either.

At 6 P.M. we shut her down, mixed gin and tonics and sat on the deck cabin watching the colorful pageant going on as the sun sank behind James Island. This is the only haven between Grays Harbor and Neah Bay, up around Cape Flattery, and during the summer fishing season it is Chaos. As evening fell, boats were still coming in, somehow finding places to park.

Morning came wet and foggy. By 5 A.M. the parade reached full stream, as boats converged off the fish wharves and threaded their way down to the bar. We wriggled into the traffic, coasted on downriver and through the outlet to the open sea, then headed northwest into the moon's path, and into haze and thin fog.

Cake Rock, a large landmark offshore to the north of James Island, stayed in sight for most of the morning. The fog patches became more frequent, so I turned on the radar for practice. The screen showed the coastline precisely, and I soon picked up the reflectors on the buoys at Umatilla Reef. There is a red buoy inside and another offshore a mile or so, about where the Umatilla light-ship used to be. The buoys are easy to pick up on radar, but the dangerous reefs here are hard to identify from the sea by visual means.

I had originally installed the radar dome on top of the trunk cabin, from which height I only get a maximum of four miles range, instead of the twelve or sixteen the rig is capable of. Of course, even in this low position, high cliffs and mountains can be detected at maximum range.

At 7 A.M. a dense fog bank lay offshore, and also shrouded the Olympics inland. The temperature was 50 degrees, humidity 95 percent, barometer 30.0—a typical summer morning for approaching Flattery. But as the morning wore on, the ocean settled down to an undulating oily calm with no wind. The sun began to burn through on the mainland, leaving the dense wall of fog offshore. The coastline became more rugged behind the crescent-shaped Makkaw Bay, with the headland of Flattery looming up in the distance.

We now were in an area of mild rips and currents, with frequent ball-ups of bait fish and salmon leaping. Some Indian canoes had come off the beach and were working along shore. Farther out a number of commercial boats could be observed, moving in and out of the fog. Crossing the mouth of the bay, the fog began moving shoreward on a breeze. Within minutes, Flattery and Tatoosh Island were obscured. The radar screen, however, showed them up with almost chartlike clarity—including some of the larger boats. The depth sounder kept us well out in the clear. We continued through the soup until we began hearing the loud horn on Tatoosh, keeping it to starboard and checking the screen frequently. The reflectors on the buoys showed up clearly, so clearly that we had no hesitation passing between Duncan Rocks and Tatoosh through the tide rips.

Then, suddenly, we came out of the fog bank into brilliant sunshine, with the Strait of Juan de Fuca opening up to the east, sparkling blue, and Vancouver Island partially obscured by its own fog bank to the north. Just opposite the slot between Tatoosh and

127

Flattery we got a fleeting glimpse of the rarely seen Fuca Pillar
—rarely seen because you must be at just the right bearing to catch
it. Some local boats were passing through the Hole in the Wall slot,
although the charts show it as being hazardous with reefs and rocks.
The light station and buildings showed clearly close by. The promontory of Flattery, once heavily timbered, has now been virtually
scalped by logging operations, and eaten into by roads.

Tatoosh was the name of an early Chinook chief. Flattery and
surrounding lands are on the Makah Indian Reservation. The light is
one of the major ones on the Pacific rim, and its history goes back to
the early Spanish explorers. A lighthouse was first proposed here in
1842, but work was delayed by hostile Indians, of whom there were
at times about 250 living on the rock, which apparently was an
ancient fishing and trading spot. An English trader, Captain John
Meares, described the rock in his log of June 29, 1788: "The island
itself is a barren rock, almost inaccessible, and of no great extent; but
the surface of it as far as we could see, was covered with inhabitants
who were gazing at our ship. . . . The chief of this spot, whose
name is Tatooche, did us the favor of a visit and so surly and forbid-
ding a character we had not seen. . . ."

The Indians occupied the rock only during the summer season. They made life miserable for the construction crews, who had
to build breastworks to stave off arrows and spears. This situation
continued for years after the light was in operation, which made it
difficult to obtain lightkeepers. The Indians continued their depre-
dations until well after the turn of the century, when they gave up
and took to supplying wood to the station under contract. There was
no water problem. Tin roofs collected rainwater and piped it into
cisterns. With a rainfall of almost 100 inches a year, and an average
of 200 days of rainfall a year, the tanks never went dry.

The worst hardship today would seem to be living under that
horn, which even at a distance offshore vibrates the eardrums pain-
fully.

Once out of the fog, we passed through, and encountered a
hundred or more sport fishing and commercial trolling boats, including many kicker boats out of Neah Bay, five miles on. We picked
up the light on Waadah Island, bore through some rough rips, and
rounded up to look into Neah Bay. It was still only 10:30 A.M., so we
decided to go right on down the Strait of Juan de Fuca to Port
Angeles. We carried a light breeze behind us, and I raised the
number 3 genoa, much to Lacey's disgust. Then, with the engine on
slow bell, we rode along on the following seas at nine or ten knots.
When the wind built up later to fifteen knots, we surfed joyously.
Even Lacey thought it was fun, but wouldn't shut down the engine.

In the afternoon we caught another fog bank and kept the

radar on for an hour or so until we came out of it. Later, as the afternoon westerly freshened, we had Port Angeles in sight. I hauled down the jenny and we motored the rest of the way against the adverse tide and with a rising gale. We rounded the tip of Ediz Hook amid the sport fishing boats, and turned up into the three-mile-long harbor at 5 P.M., plunging into the waves now on our bows, through the fleet of gill-netters headed out for the night.

We tied up securely, wound up a thirteen-hour run with ice-cold drinks, then taxied into town for dinner at a fancy waterfront restaurant. The next morning we got away on a placid sun-reflecting sea, and put into Port Townsend at 11 A.M., to start the summer game of musical moorage slips.

Wild Rose was back again at her new home.

18.
Old Port Townsend and a New Base

Port Townsend, Washington, adorns the tan cliffs and waterfront of a headland on a shallow bay facing the Strait of Juan de Fuca and Admiralty Inlet, where the currents meet at the changing of the tides. It is at the tip of high, wooded Quimper Peninsula, named for the Spanish explorer Manuel Quimper who came this way in 1790. The peninsula itself is covered with dense stands of fir, hemlock, cedar, alder, and orange-barked madrone. The undergrowth of salal, vine maple, Oregon grape, and blackberry still resists development of the interior parts. Farms and homesites often have to be hacked out of the jungle.

Along the west shore Discovery Bay indents the land, a beautiful, placid inlet, with Protection Island at the entrance. The Vancouver expedition wintered at anchor in a small cove here in 1792, making forays of discovery into other parts of the inside passages.

Captain Vancouver named the bay around the corner, on the tip of the peninsula, after the Marquis of Townshend. Lieutenant Charles Wilkes also came this way, during his expedition in 1841, and dropped the *h* from the name. The town was settled in 1851 a year before Seattle. In fact, one of the founders of Portland, a New Englander named Pettygrove, had also been a founder of Port Townsend, which is on the same longitude and about two hundred miles north of Portland as the seagull flies. By 1860, Port Townsend had a population of more than twenty thousand and bustled with ships from the world over, with the principal industries being lumber and salmon. In addition to being the base for the schooners that raced to the sealing grounds in the Bering each spring, she was also a wicked city, with Water Street so rowdy that respectable citizens built a suburb atop the hill to get away from it.

A genteel lady chronicler, Caroline C. Leighton, who had traveled widely in the Northwest territories, wrote on April 20, 1869, from Port Townsend:

We were surprised to find so many New England people about us. Many of those who are interested in the sawmills are lumbermen from Maine. The two men who first established themselves in the great Wilderness, with unbroken forest and only Indians about them, are still living near us. They are men of many resources, as well as endurance. A man who comes to do battle with these great trees, must necessarily be of quite a different character from one who expects, as the California pioneer did, to pick up his fortune in the dust at his feet.

There were lumber booms and salmon booms, and the Alaska-Yukon Gold Rush in the late 1890s, kicked off by the arrival of the steamer *Portland* in Port Townsend, laden—the newspaper headlines screamed—with a "ton of gold!"

There were slumps, too—inflation after the Civil War, a land boom and bust in the 1880s, and the crash of 1893. Life picked up again in the World War I period, with the construction of the Fort Worden and Fort Flagler facilities; then a postwar relapse, a boom in the 1920s, followed by the Great Depression, followed by World War II, followed by another postwar slump. Port Townsend never did become the West Coast terminus of the nation, as early investors believed it would. As often happens, the major cities—such as the Pugetopolis of Seattle and Tacoma—rose inland where they could be more easily reached by railroads. But people and communities somehow survive such commercial contretemps and come out of it with a unique character that in itself becomes an irresistible attraction.

By the 1960s, Port Townsend was being "discovered" again. Visiting artists and writers found the scene picturesque and moved in to stay. Local patrons sparked a restoration of the waterfront and the magnificent old Victorian homes on the hill. Once-bawdy waterfront areas became filled with galleries and boutiques in the old restored brick buildings.

When we began to consider this as a place to live someday, Port Townsend had become an exotic mixture of mansard-roofed gingerbread mansions and a nineteenth-century waterfront with modern port facilities and chain supermarkets. We liked the idea of there being four bookstores in a town of only five thousand inhabitants, in a county as large in area as Connecticut, with only twelve thousand people, and where the two biggest events of the year are a salmon derby and a rhododendron festival.

When we arrived with *Wild Rose*, Port Townsend had a pleasant air of prosperity and sophistication. The small-boat harbors were jammed with charter vessels, commercial gill-netters, and trollers from as far away as Alaska, and there was summertime ferry service to Whidbey Island. The waterfront street seemed a little too crowded on shopping days, and although this is a place you don't drive *through* on a highway trip, as it is off the main throughways, we feared that it might someday lose its charm to urbanization. In the meantime, though, it was an ideal base for cruising the entire northeast rim of the Pacific.

Over the years we had acquired the homesite on the side of Cape George (named for George Vancouver), with its striking views, and a wooded homesite in Port Ludlow, which included membership in the marina, clubhouse facilities, and golf course.

We reckoned that we would thus have the best of two worlds, come the day when we'd no longer be tied to the corporate rat race.

When it came time to find a permanent base for future operations, however, we collided head-on with the worldwide shortage of moorage space.

We found that a permanent slip for *Wild Rose* anywhere north of the Columbia River would be next to nonexistent. For example, the Northwest's largest marina—Shilshole in Seattle, with 1500 spaces—had a reservation list going back to 1968 and an estimated five years' wait. New slips were being added to increase capacity by 500 boats, with 1500 already waiting for them, and a cancellation rate of only 5 percent a year. It was estimated that in the Seattle area alone, it would take at least three Shilsholes to meet even current demand.

Although a Port Ludlow Yacht Club member and a property owner, I found that a permanent berth was priced out of our reach.

Port Townsend had two small-boat harbors: a private one at Point Hudson close to the downtown waterfront, and the port of Port Townsend's boat haven a mile the other way.

The boat haven had a capacity of about five hundred boats with expansion possible, divided between commercial fishing boats and yachts. It was encouraging to stand on the strand and see a forest of masts outnumbering power boats 2 or 3 to 1. On the adjoining port property stood several yacht-building firms and related chandleries, surrounded by yards full of salty hulls in various stages of completion, including one line of authentic Herreshoffs in molded fiberglass; and various deep-sea fishing models.

We had played the game of "musical slips" all over the Northwest without finding a marina that would even talk to us about permanent moorage, when finally, after months of looking, acquired a home in a forty-eight-foot slip next to a three-masted schooner just back from a summer of cruising the Queen Charlotte Islands. The price was only $32.50 a month plus a $2 minimum for electrical power, and by paying a year in advance we got one month free. The luck of *Wild Rose* continued on course.

19.
Sailing the Inside Waters

Once you have your dream ship, where do you journey on it?

Around the world, across an ocean, down the coastline, or right in your own neighborhood? It seemed odd that I apparently was the only builder in the world who did not dream of a circumnavigation.

To me, Shakespeare's lines in *The Winter's Tale*, "To unpathed waters, undreamed shores," applied just as well to cruising in sight of the Northwest Coast as to making a long bluewater passage, which is only many more days of repetitious on-board life, with the uncertainty of weather for spice. On the North American continent alone, the possibilities included vast areas of Alaska, the Aleutians, the British Columbia coast—to say nothing of huge Vancouver Island—and the remote, fascinating, and almost unknown Queen Charlottes.

In the course of testing *Wild Rose*, we discovered the next best thing to voyaging across oceans. We would simply take a few days, or a week or two, and sail due west, out three or four hundred miles to the bluewater of the high Pacific, turn around, and sail back again. For those who must have the competition of ocean racing or an exotic destination, this would perhaps seem unfulfilling; but it has all the elements of an ocean passage reduced in scope, including bluewater experience.

It seemed most logical to log time first in the excellent cruising waters closer to home; certainly it was the most practical thing to do in our situation. So our first goal would be the exploration of the northwest coast of Washington State and lower British Columbia, an area of evergreen beauty, myriads of isolated islands, and every kind of tide, wind, and current condition to prepare one for the even more rugged and spectacular regions of Alaska.

Looking down upon the northwest corner of Washington from an orbiting satellite, you would see what looks like a gigantic fish's mouth about to swallow Vancouver Island for lunch. The many islands and inlets seem like teeth and tonsils, the Olympic Peninsula like the protruding lower lip. While the rest of Washington's ocean coastline is rather dull and nondescript, the inside waters can be included among the world's best cruising grounds.

The Strait of Juan de Fuca separates the mainland Olympic Peninsula from the southern end of Vancouver Island by an average of twelve to fifteen miles, and extends inland to Port Townsend, about ninety miles from the ocean. From Port Townsend, Hood Canal drops south along the east side of the Olympic Peninsula, like a fishhook. On the mainland side the salt chuck extends to the south, like a gourd hanging down, to Olympia, the state capital. Everett, Tacoma, and Seattle form an almost continuous metropolitan "Pugetopolis" on the mainland side. Puget Sound, named for Peter Puget, a naturalist and one of Captain Vancouver's officers, is the general name given to all the waters of northwest Washington, but actually refers only to that open water at the lower end of Admiralty Inlet to Seattle. The region south to Olympia is usually called Southern or Lower Puget Sound, while everything to the north is Upper Puget Sound. Geographic purists object to this casual nomenclature, but no one else pays any attention to such niceties.

Between Vancouver Island and mainland Washington lies a cluster of rocky wooded islands known as the San Juans, consisting of about twelve major and a hundred or more smaller islets. On the Canadian side, a vast group of islands is officially called the Gulf Islands, and is sometimes known as the Canadian San Juans. Vancouver Island reminds me of Nova Scotia, on the opposite side of

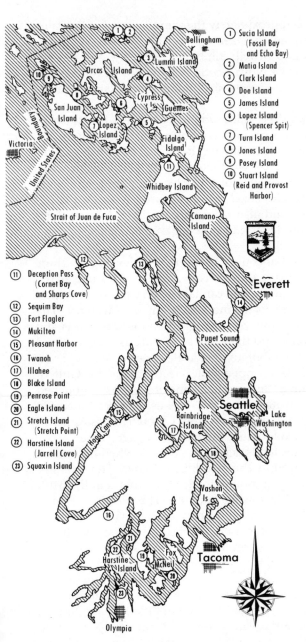

1. Sucia Island
   (Fossil Bay
   and Echo Bay)
2. Matia Island
3. Clark Island
4. Doe Island
5. James Island
6. Lopez Island
   (Spencer Spit)
7. Turn Island
8. Jones Island
9. Posey Island
10. Stuart Island
    (Reid and Provost
    Harbor)
11. Deception Pass
    (Cornet Bay
    and Sharps Cove)
12. Sequim Bay
13. Fort Flagler
14. Mukilteo
15. Pleasant Harbor
16. Twanoh
17. Illahee
18. Blake Island
19. Penrose Point
20. Eagle Island
21. Stretch Island
    (Stretch Point)
22. Harstine Island
    (Jarrell Cove)
23. Squaxin Island

HAVENS—Locations of the major Washington State marine parks are shown on map. In addition, adjacent British Columbia maintains a number of marine parks. Most of them can only be reached by water. Mooring buoys or floats, or both, are usually found at these locations, along with shoreside trails and clamming, fishing, or picnic areas. In most cases, overnight moorage or anchorage is free, on a first-come basis. Few of them have utilities or developed facilities. Most will accommodate yachts up to 45 feet, but detailed navigation charts should be consulted. Descriptive literature on the parks can be obtained from the State of Washington and Province of British Columbia travel information or marine boards.

the continent. Both are approximately the same size and in the same latitude, buttressed by the open sea on one side. Vancouver, however, is mountainous and heavily timbered, with big stuff like fir, hemlock, and cedar; while Nova Scotia is flatter, with rolling hills covered by black spruce and pole-size timber, rocks, and swampy areas.

It is about six hundred miles around Vancouver Island by the most direct passages, and circumnavigating it has become an appealing adventure to local yachtsmen. The capital of British Columbia, Victoria, with its suburbs, is situated on the southeast tip. This is the starting point of the Swiftsure, Cobb's Seamount, and Maui races. From here, John Guzzwell set off aboard *Trekka* on his circumnavigation in 1955, and also from here, in 1901, Captain John Voss and Kenny Luxton departed in the log canoe *Tilikum*, to emulate Slocum.

The east shore of Vancouver Island is well developed. There are areas devoted to industry and tourism, and a road leading all the way up to Kelsey Bay, whence one can take a ferry to Prince Rupert on the northern mainland, or connect with an Alaskan ferry. The west coast of the island, however, is rugged and isolated. It is still primitive cruising country and therefore adventurous. Puget Sound is the origin point of the fabulous Inside Passage to Alaska. From Juneau, the capital, it is an open-water leap across the Gulf of Alaska to Prince William Sound, perhaps one of the most untouched and awesome cruising waters on earth. It is as far from Juneau to Dutch Harbor, in the Aleutians, as it is from Chicago to Los Angeles. It would take years to explore just the Inside Passage alone.

So why sail off for lands across the oceans when there is so much to see and do around the Northeast Pacific? The summer months are regarded as the period of the best weather, but the truth is that this is year-round cruising country. The weather is mild enough, even in Alaska, to make it unnecessary to haul out for the winter, and there are frequent periods, in the very worst months, of sunshine and surprisingly warm temperatures. In the winter of 1938–1939, I lived aboard a thirty-foot troller with two other guys, in the Juneau, Alaska, boat harbor. In fact, in that same harbor at least half the boats had live-aboards. We did not find it uncomfortable.

For the present, we decided to gulp in little bits at a time of the most accessible southern waters, on short trips, while winding down our onshore obligations. Of immediate interest were Puget Sound and parts of lower British Columbia, which we hoped to follow up with a circumnavigation of Vancouver Island, then one of the Queen Charlottes, and thence on north to Alaska.

The waters of Puget Sound are deep, averaging six hundred

feet or more, with steep-to shorelines, dropping rapidly in depth and often rising to high forested cliffs and tan bluffs. There are some low beaches, expansive tide flats off river deltas, and occasional shoals and reefs which make anchoring an art in these waters. Dock and marina space is limited.

Winds are generally strong and predictable, and gales are not uncommon even in midsummer—as we were to discover the hard way. But the region's tidal characteristics are of more concern to the small boater than almost anything else. Tide ranges are wide and tidal currents make up to ten to twelve knots in places, with dangerous rips a common hazard. For a six-knot boat, if one wants to go anywhere on some kind of a schedule, it is essential to "play the tides"—Puget Sound's most popular water sport.

Flood tides enter through the Strait of Juan de Fuca to the west and the Strait of Georgia to the north. They cause swirling currents through the islands and around peninsulas, in and out of inlets, and up rivers. They affect all marine life and shoreside activity. On the ebb tides, the reverse happens, although the currents are not as severe as on the floods. Add strong winds to either the flood or ebb and you have some awesome complications.

Most watercraft, except full-powered vessels, try to ride the tides, although it is seldom possible to gain an advantage over any long cruise. Sooner or later you will encounter an adverse current. Each of the island groups has its own set of current characteristics, and the experienced skipper tries to analyze them to his own advantage. For a boat that cannot outrun itself, however, this is all academic. The best practice is not to be in any hurry to get to any specific place. On *Wild Rose*, we adopted the policy of going anywhere we felt like, any time we felt like it, and taking weather and sea conditions as they came. I am convinced now that every trip, no matter how short, should be preceded by a thorough briefing on tide and current conditions, as well as wind and temperature predictions. Especially, one should be careful to arrive at passes on or near the slack water periods.

The meeting places of tidal currents create tide rips, most of which are predictable in normal weather but extremely dangerous even to large vessels during gales and storms. These rips range from patches of "busy" water to stretches with overfalls, whirlpools, and sharp ridges. Often these places are full of debris, sawmill waste, and logs and trees. Traveling at night is unwise, for collision with floating logs or deadheads is a constant hazard for all but large commercial vessels. Kelp and debris from sawmills also can cause difficulty with water intakes and props.

Sailing has long been popular on these waters (how else was

this country explored before the internal combustion engine?), and is even more so today. I am not sure I know why, for sailing is hampered by variable winds, tide rips, fastwater passes, and many islands. Sail management on a large vessel with a minimum crew can get to be work. It is common to see sailboats of all sizes using both the engine and the Dacron breeze, which suggests that for year-round cruising in these waters a roomy power boat with a speed of ten to twelve knots would be more practical.

But unlike many other cruising waters of the world, these offer, in addition to scenic views, mild weather, and a sense of discovery, some quite practical diversions as fishing, clamming, crabbing, and scuba diving. Salmon and bottom fish are usually available. You can rake clams right on the beach in many locations, and I would not anchor anywhere without putting down a crab trap. One should not go without a crab and shrimp trap, some suitable fishing gear, and perhaps scuba equipment. For the latter, a wet suit is required due to the cold water.

The first summer that we operated out of the Port Townsend boat haven could be called chaos, but even in chaos one finds some kind of a pattern. There were five hundred moorage spaces available and at times a thousand boats wanting them. Due to strikes and fishery problems that year, many of the commercial trollers and gill-netters from as far as Alaska had returned to sit it out. Weekends invariably brought yacht club and Power Squadron cruises to the area, with fifty to one hundred boats all trying to find nonexistent space in the harbor at the same time.

It was apparently the custom of the port to sublet permanently rented slips, if empty, to any transients that came along. This was lucrative, and if the owner didn't return and catch the interloper, it benefited everyone concerned. However, the system often broke down into a game of "musical slips" upon the onslaught of visiting boats which grabbed the first slips they found and to hell with everyone else.

We found the same situation all over the region, especially at the most popular ports. The pattern is this: The stranger, racing the cruising fleet into a port for the night, and usually beset by a strong afternoon westerly, squeezes into the harbor. His nerves are perhaps a little ragged and he is looking forward to a quiet tie-up and an iced highball. He finds no informational signs to guide him into and through this jungle of masts, no one to direct him to an available slip. So he either ties up temporarily to the fuel dock, which is already closed for the night (and which it is usually illegal to tie up to) or takes a chance running up and down the aisles hoping to find a slip with no name on it. In most of these harbors there are strong currents and often winds that make it difficult to maneuver. Should our stranger find an open space, invariably the permanent owner will return and kick him out, setting the game of musical slips in motion again.

Once, returning to port after a cruise, I put my bride ashore to run around and handle the lines, as there was a tricky set of currents and wind to contend with. She found our slip occupied by a 36-foot sailboat manned by two swinger-type young executives who snarled, "We'll move when you give us back our three dollars!" They moved hastily, however, when I came around the corner and used the bull horn.

No boat, of course, is ever completed, and it was not difficult to compile a new list of a hundred things that needed to be done. Perhaps the most important of these was the purchase of a new anchor windlass able to handle ten or fifteen fathoms of ⅜-inch chain, remotely controlled from the cockpit. Our first available funds, we agreed, would go into this improvement; it had not taken us long to discover that anchoring requires special equipment and techniques for cruising Northwest Coast waters—as, no doubt, it does in any waters—and that one should be prepared for anchoring out frequently, perhaps every night during the peak yachting season.

But for the time being we had a lot of cruising to get on with before our time ran out, and Port Townsend was the gateway to it all. For the first trip, we had our sights on the mystical San Juans, so we made ready, studied charts, and waited for a period of heavy fog in the Strait of Juan de Fuca to change.

Then one morning we were awakened by a horn blasting beside us. I got up to drive away the intruder and found a Grand Banks 32 alongside, aboard which was my old pal, Art Lacey, his wife, Birdine, and their house guest, Mexican exchange student Betty Arellano.

"Get the hell out of that sack, you fat slob, and let's go somewhere!" yelled Lacey from the flying bridge.

20.
The Mystical San Juans

We had just begun to adjust to life aboard *Wild Rose* when the Laceys arrived. They had rented the Grand Banks in Seattle for a week, at five hundred dollars for the bare boat, and by God they were out to get the most of it. They wanted to join us for the San Juan cruise, and they wanted to leave right now.

There was no time to go over charts and tide tables. We gathered a last load of supplies, cast off, and weaved out of the harbor with the Grand Banks on our wake. We set a course of 210 true to Point Hudson, then 320 to the Point Partridge light on the southwest tip of Whidbey Island, planning to then head up Rosario Strait to Sucia near the Canadian border. Our course from Point Hudson took us past Point Wilson and directly through one of the most awesome tide rips in the whole region. We came upon the rip rather unexpectedly, at first seeing only a patch of pointed wavelets.

Then suddenly we were in the middle of a horrifying whirlpool, with overfalls and boil-ups that grabbed *Wild Rose* and wrenched her viciously. The Laceys, on the Grand Banks, had come up abreast but a hundred yards to starboard, and thus missed the worst of it.

This rip, which is the meeting of the tides coming down the Strait of Juan de Fuca and up Admiralty Inlet, can be avoided by crossing directly and keeping to the Whidbey Island shore, or by keeping Point Wilson close aboard until well past, then crossing directly over to Point Partridge. Sometimes, even without a wind, the seas in the tide-rip area are so confused and dangerous that even tugs and commercial vessels get into trouble. It is best to avoid this if possible.

The area is further complicated by the Traffic Separation Zones that converge on an intersection immediately to the northwest of Point Wilson—no place to be in a fog, what with all the ship and barge traffic.

As we drew closer to Point Partridge, I could see a dense fog bank far up the Strait, and I remarked that I was sure glad we were not heading out to sea this day. Within five minutes we were entirely surrounded by the fog, with visibility reduced to a hundred feet, and bouncing in a vicious chop. We tried to raft together, but the difference in our rails and side strakes made this too hazardous, so we decided to go back to Port Townsend and start over.

At 4:30 the next morning Lacey was at our slip pounding on the hull. We got up to see a gloomy, dark, wet day coming. During the night, the wind had shrieked through the rigging, but here in the moorage there seemed to be a calm, and the smoke from the nearby pulp mill stood straight up.

We let ourselves be persuaded to embark again, this time going up past Point Wilson to make a clockwise run around the infamous tide rips. But this put the weather coming down the Strait directly on our beam, and by the time we got past Point Wilson, it had worked up to gale force. We saw one other craft, a large sloop with a three-reefed sail, plunging and wallowing ahead of us in eight-foot swells, with winds gusting up to forty-five knots. Lacey was leading this time in the Grand Banks and making heavy weather of it, yawing off and pitching and wallowing sometimes almost out of sight. My bride had never been in any kind of weather like this and now was a little frightened.

"You better take the wheel," she said, and also suggested we go back.

"Don't worry, *Wild Rose* was built to take much worse than this." And, indeed, in spite of the huge breaking swells rolling down abeam, we did not even take any spray aboard and were not uncomfortable.

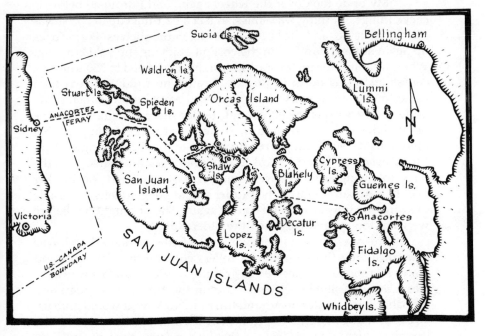

THE SAN JUANS—*Principal islands of the San Juan archipelago are shown in this sketch map. They were the scene of Wild Rose's earliest cruises after leaving the Columbia River and sailing north. The island of San Juan is only 15 miles long, which gives one an idea of the scale. Sidney, on the east coast of Vancouver Island, is also a popular yacht stop, convenient to Victoria.*

My bride took over the wheel again, and I dropped below to check things. Nothing was amiss; in fact a half-full cup of cocoa was still on the table, and the books were still in the shelves. I came back up again and sat bundled in the cockpit enjoying the wild crossing. When we came abeam the Partridge light, we turned to 350 true on a course taking us north in Rosario Strait. The wind and seas then came to our stern quarter and steering became more difficult. My bride, not yet experienced enough under these conditions, at one point allowed the vessel to turn 90 degrees to port, crying out that there must be something wrong with the hydraulic steering system. I took over and found it hard to bring her back on course with the huge following seas. We were lying almost a-hull. By kicking her over to starboard as far as the rudder would go, gradually I was able to swing the bow around on course again. Then I caught her before we went too far and corrected the other way.

This was the worst following sea I had experienced with *Wild Rose*, including those enormous rollers crossing the Columbia and Grays Harbor bars. It seemed to grip the rudder in such a way as to create an undesirable back pressure on the hydraulic system, and probably some cavitation around the rudder. A swell would grab us, swish us along at surfing speed, then drop us off the crest into the trough suddenly. I soon learned that by correcting the helm quickly, never letting the bow swing more than a few degrees one way or another, and quartering before the swells, I could keep the ship on course. After that we had no real problem.

Wild Rose under these conditions became a frisky wild colt, but there was no danger of broaching, as she would easily lie a-hull anyway, taking a minimum of slop over the rail. Once, when my bride was not looking, a small rogue wave jumped aboard and threw several gallons of water into the cockpit, but that was the first and last time I ever saw this happen.

We came abeam Smith Island off to port, and then Lawson Reef, meeting and passing a number of commercial vessels throwing spray. Entering Rosario Strait proper, we came under the protection of the San Juan group, and the seas and wind moderated. Ahead of our two-boat flotilla lay an isolated world of islands and reefs. We now saw a number of sailboats in the distance. The skies seemed to clear and the waves reduce to small whitecaps. It was still early afternoon, so we had plenty of time. We kept in contact on Channel 6 low power, and when we wanted to talk, one of us would hang a towel on the rail.

Now I called and suggested we make the first night stop at Blakely via Thatcher Pass, one of the main routes into the interior of the archipelago. It is an opening about a quarter of a mile wide, with a reef in the center and a channel on either side. The pass looked crowded with sailboats. As we approached, I could see the Anacortes–Sidney ferry plowing toward us from Fidalgo Island to the east.

I called Lacey on the horn: "It looks like we, thirty-seven sailboats, and a ferry are going to arrive at the entrance all at the same time."

This indeed happened. The ferry had to slow almost to a halt. The sailboats had to tack frantically. We were able to ease close to the rocks to make room. Once the ferry came through, we all closed ranks again and headed up a large, soundlike body of water as calm and serene as a lake. The number of boats was incredible, boats of all kinds—sailboats, powerboats, houseboats, runabouts, skiffs, plus a ferry coming or going every half hour loaded with tourists and commuters to island homes. The ferries usually stop at Orcas, Shaw, Lopez, and Friday Harbor on San Juan during their runs to and from Anacortes and Sidney, B.C. During the summer there is normally a five-hour wait at main terminal points.

We had penetrated into the heart of the San Juans during the peak of the summer season, and even I was surprised at what we found there.

The San Juans were named by Francisco Eliza, commandant at Nootka in 1791 and one of the early Spanish explorers who left their names, if not their mark, on all this country before the British and then the Yankee traders supplanted them. For many years the island group was under the control of the ubiquitous Hudson's Bay Company, which carried on agriculture and fur trade. There is today a roadside inn at Orcas which is said to date back to 1838.

Americans came to settle the islands after the Wilkes Expedition in 1841. At the time, this country was considered all Oregon Territory by the Yanks, and British by the Hudson's Bay Company, which was confusing to tax collectors and settlers alike. A U.S. revenue cutter took up station in the San Juans, which the British considered provocative. There were many incidents, including armed forays. The British Columbia gold rush in the 1850s brought many travelers through the islands. By 1859, there were twenty-five permanent American settlers. One of these, a gent named Lyman Cutter, shot an HBC pig he found rooting in his garden, thus precipitating the famous "Pig War," which lasted eleven years with a British encampment at one end of San Juan Island and an American fort on the other. The only blood shed, however, was that of the pig.

For a time there was a joint occupation, characterized by much good feeling, and many social gatherings and sporting events. Both American and British military personnel considered the San

Juans the best duty in the world. Finally, on November 25, 1872, the boundary question was arbitrated by a panel consisting of the king of the Netherlands, the president of the Federal Council of Switzerland, the kings of Sweden and Norway, and Kaiser Wilhelm I of Germany, who handed down the final decision.

The San Juans from the first became way stations for smugglers. Opium and diamonds were staples in the trade. Then wool became contraband and the islands became known for the astonishing amount of wool they produced, especially considering the few sheep being tended. During Prohibition, rum running prospered, along with hijacking and pirating. At one time there was a brisk trade in smuggling Chinese; and as the story goes, if American gunboats approached, the Chinese would be thrown over the side in sacks—a story that used to be popular back in Captain John Voss's day, but is not as believable today.

During one period, a gang of pirates inhabited the Wasp Islands and preyed on smugglers going through. These pirates, according to local legend, were cleaned out and those not killed fled to Alaska.

The violent 1960s saw the rise of drug traffic and the islands became overrun with counterculturists. Private boats and yachts were used by some for smuggling, and some have been involved in hijackings. All this has led to a heavy concentration of customs and narcotics agents.

The islands are either heavily wooded or rural-agricultural, and are the site of such business activities as logging, commercial fishing, quarrying, and cattle raising, but mostly they seem to endure best as recreational retreats. The major industry, after the Hudson's Bay Company left, was a lime and cement operation on the northern tip of San Juan Island around Roche Harbor, founded by a benevolent industrial tycoon named John H. McMillin. The Roche Harbor complex became a company town, almost an economic surfdom, with employees living in company houses, working long days at minimum wages, but "looked after" by McMillin, who considered them family. He had his own fleet of ships, an army of private guards, and companies of barrel makers brought in from Japan.

Included in the complex was the famed Hotel de Haro, built on the site of the Hudson's Bay post to entertain illustrious visitors such as Teddy Roosevelt in 1906. His signature for Room 2 is still on display in the lobby overlooking the yacht harbor.

Today, from May to Labor Day, the islands and surrounding waterways at times seem like ant hills crawling with visitors, but they leave all at once, in one great evacuation. From September to

DECEPTION PASS—A yacht leaves a foaming
wake in the turbulent tidal race of Deception
Pass between the north end of Whidbey Island
and Fidalgo Island. View is from the bridge over
the narrow gut, looking eastward. Many boats
use this route to and from Seattle and the San
Juans. Others avoid it by taking the Swinomish
Canal and Guemes Channel.

May, the resorts close up, the locals come out of hiding, and the islands return to the singular tranquillity for which they are known. The group is situated in a sort of weather pocket which consistently is warmer and dryer than the surrounding region, with a rainfall of only about seventeen inches a year compared to a hundred inches in places not more than a hundred miles away. September and even October are often better months for cruising than August—and the people are gone. Cruises to Friday Harbor are made all winter long, although snow and ice are not uncommon in December and January.

The San Juans were once the ultimate destination of yachtsmen. Now they are more like steppingstones to the Canadian Gulf Islands and the Inside Passage to Alaska. At least 90 percent of the visiting boats are small craft—many of which are attached to trailers and brought in on the ferries—day sailers, and rental boats from Seattle and Anacortes. A person who wants seclusion and quiet anchorages will avoid the San Juans in midsummer, especially August.

One reason I changed our destination from Sucia Island to the north, and entered Thatcher Pass, was to put in at Blakely and see if I could straighten the sail track so the slides would not hang up all the time. Blakely Island was owned by a friend from my flying days, Floyd Johnson, who bought it for the landing strip and then developed it into a private residential retreat, mainly for flying families, but also for yachtsmen after the marina was built.

Oddly enough, although I was an enthusiastic flyer, I turn rigid with fright atop a six-foot stepladder. How I was to climb a fifty-foot mast in an emergency was a nightmarish problem I put out of my mind during the construction of *Wild Rose*. But when I built the mast, I went to a great deal of trouble to be sure everything that had to go on it was on it when we stepped it, including even flag halyards. Later, I discovered that some of the lines and halyards had become displaced or entangled during the stepping, and someone would have to go up and straighten out the mess. By studying the problem, I could see that if I put a weight on the lower tackle I would be able to raise it to the level of the spreaders, then swing it through and down the other side.

I tied on a small dinghy anchor and raised this to the spreaders, only to have the wind roll the ship at the wrong time, winding the anchor securely around the upper mast. I next tried raising a Purex jug full of water. This, too, got caught in the upper rigging and I could not raise or lower it. Then I tried to send up a hammer (which happened to be the one I used most frequently) as a messenger, and this also became entangled. To tell the truth, I can't recall now just what plan I had in mind, but in those days I was in a perpetual state of hypertension.

Just as I had given up, I turned to find a crowd of harbor rubberneckers watching my antics incredulously. Never before had they ever seen a mast rigged with a Purex bottle, a hammer, and a dinghy anchor.

I waved to the mast and announced to the crowd, "All part of the christening ceremonies," and disappeared below for a cold beer.

Later, it took me and a high rigger I hired at eight dollars an hour to untangle the mess and straighten out the halyards and running rigging. After that, I discovered I was too big and heavy to raise myself on a bosun's chair, and had no one to help me. So I smartened up, as they say, and installed aluminum mast steps. By fighting my fear of heights and shaming myself into it, I managed to get myself up as far as the spreaders, hiring a rigger to install the ones on the topmast. By the time we had moved the vessel to Port Townsend I could almost casually climb halfway to the spreaders. I was still working on the additional height. Climbing to the top of the mast had become a goal as meaningful to me as Everest was to Hillary.

As we rounded the point and coasted into the shallow bay of Peavine Pass, we found the marina full of yachts. We drifted around for fifteen minutes while I glassed the moorage and fuel dock, seeing no chance of getting in here for the night.

I called Lacey on the horn, "Let's go on up to Rosario and spend the night. There's a world-famous resort there and we can clean up and have an evening ashore."

We should have gone to Sucia.

21.
The Winds of August

So here we are in the enchanted islands and finding many things not so enchanting. I head up East Sound on Orcas for Rosario, with Lacey and the Grand Banks following. Rosario is about five miles upsound, in an open bight facing the east, with a small harbor, fuel, and transient space, built around the converted estate of an early industrial tycoon, Robert Moran, a New Yorker who came west and made it big in Seattle, even becoming mayor. He fell in love with the San Juans and bought six thousand acres on Orcas, under the lee of Mount Constitution, for a summer home. Most of this has become a state park, but Rosario—including the old mansion with its plate-glass windows, solid mahogany doors, and teak parquet floors—is now a luxury resort.

The little cove is called Cascade Bay, and it faces the east. The water drops abruptly from the rocky shore ledge to depths impossible for anchorage. Close in, some mooring buoys are maintained for smaller vessels. I should remember all this but don't, in my haste to get anchored and squared away for the night. We run down the sound with the wind at our backs, which is unusual. This time of day and year, the prevailing wind is westerly. But a front is beginning to move in, a low-pressure system which always brings winds from the southeast, as I also should remember.

Cascade Harbor, we find, is a lee shore. Moreover, it is jammed with small sailboats and jerks in high-speed runabouts showing off for the audience on the verandahs overlooking the harbor. Seaplanes come and go, adding to the confusion. The wind makes maneuvering difficult, the water depth makes anchoring impossible. Lacey lets out twenty fathoms of chain without holding bottom, and blows a fuse in the anchor windlass panel. Having no extras, he wraps the old one with aluminum foil, burning his hand.

Meanwhile, I have twenty fathoms of rode out, mostly nylon, which stretches so much I find myself in among the mooring buoys, with boat owners shaking fists at me but not offering any help, which is normal. Up at the lodge, an audience of tourists and smart-alec onlookers gathers for the impromptu demonstrations of poor seamanship. We spend about an hour trying to anchor under these conditions before I give up and head into the wind back toward Blakely. At the little village of Olga in Buck Bay I turn in, seeking shelter. We find anchorage off the public float leading up to the country store, just outside a large field of crab-pot floats, in thirty feet of water, mud and sand bottom. The Laceys arrive in a few minutes and drop their anchor. We drift some with the tide and wind, but a second anchor also digs in and we are secure for the night.

Buck Bay is a good anchorage, but also exposed to the east. Just before dark, though, the wind dies down, the bay becomes placid, and then the lights begin to wink cozily through the trees on the hillside. We put crab traps over, baited with scrap fish caught by jigging, and harvest several dozen.

Next day we are up early watching the morning come on dark and overcast, cold and humid—which a wiser sailor would recognize as part of the advancing low-pressure system. At 8 A.M. we heave the anchors and head via Upright Channel for Friday Harbor on San Juan Island. Traffic is light, for most cruisers sleep in of mornings in these parts, wasting the best part of the day.

Beyond the pass, we turn up San Juan Channel through some heavy tide rips, bucking the current the last two miles. Friday Harbor, a deep bay facing north and partially protected by Brown Island, is the most populous town in the group, with about six hundred permanent residents, a small shipyard, and the University of Washington Marine Biology Station. It is also a major port of entry, a shopping center, and ferry terminal. We need to do some shopping and I want to show the Laceys around this quaint island community.

The harbor is jammed with yachts of all kinds and sizes, seaplanes and ferries are coming and going, and the marina is bouncing with continuous wakes. We try to get to the fuel dock, but are warned off by some local kids—the dock is too shallow for our depth. We tie up at the transient float, squeezing in behind a California yacht and a Seattle houseboat. This is a mecca for California yachts, drawn here by all the high-blown publicity in the boating magazines. The San Juans' most famous resident, Ernest K. Gann, who has an estate in the valley behind the tow, has tried to discourage this by running down the place whenever possible, without any success.

Friday Harbor has new facilities, but we are told there is a week's wait to get in. We fix a light lunch aboard and walk uptown to shop through the vacation mobs. We do not see a rabbit on the main street, but on past trips we have seen them going up and down the streets, and overflowing the yards of homes. In fact, rabbits have overrun San Juan for years. The problem started when a local farmer imported a pair of Belgian hares. They escaped, and as such critters proliferate, the island was soon almost knee-deep in them. Hunting them became a year-round sport and business, but the rabbits continued to increase. Next, farmers imported foxes in the hope that they would soon clean out the rabbits. But then the island became knee-deep in foxes as well as rabbits. The foxes later developed a fatal virus and were wiped out, leaving the island once more to the rabbits.

For many years the rabbit hunting attracted outsiders until it became hazardous to life and property. No Trespassing signs went up, guns were banned, and a new sport developed—rabbit netting.

Two of you sat on the front fenders of a car as it was driven at night along the roads and across fields. The headlights blinded the rabbits and you simply scooped them up with a salmon landing net. Some years before, I had accompanied a friend to Friday Harbor to get the story of this unique hunting. We slept aboard his 18-foot runabout at the float. One night, some of our new hunting companions came down after we were asleep and dumped several gunny sacks of live rabbits into the boat. We awoke to find two dozen furry animals crawling all over us.

Now, we and the Laceys finally flee Friday Harbor, heading on up San Juan Channel toward Roche Harbor through heavy sail and motorboat traffic. We come up on Speiden Island, and through the 7 × 50 binoculars I scan the grassy slopes. Grazing about half-way up is a herd of African animals. Speiden, now called Safari Island, is private property once owned by a wealthy family of big-game hunters who stocked it with exotic creatures from all over the world.

We enter Roche Harbor, turn left through the pass, and come up in the heavy congestion off the Hotel de Haro. I sweat into the fuel dock and take on twenty-eight gallons of diesel. The chaos in the harbor, however, is too much, so instead of going in behind the log boom, which would have been out of the wind during the night, I follow Lacey and the Grand Banks across the bay to a small cove on Henry Island. There is another Grand Banks anchored in the cove, and a small sailboat close in toward the beach. Lacey drops his hook and it holds. Next follows two hours trying to get me anchored in the sand and weed bottom with the wind freshening from the east. Because of my draft, I cannot get into the cove far enough to find shelter from the wind. It takes three anchors finally to keep me from drifting, including a twenty-pound Danforth off the stern to keep *Wild Rose* from sailing around.

In the morning, the front can be seen approaching. The bay is covered with frothing waves. The sky hangs dark and rainy. We are underway at 6 and out the pass into Speiden Channel. The rain now beats down hard. The wind against the rips throws us around. In an hour we are abeam Green Point. Instead of heading north down President Channel to Sucia, we change our minds and start across to Jones Island. The barometer is 29.8 inches; the temperature 50 degrees, the humidity 78 percent. We meet the wind coming full bore from the southeast up San Juan Channel. We are glad later that we did not go up to Sucia this day, for the boats caught there had a hard time of it in the storm. The changing tide brings furious rips. It is a rough crossing, with seas of four to six feet breaking on our starboard quarter. Once behind Jones Island we hope to find a protected anchorage in the marine park. We find it jammed with boats so we continue on through the pass, rounding up behind Fawn Island in Deer Harbor.

Deer Harbor is a popular protected harbor—except in south-easterlies. The wind is now gusting to forty-five knots. The moorage and fuel dock are jammed with boats and a number of others are trying to get in for shelter. One sailboat is already aground on the beach, and another looks about ready to wind up the same way. Since Lacey has a remote-controlled windlass, I call for him to find us anchorage.

"Don't put the monkey on my back!" he yells.

I head up under Fawn Island and drop the hook. It is a rocky bottom, and we are poorly positioned. I have to haul up again. Meanwhile we are drifting fast onto the rocks. Lacey yells over to follow him. I grab the wheel and advance the throttle.

He heads directly for Pole Pass, which is supposed to be dangerous under these conditions. We leap through the breaking seas and whirlpools in the narrow slot. Lacey finds an anchorage in a bight close up on the north side of Shaw in Wasp Passage. He has no trouble anchoring and is soon fishing. I cannot get our anchor to hold. It is deep and steep—right up to the shoreline.

Exhausted from hauling anchors and trying to control *Wild Rose*, and angered at seeing the Laceys lounging in the cockpit fishing, I give it up. I yell as we pass that we are headed for Orcas. Out in Harney Channel, we again run into breaking seas, and I see the Laceys coming up behind us. There is a ferry at the Orcas landing, and the fuel dock is jammed with yachts. I continue on past and cross over again to Shaw and a large open bay called Blind Bay on the chart. It seems to have good depth, although there is a reef at the entrance, and it has a westerly exposure, protected by a small island.

Blind Bay has a bad reputation, but we find the entrance easily in the storm and motor up to the head of the bay where at least fifty yachts are anchored in water less than twenty feet deep. We drop the hook on the outer fringe. The Laceys come up and anchor off us. I put down the four-pronged Squid and back off to a five-to-one scope. The bay opens to the west, but the easterly is coming over the low gap in the land behind and swooping down furiously, as through a venturi tube. We drag and drag, and when we hold, *Wild Rose* sails around the anchor and loosens it. We are in the middle of the bay when I get her holding with three anchors down. Instead of a stern anchor, though, I set up the Wind Wand vane, which stops the sailing around the anchor. We are dug in securely at last.

The wind is gusting now to fifty knots. Then the rains come, a deluge not of drops but of shafts of water driven downward by great force, enough to wash the decks of the Roche Harbor mud. The windows and ports fog up. I go up on deck to see the Laceys dragging down on us as Art hauls the anchor. Then they circle us and hail across that they are leaving.

Now we are alone. When the rain lets up, I get out the big Danforth landing craft anchor, surplus from World War II South Pacific operations. I rig this with ⅜-inch chain and get it ready to put over. But then, toward twilight, the wind dies down, the sun peeks out, and suddenly we are becalmed on a mirrored bay with the most gorgeous sunset of the summer. I put the crab pot over and in a few minutes have eighteen red and dungeness crabs. Jigging for bottom fish, I hook an eight-pound "blackmouth" or small chinook salmon.

During the night the wind comes up again and we are lashed by waves and pounding rain, but the anchors hold and the rocking of the boat and the slapping against the hull even become soothing. At dawn I get up to find the bay again mirrored and this time a most spectacular sunrise. There is peace all around us. As usual, none of the other boats have their eyes open. We have all this glory and peace to ourselves. I haul in the trap and find a half-dozen more crabs. We don't need any more so I release them—it is just nice to know I can catch them when I want to.

We decide to linger awhile, and being at last alone, we feel under no pressure to do anything or go anywhere. I think at last we have learned the first lesson of cruising these waters.

22.

Sucia Means Foul

Before leaving the San Juans, we returned to Orcas Island and visited the Rosario resort under better circumstances. The main lodge, which was the original Moran mansion, was worth the visit, and the dining-room fare was outstanding. But looking over the marina, we could see it was not for the likes of *Wild Rose*. There was also at the time a charge of twenty dollars a day in return for which one was given scrip good for exchange at the other facilities.

We climbed to the top of Mount Constitution, which rises 2,409 feet above the island group and from which we could see Mount Baker, the volcanic peak to the northeast; Mount Rainier to the southeast; Vancouver Island to the west; the Olympics to the southwest; and all of the hazy Pugetopolis on the mainland. The summit is now an antenna "farm" for television stations and communications systems, including a repeater station for the amateur

VHF/FM band, which we found more reliable in our cruising than the marine channels.

For years I had wanted to visit the tiny, remote islands to the north in the Strait of Georgia—Matia, Sucia, and Patos. They are up there by themselves, and until recently they were seldom visited and almost unknown. In the old days they were bases for smuggling and other fringe activities, and all the legends surrounding them.

Today Matia is a bird sanctuary and has a marine park with camping facilities for small-craft visitors. It is home to seals and bird life of all kinds, including the rare sea parrot. Sucia, the larger of the group, takes its name from the Spanish word meaning "foul," as in foul ground, for it is surrounded by rocks and reefs. There are two havens, both of which open to the southeast: Fossil Bay and the larger Echo Bay, finger inlets with deep water and rocky wooded shores.

In the 1920s, Sucia was used as a fox farm. Sandstone was also quarried on the island for many years, and occasional families lived there. In the 1950s, an energetic yachtsman and community-minded leader, Ev G. Henry, organized Puget Sound boating groups into an association to buy the island and turn it over to the Washington State Parks and Recreation Commission for a perpetual state park. Today there is a marker and plaque dedicated to Henry and the Puget Sound Interclub Association at Fossil Bay.

During the recent storm we had wisely not gone to Sucia, where the anchored yachts had been scattered by fifty-five-knot winds roaring up Georgia Bay, but today we sailed out of the San Juans through Peavine Pass and around the east side of Orcas to Sucia in placid weather. Floats and water were available in Fossil Bay, which was also full of yachts. We went around to Echo Bay, finding more room there for a large vessel, and were greeted by a scenic view of Mount Baker to the northeast. The rock formations on Sucia are fascinating, for the geology is unique, with remnants of two separate ice ages evident in the fossils of mammoths and other creatures that have been found there. It is a beautiful place, but like other marine parks, too civilized for *Wild Rose*. We passed up Patos (Spanish for "duck") and Matia, saving them for a later day, preferably in the off-season. We also put off Reid Harbor on Stuart Island for another day, along with Waldron, the big island that is fascinating to see on the chart, because of its size and isolation. Instead, this trip, we came down Rosario Strait among the so-called Eastern San Juans, which include Lummi with its reef netters, Sinclair, Vendovi, Eliza, Cypress, Guemes, Fidalgo, and many small islets. We had completed a circumnavigation of the main group of San Juans.

On one occasion in Haro Strait we witnessed a most unusual

drama. One morning, just off to starboard, we saw a company of at least a dozen tall dorsal fins congregating in a pod—killer whales. As we watched, they began moving out, with the tallest fin in the lead, followed by progressively smaller fins in single file. The file took on more speed, sometimes the glistening backs coming awash, then in a sudden burst the file began circling what must have been a school of salmon a good city block in size. There came then an awesome thrashing as the killer whales broke formation and moved through the school of salmon, which was decimated in a matter of seconds. Although I knew that these salmon runs now exist only through artificial fish management, I could not help being impressed by a demonstration that Mother Nature was still the greatest of ecologists.

There came a day when we discovered that even with large tank capacity, unsparing use of freshwater supplies soon demands a reckoning. In our perambulations among the islands we had used up most of the main tank, so we decided to go into Anacortes for a weekend stay. We made Quemes Channel on a lovely Saturday morning, sailing slowly against the tide, with at least fifty other yachts strung out behind us, all seeming to converge.

Rounding the hook on Fidalgo Island, we entered the almost landlocked boat haven. We turned right through the entrance. There in the first aisle was an open guest slip. We tied up and I went in search of the harbor master. He turned out to be a busy but friendly gent, who made us move to the other side of the double slip, however, saying he had another vessel coming in with a prior reservation. But we were glad to be tied up early on Saturday with no hassling. We were also astonished to find modern 30-amp shore plugs that did not need adapters, convenient faucets of cold sweet water, clean garbage facilities, and, nearby, chandleries and ice machines. By noon the transient slips were all full, and the fuel dock and boat haul out jammed.

Anacortes is an important lumbering, fishing, and oil refining center on Fidalgo Island, which is separated from the mainland by the narrow waterway called Swinomish Channel. This is certainly one of the finest boat harbors in the Pacific Northwest, and the most sheltered. We hiked up to the supermarkets and shopped for some fresh fruits and vegetables. I filled the main water tank and the two five-gallon jerry cans, replenished the block ice in the chests, scrubbed the deck and hull of mud, weed, and crud, and caught up with other maintenance work.

The harbor was busy with yacht and fishing activity, but we enjoyed the bustle for a change, and the weather could not have been better. A local expert, who was completing a Miller 44 nearby, ambled over to talk. It was he who, hearing our recent anchoring tales, told me that Blind Bay had a lot of solid rock underneath it, and that probably was why we drifted so much.

Unlike what those pretty diagrams in Chapman's and the yachting press lead you to believe, anchoring in these waters requires special techniques, he said. His standard formula for anchor gear included six fathoms of 3/8-inch chain for every situation, plus two fathoms of chain for every fathom of depth, plus a 5/8-inch nylon rode to suit. The chain gives the necessary weight, and the nylon the elasticity to take up shock. Anchors should be heavier than the tables given in the books per length of boat, regardless of their design.

There are few really good anchorages in this region. Often the water drops from ten or twelve feet along shore to five hundred feet or more a few yards out. Where there is shallow water, there is also likely to be kelp. Moreover, the bottom is often rocky or sandy with weeds. All the good anchorages are seemingly always too crowded for proper scope and swing, which makes anchoring difficult. Most vessels will have the anchor chain dropping almost vertical from the bow, with no scope at all. Under these conditions, not only is heavy tackle needed, but also a heavy-duty windlass for handling the tackle, remotely from the cockpit if possible.

Further north, where steep-to conditions are even more prevalent, the best technique is to move in close to shore, using the depth sounder to find the ledge, and then turn around facing outward so the hook can be dropped in deep water. Next, you back in close to shore to put down a stern anchor or a line to a tree, and adjust the bow rode and the stern line so that the bow anchor hooks into the *side* of the underwater ledge. If the stern line is secured around a tree, you bring the bitter end aboard so that slack can be adjusted for the range of the tide.

For some time I had been feeling intimidated by Deception Pass, the infamous slot between Fidalgo and Whidbey islands. I had sailed by it several times, inspected it from the high bridge over it, and read many accounts of passages through it. I had always been impressed, knowing from the first time I saw it that sooner or later I would have to go through it on a boat. As frightening as it seemed, it was almost too much of a challenge to ignore.

The very first time I saw it was on a motor trip when my daughter, Becky, was only about five years old. We had stopped at the picnic area on the center island and walked down a trail through the dense woods to find a spot where we could take pictures. Becky had been skipping ahead, full of wild abandon, pushing through the bramble and undergrowth that obscured the view of the trail ahead.

Suddenly I had an intense feeling of danger, and yelled at Becky to stop immediately. For once she did. I caught up to her, pulled her around behind me, pushed through the next clump of underbrush, and there the trail ended in a sheer cliff that dropped several hundred feet into the maelstrom below.

The pass is a well-traveled route from Seattle and the east side of Whidbey to Rosario Strait and points north and west. The approaches are marked by tide rips that can become dangerous in bad weather. There are refuges, however, on both sides of the pass, the best one being Cornet Bay, just east of the inside entrance. On the big springs, the currents reach more than nine knots, with big whirlpools, upheavals, back eddies, and overfalls. In a six-knot boat it is best to wait for a slack, but I have seen powerboats of all sizes running through on any stage of tide both ways. Local yachtsmen hardly give it a thought, but to a stranger it can be frightening.

Deception Pass not only intimidated me, but I regarded it now as good practice for running passes and tidal rapids on the Inside Passage to British Columbia and Alaska, where in some places Deception would look like a meandering river by comparison.

Having been watered, rested, fattened up, and renewed in pleasant Anacortes, we decided to take on Deception Pass Monday morning. I had spent some time studying charts and tide tables, and so we timed our departure to arrive slightly before high slack, as given in the local tide book. We estimated a speed of six knots, but running down Guemes Channel we were carried along on a strong ebb at about twelve knots. Rounding Fidalgo Head, we slipped through the pass between Burrows and Fidalgo, still riding the ebb, and sailed south through scattered rain and fog down Burrows Bay and around Langley Point. We were overtaken by dozens of power cruisers streaking from the San Juans toward Deception. We worked through the fishing boats off Reservation Bay, meeting more cruisers coming from the pass and heading for Rosario Strait.

We could now see the high soaring bridge over the narrow gorge. I kept telling myself that if a friend of mine could negotiate the pass under water in scuba gear, then we certainly should have no trouble with *Wild Rose*. Lined up with the bridge, we could look through it and see the little island on the other side. The level of the water seemed noticeably higher there, as if we had a hill to climb. My bride looked at the whirlpools and overfalls, and said quietly, "Maybe you'd better take it."

The wheel felt limp to the touch, then alternately moving with rudder pressure. The tide, instead of being high slack, was running out at a good clip. But we were committed and, knowing this, my nervousness left me and I concentrated on picking a good path through the bad spots. I increased the engine speed from 1,600 to 2,000 r.p.m. and *Wild Rose* leaped from one roll to another, swerving violently off each whirlpool. We were actually climbing, until we got under the bridge, and then riding the center bulge of water which fell off into swift troughs alongshore. I steered between two giant whirlpools, and now we were through and bucking only the current. Passing Cornet Bay, I reduced engine speed again. We had sweated it some, but there had been no real difficulty. We both felt taller and straighter for having responded to the challenge, and no more would Deception Pass intimidate me.

We cruised on south along the east side of Whidbey toward Hope Island and Skagit Bay, pausing off Hope Island to join a couple of dozen fishing boats, dropping lines with herring-baited hooks and attractor blades. We trolled through the rips slowly, the blades working the bait. At one time Hope Island was the most famous place in these parts for giant chinook "hogs" in the fifty- to sixty-pound class. For years, every record chinook seemed to come from Hope Island. But no more. Overfishing by commercials, pollution, loss of stream spawning beds, and other evils have seen to that. A fifty-pound chinook would be a "seven-year fish," with five of those years spent in the mother ocean. Today most runs are managed with propagation programs, and the big fish with the proper genes are gone now.

Toward noon we hooked one on my bride's pole, a bright twenty-two-pounder, which was quickly netted, cleaned, and stowed in the ice chest. In prime meat there is no equal to a fresh chinook. In value, at current prices, this fish was worth forty dollars on the retail market counter.

We picked up then and headed south, not having any particular goal destination except to circumnavigate Whidbey Island, the largest of all. As we approached the southern end of Swinomish Slough, also called Swinomish Channel, we saw a stream of yachts coming and going between the close-spaced markers. We had also entertained the thought of avoiding Deception Pass by making the shortcut from Anacortes and Padilla Bay to Skagit Bay, thus circumnavigating Fidalgo as well. It had only been the challenge of Deception Pass that influenced us not to take this shorter inland route—I won't say "easier," for it is a narrow, restricted channel with only a guaranteed nine-foot depth and a strong current.

But the channel had recently been dredged and improved, and local people had told us we should not pass it up, so I had bought the large-scale chart, N.O. 18427, just in case.

Now, heady with victory over Deception Pass, we approached the southern entrance to Swinomish off Goat Island, and lined up with the channel markers. The channel was well worth the trip, as we moved up through the flat agricultural lands of the Skagit delta, past Indian villages and the quaint old fishing and farming community of La Conner, and tied up to a float near the new boat harbor securely against the heavy current.

La Conner had changed since the last time I had seen it, back in the middle 1930s, but not much. Then, in my late teens, bumming around with two high-school chums, in those Depression days looking for work, I got a job here harvesting peas, a two-week run of ten-hour days at a pay of three dollars a day plus room and board. Now, having passed through the Swinomish we found ourselves at Anacortes's Cap Sante Boat Haven and could not resist another sojourn.

We then headed north toward Lummi, cruised around Cypress and Guemes, visiting Strawberry Bay off Cypress and anchoring for clams and crabs off Dot Island near Saddlebag. Salmon fishing is especially good north of here in the main route of the migrating fish. The reef netters were still operating off Lummi, but we did not pause there.

The waters around Guemes and off Padilla Bay, however, were productive for clams and crabs. We carried a single crab trap, sufficient for supplying our needs, and baited it with heads of bottom fish caught by jigging or with a can of strong cat food with holes punched in it. The latter is also good for trapping shrimp in the deep holes.

The two most common crabs in these waters are the familiar dungeness, or *Cancer magister*, which is found from Mexico to Alaska; and the red cancer, or *Cancer productus*, which is excellent eating but seldom tasted, as there is no commercial fishery for it. Another species, the rock crab, or *Cancer antennarius*, is also found here. The king crab or box crab are rare but are occasionally taken by scuba divers.

We process crabs the Puget Sound way. Instead of dropping them alive in hot water, we clean them first. This is done by grasping the crab from above, folding its legs back, and prying off the back shell against some firm object. The crab is then broken in two by folding the legs in toward each other. The viscera is shaken out, and the gill filaments pulled off. Then, after being washed in clean fresh water, the remaining parts are boiled for fifteen minutes in sea water. Afterwards, the clean cooked and edible parts are placed on ice, to be used for cocktails, salads, grilled crab and cheese sandwiches, and baked crab in ramekins, in the special way my bride fixes them.

Our time was now slipping away rapidly, and we had to turn

south again in the general direction of home. We could have gone the short way, down Rosario Strait, but that would have been too short, and we would miss the inside passage down the east coast of Whidbey, so we once again passed down the Swinomish Channel to take up where we had left off—by going aground on the Skagit flats.

23.

A Small Emergency

We have now entered the final phase of the summer's cruising, and are heading southward along the east shore of Whidbey Island with the intention of stopping overnight at Everett.

The passage is crowded with boats, from fifty to a hundred of them. There is a natural tendency to ease over toward the Skagit flats, which at high water looks like a deep bay but isn't. Moreover, the buoys are often misplaced or out of service. We should have done what all the books recommend—stay in the channel close to the Whidbey shore. We soon slither to a stop on the sand and, for the third time, *Wild Rose* has gone aground: once after launching, once on the Kalama River bar, and now here—after all she has been through, including a safe passage through Deception Pass and the Swinomish Channel.

The wakes of the passing vessels soon raise *Wild Rose* off her

keel and we quickly turn in toward deep water. We round Strawberry Point, cut across to Rocky Point on Camano Island and sail
along this fine stretch of water under a bright sun. Altogether this is
one of the loveliest days of the cruise.

Coming down Saratoga Passage we see the stacks of Everett
across the sound, with Gedney Island coming up to starboard. The
afternoon westerly is beginning to build, raising whitecaps. At 3:45
we are approaching black Buoy 3 off the Snohomish River bar before
a fifteen-knot wind with swells of three to four feet. We are in the
midst of fifty or more yachts, most of them sailboats waltzing
around in the fresh breeze when the engine suddenly races and the
shaft and gear make a horrible racket. We must have struck something, but there has been no thump.

The first thing to do is shut down the engine; the second is to
raise the international distress flag; the third is to call the Coast
Guard on Channel 16. Seattle responds, although there is a Coast
Guard station and cutter in Everett Harbor, not three miles away.
Seattle patches us through to the auxiliary cutter of Flotilla 18, the
Tatoosh, which is on another call off Mukilteo. The *Tatoosh* says to
stand by, they will be there in fifteen minutes.

Meanwhile we see the rocks and pilings of Port Gardner
downwind and wonder how soon we will be upon them. Not a
single boat around us seems interested in our emergency, although
the big flag is hanging in plain sight. *Wild Rose* drifts a-hull, broadside to the wind and waves, riding easily on the swells. She has
found her natural position under these conditions. It is forty-five
minutes before the *Tatoosh* gets to us, and just in time. Circling, they
throw us a line and it falls short. On the second pass, I catch it and
make it fast. The *Tatoosh* tows us across the bar and upriver through
all the traffic and into the boat harbor. Now the wind is twenty-five
to thirty knots. Everything is closed, so we are brought up to the fuel
dock, where we secure.

We spend a glum night and at 7 A.M. make arrangements with
the Fishermen's Boat Yard to haul us out. The head mechanic immediately diagnoses the trouble as a broken reduction gear, caused,
he says later, by improper installation at the factory. We find, however, that the bottom, after more than two years, is almost as good
as new and free of growth.

Disheartened, we prepare for a long delay, but with only a
little prodding a replacement part is brought up from Seattle, and by
the third day, a Wednesday, we are on our way. The people at the
yard are courteous and cooperative—indeed, we find Everett the
friendliest place we have yet visited. When we prepare to leave, the
bill has not yet been computed, so the officer manager says not to
worry, they'll send us a bill later. I volunteer to pay $100 on account.

When received, the final bill totaled only $225, including the towing and hoisting.

By 1 P.M., on a high tide, we ease out of the crowded boat harbor and cross the bar under a bright sun, the sound calm and glassy. At 2 we are abeam the Mukilteo ferry landing, and turning to 203 degrees true for Possession Point. At 3:30 we are passing through a couple of hundred salmon-angling boats off Point No Point, and at 4:00 we turn 233 degrees with Port Ludlow in sight. At 5:00 we are tied up at the outside float of Port Ludlow and connected up again with 30 amp shore power. The relief valve on the hotwater tank had blown off Point No Point and put five gallons of water into the bilge.

We had called ahead for a reservation, although there proved to be plenty of space, since many of the transients had anchored out in this sheltered bay. We find out why. The night's moorage costs us $7.50, compared to $3 everywhere else. We had hoped for some special privilege, since we are members of the Port Ludlow Yacht Club, and also of the property owners' maintenance commission. Not so.

In the morning we sleep in, and after a late start head for Port Townsend, to complete a circle of Washington's sounds and out islands. We have considered going through the Port Townsend Canal, which would save some time, but we are apprehensive about the depth and the overhead clearance, and have already had all the episodes we want for the summer. Besides, we are in no hurry, so we choose the long route around Marrowstone Island and up Admiralty Inlet.

Off Liplip Point, we encounter adverse currents and some heavy rips. We stay in one spot for half an hour, while running at six knots, then turn in close to shore and run along the sixty-foot curve to avoid the currents and head seas out in the channel.

Approaching Marrowstone Light we can see the fog coming down the Strait of Juan de Fuca. I check the charts and turn on the radar. We pass several fishing boats hove to off the light station. We plunge into the fog, holding course for five more minutes. Using the screen which shows up most of the boats, the buoys, and the Victoria ferry—as well as the shore outline of Marrowstone and the hills behind Port Townsend—we change course 90 degrees. Port Townsend bears ahead and two miles away. It is a perfect radar approach. Soon we are out of the fog and in the sunshine. We enter the boat haven and, at 11:45 A.M., tie up at the fuel dock.

Wild Rose is back home.

In September we ran out the Strait of Juan de Fuca to crowded Neah Bay for the fall coho salmon fishing. We made a delightful weekend voyage to nearby Discovery Bay, anchoring one night within view of our homesite on the side of Cape George, and on the same spot where Captain George Vancouver had moored the *Discovery* for the winter in 1792. We fished and dug clams, and I searched the bottom with a depth sounder, looking for a spot that might make a permanent mooring at some future date.

We explored Protection Island, which guards the mouth of Discovery Bay and for centuries was a sanctuary for numerous birds, including the rare rhinoceros auklet. The west end still remains a reserve, but the rest of the island is being developed for residential use.

We made other trips into the South Sound waters, Hood Canal, and around Bainbridge. We ran the currents under the soaring Tacoma Narrows Bridge, successor to the "Galloping Gertie" that I watched collapse during a windstorm in the late 1930s. Port Madison, on Bainbridge across from downtown Seattle, proved to be one of the finest natural anchorages in the whole region. Our favorite place, however, turned out to be quaint, secluded Gig Harbor.

In the end, we were satisfied that we had given *Wild Rose* a most thorough shaking down—to say nothing of her captain and first mate. From this point on, we felt, the dream had come to an end and the reality was just beginning.

We do not sail off into the sunset for distant and exotic lands, but a number of truths, practical as well as spiritual, have resulted from our experience. One is that, it is possible, provided you have patience, fervor, and a steady source of income, to turn a dream ship into a reality. I started with $100 and wound up with a $60,000 yacht without leaving any bills behind.

But cost is only one consideration. The most satisfying revelation was how *Wild Rose* changed both our lives.

In the past my bride had shown no interest in boating. But from the moment she took the wheel, she went through a spiritual metamorphosis in which she was transformed from a person rooted in a solid, suburban existence into a free creature whom I almost had to drag home after every cruise. She even learned to exult in stormy weather.

Each time we left home and jobs to spend a weekend, or a week or two aboard, it became harder to return to life ashore. We even found that we could "escape" without leaving the moorage, just by fooling around with ordinary chores. Our little ship was a world in itself, self-contained and life-sustaining. One day, after a couple of weeks' cruising, we woke to discover we had never felt so close to each other.

Aboard *Wild Rose* my physical and mental well-being improved noticeably. Having been an aggressive and competitive man all my life, with a low boiling point, I note the transformation with satisfaction.

This the supreme lesson: I think that I have, at long last, learned to live one day at a time.

APPENDICES

How to Get
Your Dream Ship

Once a person is bent on owning a boat, virtually nothing will stop him until he is somehow afloat. In most cases a lifetime interest will result in a succession of boats, sometimes running the full cycle from a rowing or sailing skiff to a large yacht and back to a skiff again. In my own case I have owned or built fifteen or twenty small boats, and in addition spent about four years in the shipbuilding business.

But if you're relatively new to the field, it pays to know as much as you can about what you're getting into before you actually acquire that boat you've always dreamt of.

What to Look For
If I had it to do all over again (and pray God I don't!) I'd open my mind to every possible kind of vessel available, and determine truthfully just what my principal purpose is. If a boat is to be used for

175

ordinary coastwise cruising or cruising-racing, it would be silly to invest in a semi-submarine, such as famous circumnavigators Bill King and Bernard Moitessier built for the high southern latitudes where knockdowns and capsizings can be routinely expected. If one's interest is in racing, he shouldn't get a cruiser, and vice versa. For coastal waterways with flukey winds and tidal currents, perhaps one should think in terms of a suitable power cruiser, not a sailboat. Ray Kauffman, who in the 1930s built the ketch *Hurricane* and made a successful circumnavigation, in his retirement years bought an Alaskan 49 deepwater trawler yacht for coastal cruising. Carleton Mitchell, for thirty years a famous ocean sailboat racer, similarly retired to a passage-making power yacht. It's been my observation that most sailing auxiliaries in coastal waters are either under power or using both engine and sails about 80 percent of the time.

Maybe you don't want a sailing auxiliary at all. For a fascinating study of this subject, see *Voyaging Under Power* by Robert P. Beebe, which details his experience in designing, building, and motoring on long passages around the world.

If you lack the months and years necessary for a world voyage, and plan only on a vessel that will get you away from the office for a few days, or simply a vehicle to enjoy in retirement, perhaps the so-called cruising houseboat is the answer. They are roomy, luxurious, shallow draft, and surprisingly handy. We encountered many of these while cruising northern waters.

If your primary purpose is bluewater voyaging, then for safety's sake, if for no other reason, you need a vessel capable of taking on any weather or sea conditions encountered, as you cannot outrun anything on the open sea in a small craft. In my opinion, such a yacht should be of conventional design and workmanship, with safe, clear decks, comfortable accommodations, plenty of storage space and tank capacity, capable of easily heaving-to or running before the wind.

In long or foreign voyages, living aboard is a fact of life. As Moitessier noted, even the most dedicated sea dogs will spend up to ten months of a year in port or in anchorages, and for this, comfort and the amenities are most important. I have read many articles in the boating press by couples who claim to live year-round on 30-foot and even smaller vessels, often raising a child or two aboard. I doubt very much if there are many couples who could be satisfied with this kind of sardine-can living. If you are thinking of this, mark out on the living room floor a space about eight by ten feet and then try to put into it all the clothes, groceries, toiletries, and recreational items necessary for a month-long stay.

Anyone who has had much experience in living aboard house

trailers and motor homes or campers, where one can at least step out the door and use public park facilities, would think seriously before cramming himself, for any considerable amount of time, into a small boat cabin. That isn't living—it's confinement.

Some of the most experienced live-aboards in the world are the members, or "commodores," of the exclusive Seven Seas Cruising Association. A study of their monthly bulletins reveals that practically all their vessels are of generous size and equipped with modern plumbing facilities, electrical systems, and dependable engines for making life easier in confined spaces.

My own decision was influenced by practical considerations. To me, the investment of sixty thousand dollars in such a project called for common sense. I wouldn't spend that much on a vacation cottage and then leave out the plumbing and electricity. Oil lamp lighting (which I grew up with on the prairies) and an outhouse are not my idea of living anymore.

On the other hand, it isn't necessary to spend thousands of dollars on cosmetics and frills. The gorgeous full-color ads in the magazines should not blind one to basic hull construction, which is often pretty shabby underneath. It is better to leave the interior plain but functional, with all wires and plumbing visible if necessary. For one thing, it takes months to really shake down a new vessel and turn up defects such as leaks. It is easier to repair these, or make changes in the accommodations, if you don't have to rip out a lot of upholstery. There will be plenty of time later to complete the interior decorations. It is surprising how easily you can adapt to a plain "commercial" interior, and how quickly you can become bored with one of those chic decorator jobs.

To Buy or Build

If I were doing it over, and had the cash in lump sum, I would without hesitation buy a new or used dream ship outright. I would never contract for a custom job without having an iron-bound agreement as to cost, quality, and a firm delivery date, with penalties for delays and broken promises, and every possible builder's loophole or escape hatch plugged. Under these conditions, of course, you would not likely find a builder willing to sign. The prosperous ones wouldn't touch it; and the fringe operaters, who might, are unreliable and often immune to retribution. I certainly would not advance any money without knowing the financial condition and credit rating of the firm. And no deal this big should be made at all without qualified legal advice.

Shopping around for a new or used boat can be just as much fun and just as soul-satisfying as building your own—and a lot easier. Shop carefully and at your leisure. With so much money involved, it pays to make trips to the big yachting centers such as New York, Miami, Los Angeles, Seattle, and Honolulu, to run down leads. Often such way stations as Panama are fertile hunting grounds. Armchair hunting can be done through the broker sections of the boating magazines and the classified ad sections of major Sunday newspapers. Searching for a dream ship, in fact, can often be an excuse for a vacation trip.

Buying a boat is a complex personal experience, and once the deal is made you should be prepared for a heavy emotional and spiritual letdown. At this time, all your previous judgments will come under severe self-examination in which you will be asking yourself one major question: *How can I sell this tub when and if I change my mind?*

I don't think I enjoyed anything so much as the several years of prowling the waterfront and studying the boat ads before I made the decision to go the kit-boat route.

The Uncompleted Dream Ship

I am convinced that the buyer without enough capital to purchase or finance outright is best off completing the so-called kit boat, most of which now are in fiberglass or G.R.P., as the British call it. For a minimum down payment, you get a professionally designed and molded basic hull and deck, built to required specifications with a material that has been proved in over thirty years of ocean experience, and requires the least maintenance. This can be purchased for from about five to ten thousand dollars and will eliminate the most exacting and time-consuming part of the project. It will also give you the opportunity to complete the yacht to suit your own ideas and requirements, within reason; and the work can go forward as fast or as slow as you can complete it or pay for it, in your own backyard or at a convenient moorage.

In no case should you attempt such a project unless you can pay your way as you go along. Going into debt for a boat is the worse kind of financial folly. Anyone who cannot pay as he goes, should consider the only alternative: building from scratch—in which case he has my sympathy and earnest expressions of good luck.

If you decide to go the kit-boat route, choose the largest size design you will ever want, can pay for, and complete in a reasonable time. Don't select a smaller size with the idea of later "moving up." Once is enough for this kind of project.

If possible, choose a reliable builder as close to home as possible, so you can avoid enormous hauling charges and also be close to the factory where parts and advice are easily obtained. Some builders have space in the yard where buyers can complete their boats, and usually parts and materials can be obtained at a discount—I was able to get as much as 40 percent off the retail price on some items. The builder should also be vulnerable to any possible warranty problems.

If you prefer to bring the hull home, or to rent space close by, be sure the space is going to be available over the three years or so you will spend completing the boat. If the landlord has you at his mercy, you can be sure he will take advantage of this sooner or later.

You will need a source of electrical power, rest room facilities, and security from theft and vandalism. Some sort of shelter is also needed, especially in the northern climes. Almost as important is the need for protection from visitors. Slocum wrote how delighted he was to have the old mariners "work up along" the bridge and stop by to watch the progress, and he was never too busy to stop and have a gam. Personally, I found that these visitors and gawkers nearly drove me up a tree, and I discouraged them as forcefully as I could.

Take the hull in as factory-completed condition as you can possibly afford. At the very least, the bulkheads and deck beams should be in before the hull is removed from the mold, in order to assure integrity of model. I would recommend that you consider, as minimal conditions of completion by the factory, the following: a hull with bulkheads, deck beams, floor timbers, chainplates, stern and rudder tubes, engine mount, and skeg already installed. To have the water and fuel tanks, bunks, galley, and head finished would be highly desirable, and deck installation completed would be even better. This will still leave one helluva lot of work to be done.

Always take advantage of the builder's option packages, such as head and shower compartment module, integral fuel and water tanks, galley modules, bunks, deckhouses, and other standard parts. You cannot build these any cheaper yourself, and the factory job looks more professional. Do not, however, agree to any casual or unnecessary *custom* work at shop prices, unless you really want to get ripped off. If the hull is in the shop or on the builder's lot, make sure you have a firm agreement on custom work. Your best bet is to give the builder a letter stating that no work be done unless specifically ordered or unless you are there to supervise it entirely.

Do not make any major alterations of hull design or configuration without the designer's approval. One Cascade 42 builder lengthened the hull two feet by extending the transom; another had the basic hull spread a foot for more beam. These were approved by the builder, but bizarre changes may not only result in a dangerous vessel, but are likely to reduce the resale value.

Shop diligently and thoroughly for parts and accessories. There is an enormous amount of just plain junk being peddled as "marine-quality." The brand name no longer means anything, either. Some of the worst equipment I purchased came from old-line firms. Unpack and examine every part that comes in, to make sure it is complete (leaving out a few fastenings is the standard rip-off these days) and that it fits and works. Sometimes it is months before you actually install the part, and by that time the warranty may have run out. On most items, you will find the instruction manuals semi-illiterate, and parts lists nonexistent or not applicable to the model you have purchased. I spent many a sleepless night, after an eighteen-hour day, trying to decipher an operating manual written by some pointy-headed subgrade factory engineer.

Building from the keel up can be done by experienced and patient craftsmen for about one-third the factory price. Completing a kit boat can be done for, at best, about two-thirds the factory price. But for most dream-ship people, it is still the most practical way to go.

Tools
After you have completed a kit boat, or built one from the keel up, you will automatically become at least a semiskilled professional boat builder, with a shed full of tools borrowed, bought, or stolen.

I soon learned which tools were practical to keep aboard. During the confusion of construction, I found it cheaper to buy small tools from the bargain bin at discount stores than to spend time looking for lost ones. The most frequently used tools are screwdrivers, of which you will need a wide variety in the different tips such as conventional slotted, Reed & Prince, Phillips, and others. Next in frequency of use are the drills. Power drill bits will be needed by the dozen for the various materials such as fiberglass, wood, aluminum, and stainless steel. In the latter case, the best-quality precision bits are needed, some of which cost as much as ten dollars each.

You will also need handsaws, power saws, wrenches by the score, clamps, pliers, assorted electrical and plumbing tools, putty-ing and painting tools, and a small vacuum cleaner to get the dust and chips out of bilge and crevices. It is amazing how much sawdust and chips will accumulate inside a boat. I am still finding little pockets of it, four years after the launching.

Unless you plan to continue in the boat-building business, you will find that most of these will be surplus after launching and christening. After launching and construction are done, carefully select an array of tools to keep aboard. These should include large spanners for the tailshaft packing nuts, screwdrivers and socket wrenches that will fit every nut and screw on board, in various shapes so that all these can be reached easily. You should also keep a set of engine tools near the engine, especially on a diesel, where bleeding the fuel lines is a common chore.

I keep in separate plastic (or fishing tackle) boxes tools for electrical, emergency, engine, rigging, and routine maintenance.

My electrical tools include: a soldering iron, wire cutters, screwdrivers, small socket or drive wrenches, terminal lug tool with lugs, friction tape, assorted lengths of wire, fuses, staples, and clamps.

Engine tools are kept with or close to spare parts such as filters, water pump impellors, injectors, tubing, gaskets.

Rigging tools and bosun's stores are kept separately. These include screwdrivers, wrenches, pliers, knives, sewing kits, rope kits, shackles, cable clamps, assorted ropes.

I keep a separate box of tools for maintenance, including tools for plumbing jobs, fiberglass repairs, painting, and damage control. Also on hand is an assortment of fiberglass cloths, patches, gels, and resins.

In addition, at the navigator's station I have a special drawer for fuses, vinyl tape, light bulbs, often-used screwdrivers and wrenches, rigging knives, and anything else that may be needed in a hurry.

I also keep handy a can of acetone and a spray dispenser of WD-40—the best friends of the boat builder. Both are often used, and the latter especially seems to be the proper medicine for almost anything, including unsticking lids and nuts, cleaning corroded fuse connections, protecting exposed parts, killing wasps, freeing plumbing fittings, loosening curtain snaps, and even deodorizing. We used it so routinely that it became second nature. Once, while I was on deck struggling to get out of some foul-weather gear without removing my shoes, my wife yelled up, "What are you cussing for?" "I'm trying to get these damn pants off!" I retorted. "Have you tried WD-40?" she suggested absently.

Another indispensable item is old-fashioned Vaseline petroleum jelly. It can be used (medicated) in the medicine chest for burns, rashes, and so on; and on electrical terminal blocks, as protection for seals, for lubricating small parts, for greasing the sail slides, and for waterproofing persistent leaks. It is not greasy and leaves no stains. It can even be used for preserving fresh eggs. Without cleaning the outside of the egg, smear it with a layer of Vaseline and it will keep without refrigeration for weeks.

For emergency use, I keep special tools to fit the stern tube packing nuts, the engine fuel injectors, oil drains, and hose clamps stowed within reach of where they will be needed, along with a flashlight.

In addition, I keep a cloth bag of tapered wooden plugs to fit every hull connection, along with a hammer and some cloth, near every fitting. An assortment of cable clamps is also kept handy, and above each bank of batteries I keep a plastic bottle full of battery water.

Power Tools

Power tools are great savers of time and soothers of frustration, and these days the discount stores offer such bargains that one cannot afford not to use them. In the early 1970s, I was able to buy drills, saber saws, and small orbital sanders for less than ten dollars. It is not necessary to buy expensive high-power tools for such a relatively short-term use as boat building. They come in a wide variety of stock items for the home-builder market, and are cheap because they are programmed for a maximum life of around twenty-five hours of use. This doesn't seem long, but stop and think how long it takes to drill a hole—a few seconds at most, and then the drill is put down until it is needed again. For the average home builder or hobbyist, such tools will last a lifetime; and in boat construction, for the length of the project.

Be sure, however, that you buy tools approved by the various safety and quality-standards agencies. A faulty tool can kill you. One such tragedy took Cliff Bird, a well-known New Zealand yachtsman, as he was completing a 62-foot Tryphena on Great Barrier Island. A short electrocuted him, leaving his wife, Fran, to pick up the pieces of her life and complete the project alone.

For a project like *Wild Rose*, you will need three power drills in the ¼-inch, ⅜-inch, and ½-inch sizes, with a wide selection of bits and hole cutters; a small and medium-sized saber saw, a small orbital sander and medium-sized belt sander, a grinder, and a vacuum cleaner. I also used a small, lightweight portable drill press; there are many drilling jobs which cannot be done accurately with a hand drill, such as boring precision holes in stainless tubing and counter-boring handrail bolt holes. Another indispensable tool is the portable one-inch belt sander, for which grinder belts are also available. Any larger tools can be rented for a few hours as they are needed.

A boat under construction is a hazardous place to work, even without power tools. There are many opportunities for receiving cuts, burns, and eye injuries, and for tripping and falling. Usually the electrical power is supplied through a maze of temporary extension cords and multiple outlets that proliferate as the work progresses—another dangerous situation. If the boat is in the water, there is another problem: dropping things overboard. I lost many of my favorite tools this way, and lots of parts. Screws and bolts had a way of falling to the deck, and making a single jump over the rail. Winch springs, deck plate padding, clevis pins, shackles, and blocks were other common items that jumped ship. Sometimes, in a reflex action, I almost went over, too, trying to catch them.

Sources of Supply

Building a vessel like *Wild Rose* is a traumatic experience in purchasing parts and materials. You have to make buying decisions on from five hundred to several thousand separate items, ranging from a dollar to five thousand dollars in cost. Shopping for the right part or fitting and going through the purchasing routine is time-consuming and often frustrating; at times it made me physically ill. At best, it is like Christmas buying every day of the year.

If you live near a seaport or boating center, you are lucky —not that you will find everything you want handy, but that you will be able to see the actual item before you buy it. And if you live in a large city, you will find marine jobbers and wholesalers with large stocks of merchandise which most marinas and boating outlets do not carry. Indeed, these small retailers most often do not stock any high-priced items, but merely take orders and then run down to the wholesale distributor and pick up the items C.O.D.

Marine suppliers are not the only sources. War surplus stores, trailer supply houses, hardware stores, and large trucking terminals carry an astonishing amount of merchandise that is similar to, the same as, or can be substituted for the so-called marine grade items. It takes time to shop these places, of course, but if you have more time than money, what's the difference?

There are some two or three hundred mail-order "discount" houses in the U.S. that specialize in marine equipment or related merchandise. Of these, about a dozen will sooner or later come into your life, two or three of them working out to your satisfaction. Most carry a basic stock of standard items (a majority of which are imports) and will accept orders for "drop shipping" on more expensive or less standard ones. This means that they take your order, extracting the profit, and pass it on to the manufacturer for shipping direct to you. Pricing systems vary from one house to another, so that it takes careful study to find out if you're actually getting a good price. One house will stock a certain item that others do not, and vice versa.

I had a great deal of difficulty, when ordering from mail-order firms, in getting exactly what I had ordered and at the price listed in the catalogue. I would estimate that from 50 to 70 percent of my orders were in some way unsatisfactory. I would attribute most of this to the type of help these firms employ, and some of it to deliberate rip-off. I have also lost several hundred dollars through firms which went broke or kept the money and did not send the merchandise. In cases like this it would be necessary to bring in the postal inspectors and let them take over. In any boating transaction, as in normal relations with merchants and sellers, the old principle *Caveat emptor* should always be kept in mind.

Shopping is time-consuming, and if your time is limited the best thing is to keep a library of marine catalogues on hand and do your shopping first at home, resting in the old armchair, and to plan ahead, making up lists of what will be needed, and getting the best price possible. The mail-order catalogues are extremely useful reference sources, even if you don't spend much money with them. Most builders will find, however, that for about half the merchandise they need they will settle on one or two outlets which prove reliable and honest; and will pick up the rest through local outlets. When shopping by mail, use the credit-card system. This way you won't have to bother with calculating postage and percentages of discount. And, if you have any real complaints, you can as a last resort go to the card issuer for some added clout. The card also gives you a convenient record of purchases, and eliminates writing checks, which carry a bank charge.

During the course of building *Wild Rose* I spent over one hundred dollars a day for more than two years on such purchasing. I have never in my life spent money so casually or routinely, and there never seemed to be any end in sight. All my life I have had to struggle to earn and try to save money, and always it has been a life on a limited budget, in which I often went without things, and had to learn to suppress buying impulses. Then, in going through a long period when purchases involving hundreds and even thousands of hard-earned dollars were being made routinely, I found the psychological effect at times overpowering.

In the end, however, I felt a great satisfaction in having started out with less than a week's paycheck, financed and completed the project entirely on my own, and come out of it not owing anyone a dime.

Marine Insurance
With so much invested in a yacht, one should never try to get by without insurance. Only the rich can afford to do that. You would not buy a car or a house without having it covered. It is even more important not to leave your boat uninsured.

I insured *Wild Rose* from the moment it came out of the mold. Because of the peculiarities of marine insurance, I found it necessary, during the construction and final outfitting, to change companies and take out several different policies to get the right one at the lowest cost. The whole field of marine insurance seems to be changing, and for this reason you should be careful of which agent you choose and *exactly* what the policy covers. As *Wild Rose* neared completion, at various times she was covered for fifteen thousand, twenty-five thousand, and forty thousand dollars. When I finally added up all the bills I could find, the total cost came to about sixty thousand dollars. I chose to have the policy rewritten to cover an "agreed upon value" of fifty thousand. This isn't the replacement cost, but is what I thought would be the most coverage for the least money. The agreed-upon value is very important in a marine insurance policy, so make sure it is as high as you can afford.

Another important clause is an anachronistic exclusion referring to "acts of war, piracy on the high seas," or words to that effect. This is a little loophole that some companies resort to, which can under some circumstances excuse them from paying when your yacht is hijacked by a drug ring or even stolen by hoodlums at a moorage. Since this is common today, I asked one agent—a well-known boating association—for clarification. This was not forthcoming, and the staffer who answered my follow-up letter concluded by saying that she knew everything was all right, and I had nothing to worry about. Don't ever take this kind of an answer, because you *do* have something to worry about unless it is specifically taken care of in the policy.

I finally wound up with an old-line company and a policy that covered me for *all risks* within the inland and ocean waters I intended to cruise, plus comprehensive, theft, fire, collision, and liability coverage. This costs fifty dollars a month at current premium rates.

Incidentally, members of the Power Squadron or Coast Guard Auxiliary, and holders of a commercial license, are eligible for some healthy discounts on insurance rates.

Documentation
At this writing there is a strong propaganda move on by certain state and federal officials to eliminate the privilege of documenting a yacht of five tons or more. All kinds of reasons are given, most of which are not valid. The underlying purpose of the move seems to be the desire of politicians and bureaucrats for more revenue. Boat owners who don't understand the facts are inclined to accept these reasons, unfortunately.

Documentation is, however, a valuable thing to have. The

best reason is that it provides indisputable title to your vessel that is recognized in every port in the world. As far as many officials in the more backward countries are concerned, state registration numbers are worthless, and if you have no other way of proving who you are and that you really own the vessel, you are in trouble. A Yacht License issued by the United States Government is the best insurance you can have abroad, especially if someone pirates your boat.

A documented yacht also has certain customs and clearance privileges, is automatically listed in the international directories, and is exempted from state regulations and fees in some cases. As it so happens, I have to pay a nominal fee to the Oregon Marine Board, in lieu of taxes, but on the other hand I do not have to carry the state numbers on the bow. A documented vessel has to display the name and calling port only on the transom, and the documentation number and net tonnage in a permanent place below decks.

In addition, if you intend going international, it is possible to qualify for flag signal code, which is permanently listed. In my case, I was issued a flag code, which is the same as my radio license call letters: W Y Z 9 3 0 4. For signaling purposes, I obtained a set of these flags, hanked them all together, and stored them in a handy place for use.

I applied for documentation when *Wild Rose* was still in the mold, and the local documentation officer took it from there. I filled out forms and answered questions only as they came up. It was not complicated and involved no red tape. It took only time, which I had plenty of. Before *Wild Rose* was even removed from the shop, she had her papers, the number and tonnage molded into a permanent spot, and her official name and calling port lettered on the transom.

There is only one thing to remember: Renew the license each year *before* the expiration date, or you might have to go through the whole process again.

On Financing a Dream Ship

Where do you get the money to finance the purchase or construction of a dream ship? And, after you have it, how do you live, keep up the mortgage and insurance payments, and maintain this demanding mistress or gigolo?

In my research for *The Circumnavigators*, I analyzed hundreds of accounts of yacht voyages and dream ships. Almost all of them were maddeningly vague about where the wherewithal came from, and many of these accounts seemed deliberately to avoid such crass subjects. Nevertheless, finance is a cruel fact of life everyone must face, preferably *before* committing one's future welfare and peace of mind. The only exceptions are the foolhardy and the independently wealthy.

Dream-boaters fall into two classes: the older citizen with accumulated savings, or a good source of income, who is looking for one last fling or for a chance to recapture once more all the things he missed while accumulating all this security; and the young adult, who has a lot of things going for him, especially youth, but is usually of limited resources and experience.

I am sure that members of each class would gladly exchange what they lack for what the other has that they want.

The older, more settled citizen, is usually better off purchasing a new or used vessel outright, and should expect to pay no less than what he can sell his middle-class suburban home for. For younger persons without funds to do this, the only other route is to build a dream ship, which will take from two to six years, depending on their ability to scrounge and the number of willing friends at their disposal.

The method I used was a compromise: completing a kit boat, which seems to be the trend of the future as worldwide inflation gets worse. This way one is usually assured of a well designed, structurally sound vessel to start with, and from there on one can finish it to the state of luxury one wants and can afford. It requires a minimum initial investment, and can usually be paid for as one goes along.

In any case, however, I would emphatically recommend that anyone planning such a large investment first try a vacation cruise or two, or at least some weekends, on a rental or charter boat of the type that he is contemplating owning. Few dreamers will have the patience and the restraint to do this, but it is worth suggesting, and I can only say that I wish I had done it. It would have saved a lot of subsequent grief and unnecessary expense.

The cost of a dream ship of any kind will range from something just barely above the cost of the materials up to the limit or more of one's personal resources. Slocum rebuilt *Spray* for less than six hundred dollars and a year's work. Pidgeon built *Islander* from scratch for a thousand dollars and eighteen months of labor. Both were men of single-minded purpose, with enormous patience and mechanical skills. They were also unencumbered by family obligations—Pidgeon because he had no family, and Slocum because he simply foisted them off on relatives. In the case of *Wild Rose*, I lost track of what I spent when I passed sixty thousand dollars. I suspect that most who are reluctant to quote figures are either self-conscious or ashamed, or have also lost track of what they spent, or—worse yet—never bothered to keep track.

Had I been able to purchase a vessel outright, I more than likely would have shopped around and done so. This would have saved my years of agony if not ecstasy, to say nothing of valuable time. As it was, I had to depend upon some meager savings and a lucky real estate transaction or two, but mostly upon hardrock moonlighting for extra money. In my case, this moonlighting meant freelance writing, including a couple of books. My theory was that I would do better to moonlight at *my own* trade to earn the money to hire people who were expert at boat building or mechanical skills, rather than do the actual work on the boat myself. This is a nice theory; but I usually wound up doing the work on the boat as well as the freelance writing. Sadly, in these days it is almost impossible to find people who want to work for pay and who are reliable, conscientious, and qualified.

Thus, acquiring my dream ship cost over sixty thousand dollars in hard cash, and several years of eighteen-hour workdays. I have long since forgotten what it feels like to put in a hard day at the office and then go home and relax, or go out for an evening on the town, or have guests in, or take a vacation trip or a weekend at the beach. The end of my hard day at the office would be only the beginning of another hard day's work in the study or out at the boat; and on weekends the day would begin with a writing session at 6 A.M., followed by a break at noon and the rest of the day working on the boat—a sixty-mile round trip from home.

One must have a lot of single-minded purpose, or a full-blown obsession, to put up with a schedule like this for several years. In any case, it is the type of effort that most of us can endure only once in a lifetime.

During the construction of your dream ship, you will also suffer, in addition to the monetary burdens, the trauma of having to shop for and make decisions on from five hundred to a thousand different items, all on top of your regular household routine.

All this will blissfully come to an end upon the launching and completion of your vessel. In fact, there will come with this a massive letdown, physical and emotional. But, best of all, the greater part of the spending will have ceased, though there will remain the regular yacht maintenance and moorage expense, plus the inevitable changes and replacements after a complete shaking down of the vessel. In the case of *Wild Rose*, it took almost three thousand dollars to make all these changes and replacements.

Those who plan to take a long cruise, or to become retired live-aboards, should by that point have paid all their bills and have sufficient reserves to cut loose for several years. The worrying kind, or those who like to be prepared as much as possible, will also have arranged for medical insurance or prepayments, several credit cards, yacht insurance and documentation and, if going abroad, passports and proper visas.

Living aboard while working at shore jobs is fairly common in coastal centers where living aboard is allowed and where employment is available. One can usually find work in the United States and Canada and other English-speaking nations, but anyone contemplating going abroad would be wise not to plan a trip around being able to obtain employment exactly when needed.

If you have a trade—especially a mechanical or technical trade such as welder, machinist, catskinner, carpenter, electrician, plumber, chef, or musician—you will usually be able to find a job. Teachers, too, can find employment almost everywhere. Dentists and doctors can pick up fees here and there—sometimes from each other. Tahiti Bill Howell volunteered at a yacht club party to extract an impacted tooth from David Lewis. The next day, Lewis woke up to discover that the wrong tooth had been pulled. It was that kind of party.

Some famous voyagers, such as the Smeetons, had life savings supplemented by service pensions. The Hiscocks financed their voyages through the sale of real estate and through books, articles, and lectures. All of these examples, however, date to a period now gone by. In the 1970s, world cruising has become increasingly more difficult for political reasons, and more expensive for economic reasons. The irresponsible, penniless ocean vagabond is much less welcome in strange ports than in the glorious 1950s and 1960s—especially if he looks and behaves like a hairy counterculture radical. The best defense against suspicious officialdom abroad is a pair of hair clippers and a razor. Obviously, anyone who plays around with drugs, or permits any crewmen to bring narcotics aboard, deserves all the hassle and consequences such behavior will bring. For an example of this, see *Cutting Loose* by James Lipscomb.

In spite of all the restrictions and obstacles these days, however, work is available abroad, even in Polynesia, Africa, and Asia, as indicated by the reports of the cruising "Commodores" of the Seven Seas Cruising Association. Individuals and couples from the U.S. and Canada have found temporary work even in Tahiti, Samoa, New Zealand, and Australia as teachers, tour guides, performers, painters, carpenters, interpreters, construction workers, television technicians, cooks and crewmen on large yachts, and even as extras in movies on location. Of course, one must have these skills before leaving; and, also, that ugly word w-o-r-k is the one thing that most yachties are trying to avoid in the first place.

This brings us up to the one source of income which 90 percent of cruisers openly or secretly aspire to or anticipate: freelance writing. Unfortunately, this is the most difficult and frustrating of all potential sources of income, although it is almost impossible to impress this upon the uninformed or aspiring amateur. A few have made a living at it, such as Slocum, Hiscock, and O'Brien—but only *after* they had become famous as voyagers; and even then, it is a risky way to provide groceries and maintenance for the yacht.

Although there is a steady flow of yachting and voyaging books each year, and the magazine shelves bend with a wide selection of "boating" periodicals, the market is overcrowded with professionals and flash-in-the-pan amateurs, and the readership surfeited with the usual "Dear Aunt Clara"-type stories. Besides that, the pay is often so low that it isn't worth the typing, and seldom even pays for the cost of the accompanying photos. Unless the author has some truly outstanding photos, and story material of an unusual nature, he usually finds it difficult to sell his work, and at best it involves several months' time. The professional writer is in a better position, especially if his is a known byline and he has a New York agent to handle his work. Nowadays, books are usually contracted for *before* they are written, although there are a few exceptions, and are much more difficult to sell for an unknown author. Even if sold and published, few of them earn enough royalties to justify the time and effort by the author. All of the above also applies to the aspiring photographer and cinematographer.

A final note: When would you find time to do all this writing and photography? My own experience has been that there are too many other things to do on board and too many alluring distractions, even though as a longtime professional writer I am used to such conditions. Jack London, it might be said, wrote a thousand words a day wherever he was and however he felt physically or mentally—even aboard the *Snark* in storms at sea. But not all of us can be another Jack London. William A. Robinson was another who disciplined his writing time and turned out, aboard *Svaap* and *Varua*, some of the most beautiful sea prose around. Richard Maury's saga of life aboard his *Cimba* is another example to aspire to. If you are still determined to go this route, the only encouragement I can offer is that "a page a day is a book a year."

Freshwater Systems

On *Wild Rose* we molded into the forefoot of the hull an integral fiberglass water tank that was said to hold 110 gallons but which turned out to be able to hold 150. This was the source of the vessel's hot and cold automatic freshwater system. In addition, we also carry on cruises two plastic five-gallon cans of drinking water. The die-hard purist no doubt will scoff at such an elaborate lash-up, but we believe the day of the rusty, algea-filled seagoing cistern is about over. So is the need to ration out a pint of green scum a day for drinking and cooking. Any yacht capable of making comfortable cruises and passages is large enough to be provided with a modern, efficient water system. As for ourselves, we have spent too many years traveling with land yachts, such as mobile homes and pickup campers, to put up with anything less aboard any ship of ours. As a matter of fact, a travel-trailer water system is easily adapted to a

PURE WATER—A problem at many moorages and marinas is foul-tasting and chlorine-loaded freshwater supplies. Small filter units, such as this portable one, can make most of this bad water drinkable and improve the potability of coffee, orange juice, and mixed drinks. It should not be trusted to remove coliform contamination. Only chlorine, iodine, and distilling can make such water safe to drink; and only distilling units are practical for making fresh water out of salt water.

PURE QUILL—This portable water distiller is used aboard Wild Rose for an emergency freshwater source. The base is a standard stainless pan with cover and connection for mounting the finned cooling unit on top. With the pan filled with water—any kind, including seawater—the unit is placed on a heat source, in this case the propane galley stove burner. Within a few minutes, fresh, pure water comes dripping out of the cooling element. This size model will produce about a quart an hour, or about three gallons a half day. Larger models will produce about a gallon an hour. The still is made and sold by Vita Foods Company, Everett, Washington. The base pan can also be used for cooking. The unit is of course also capable of producing moonshine.

yacht and the cost is much less than a marine system (although the components are often identical).

From the main tank in the bow, water is piped first through a filter unit, then to a 12-volt d.c. pump of the *piston*, not the impellor, type. Next comes an accumulator tank to equalize the pressure. Then the water is distributed to the twelve-gallon hot water heater, and to the galley and shower room faucets. The piping is all flexible synthetic hose attached with stainless hose clamps. The water pump operates automatically whenever the pressure falls below a certain point. The Raritan hot water tank is heated automatically by the engine-exhaust heat exchanger underway, and a 115 volt a.m. shore power at the dock. It takes less than twenty minutes to get a full charge of hot water underway; and about a half-hour to forty-five minutes on shore power, starting with a cold tank. A grade of hose suitable for hot water should be used in the system.

The galley sink is also equipped with a direct seawater hand pump for rinsing dishes and other nonpotable uses. A portable sea-water pump is used with a garden hose for deck purposes away from shore power.

We find the 150-gallon supply none too much for leisurely cruising, and sources of refill none too convenient or palatable. In spite of all those sea stories about living on a pint of water or less a day, the normal human needs at least two quarts of liquid, and preferably a gallon, a day. I find that at sea I tend to become dehydrated from the salty atmosphere and the constant motion and exertion. I can easily drink two quarts a day to quench that thirst, and I find nothing quenches it so well as good cold fresh water. Although we carry the beer, soft drinks, and alcoholic supplies that one would normally stock around the house, substituting any of them for water is not only stupid, but could be fatal. For drinking and cooking, good old fresh water is used. We have found the powdered and flavored soft-drink mixers convenient and easy to prepare, and use a lot of them. Water is also used for making coffee and for cocoa mix, of course.

The first time we refilled the big main tank away from home port, I discovered too late that the moorage supply was superloaded with chlorine—to the point where I could not stand the smell, much less the taste. Even the strongest coffee could not mask it. Fortunately, I had on board an Aqua-Pure filter unit, which I immediately installed. By the time the tank was drawn down about a third, I could no longer detect either smell or taste. This, to my mind, is the answer to cleaning up yacht water supplies—provided the water source is otherwise safe, since a filter such as the Aqua-Pure will not remove bacteria or virus or saline substances.

To assure *safe* drinking and cooking water, the source must be known to be pure, or must be treated with chemicals to make it safe. One such chemical, chlorine, is used in certain forms in all municipal water supplies. In the case of boat or land recreational vehicles, unknown sources of water can be treated with ordinary household bleach, which is about 3 percent chlorine. (Clorox and Purex are two well-known brands.) Health authorities tell me that to flush out and disinfect a tank, new or old, one should use about one ounce of chlorine to ten gallons of water. Thereafter, to maintain a safe level, about one part chlorine to one million parts of water should be used. Since household bleach is only about 3 percent chlorine, the ratio is about thirty to one, or one part to one thousand, or—as one staffer told me: "Use just enough to make it smell and taste, and then back off." If in doubt, consult your local water and health experts.

Unfortunately, while chlorine solutions are effective on ordinary bacteria, they are not so effective on viruses and amoeba, and in some parts of the world these strains can be deadly. Some famous circumnavigators have commented offhandedly that they drink the water raw wherever they go, on the theory that if it wasn't safe, the local population would long since have died off. This is a misleading and irresponsible suggestion. In some of the places in question, the people you see are only the survivors who have become immune to the water-borne disease through generations. Someone coming from a country with higher health standards is not immune, and the consequences can be about the most serious anyone would like to encounter. It is foolish to take the risk.

One good way to assure pure water under the worst conditions found in backwater countries is—according to Peace Corps sources—to boil the water for twenty minutes, filter it, and then boil for another half-hour. Another method is to dose it with iodine. Iodine kills bacteria and amoeba, whereas chlorine and permanganate kill only bacteria. The formula for iodine treatment is about three liters per thousand, or just enough to tinge the water slightly or alter its taste perceptibly. Filter it before drinking.

The only sure way to kill all the bugs—and also to eliminate all salts and minerals in the water—is through distillation. There are a number of marine "water makers" on the market, most of them too large for use in yachts, although one model which makes about five gallons an hour takes up only about as much room as a large suitcase. These marine versions are efficient and use the engine exhaust heat for operation. I sailed aboard an 85-footer once which had a twenty-gallon-an-hour model. This permitted the carrying of extra fuel for the long-range cruise, and the water maker provided such delicious drinking water that I preferred it to the other refreshments aboard.

Even five gallons an hour is much too much capacity for the

ordinary yacht (unless you run the engine only an hour or so a day). During the construction of *Wild Rose* I made an extensive study of water-distilling units and accumulated considerable material. Most of the small home or trailer units, heated by electricity or a gas burner, although efficient, did not provide enough capacity for the energy they used, and were too fragile to stow aboard. The best unit I discovered (and which we carry aboard) is the stainless-steel distiller made by United Vito-Way of Everett, Washington. It will turn out six gallons of pure quill, even starting with harbor water, in about four hours. It looks like a portable moonshine still, of the kind I knew as a kid during Prohibition days. Instead of discharging a drip at a time, however, the pure water comes out in a small but steady stream. Of course, one can make *less* water than the unit's capacity, in less time. The main component of the unit, incidentally, is the standard six-gallon stainless-steel pot, which can be used for other things aboard, such as cooking crabs or making soup.

The search for sources of pure, fresh drinking and cooking water is reaching crisis proportions in a world filling up with pollution and people. A recent study showed that even the water supplies of most American cities are below safe health standards, to say nothing of the adequacy of the supply. It has been our intention to make *Wild Rose* independent and self-contained in this regard, wherever she might be.

Plumbing

I don't know of any yacht owner today who clings to the old cedar bucket recommended by L. Francis Herreshoff. Not only is this unsanitary, uncomfortable, and unsightly, but it is against the law to pollute our waters with raw sewage. The modern version of the honey pot is the portable unit with a chemical treatment compartment, which can be carried aboard for up to a week and then discharged and recharged ashore. Its advantages are that it is self-contained, uses a minimum amount of water, is safe, odorless, and requires no through-hull fitting.

Wild Rose carries one of these, but only for guests and emergency use. The main installation is a Raritan Crown Head electric macerator-chlorinator-type unit. It is also self-contained, but discharges overboard. A small amount of water, along with the powerful chemical, is used for flushing, and the tank is good for thirty uses. It uses a considerable amount of electric current (in excess of 30 amps of 12-volt d.c., which also unfortunately has to travel a considerable distance from the batteries). It is effective, noisy, and should be flushed sparingly. At sea, we flush it only when the engine is running, to prevent a heavy draw-down on the batteries. At the dock, of course, there is no such problem.

As this is written, new regulations prohibiting any discharge are being adopted. *Wild Rose*, under the "grandfather" provisions, will be able to continue using the macerator-chlorinator overboard discharge system for a number of years, but eventually must also comply with the no-discharge rule. Anticipating this, we provided a space for a holding tank, as well as the plumbing for installing it. It will be a simple matter to keep *Wild Rose* legal when and if it becomes necessary. The problem of how and where to dump the holding tank has been carefully avoided by the bureaucrats who write the regulations. As far as I am concerned, this remains their problem. Either they solve it or the boating public will ignore it, just as the public ignored Prohibition.

The only other plumbing aboard *Wild Rose* consists of the galley sink drains, and the shower room sink and foot drains. All of these are direct gravity flow, except for the shower pan drain, which is pumped by a small 12-volt Water Puppy. All piping is flexible synthetic tubing, held with stainless clamps.

Refrigeration

There is no longer any valid reason for not having mechanical refrigeration aboard even a small yacht. Inspired by the vast recreation-vehicle market, the industry has come up with a wide variety of compact and efficient refrigerators. In addition, small units are available which convert old ice boxes into automatic electric refrigerators and freezers. All these are operated by ship's battery power, and most of them will also operate on 115-volt shore power. With the development of solar cells and wind generator units, it is possible to enjoy refrigeration, and even ice, aboard engineless yachts.

Wild Rose has a Norcold fridge, which operates automatically on either 12-volt d.c. or 115-volt a.c., and is installed neatly under one side of the chart table. It will hold an astonishing amount of food, and its separate freezer compartment will make three or four trays of ice cubes in a short time, or hold half a gallon of ice cream, frozen fruit or vegetable packages, or any combination of these. At first we also carried a portable electric freezer, but we soon decided it took up too much space for the small capacity and for the heavy current draw. Perhaps on a long passage away from sources of ice, it could be fit in somewhere, but for coastwise cruising it is just in the way.

Instead of the portable freezer, we now carry a couple of those new portable ice coolers, which are amazingly effective. Block ice will last us up to ten days, while crushed ice is good for almost a week in summer. The large-size cooler is carried on the after deck and is roomy enough to hold the biggest salmon I ever expect to catch. In the meantime, it will hold cases of beer, soda pop, steaks, fresh milk, vegetables, and other perishables. It is also a source of ice for mixing drinks, without the freezer compartment of the refrigerator having to be used. To make the ice last longer, fill several plastic pails with pure water, deep-freeze them, and then place them in the cooler. This "hard" ice will last up to two weeks. As it melts, it will provide ice-cold drinking water, and for drinks you can chip off pieces with a pick.

We also find it convenient to carry one of the small coolers with ice cubes for keeping handy a small assortment of drinks and perishables.

There is no reason to be without the convenience and luxury of ice or refrigeration, unless you're a person who just likes to do things the hard way.

Dinghies

Joshua Slocum sawed a Cape Ann dory in two, boarded up the open end of the front half, and took her around the world (although he almost drowned trying to kedge out an anchor on the Patagonia coast). William Robinson picked up an Indian dugout in the San Blas and took it around the world as a tender. With the possible exception of multihulls, which can be run up on a beach, every yacht must have on it some means by which passengers can get ashore from an anchorage and back again, conveniently and quickly.

Up until the 1950s, dinghies were invariably wooden tenders built to ride on deck in some way. Today, the need for a tender or a dinghy is even greater because of the crowded moorages and the necessity of anchoring out more frequently. But what is most frequently used nowadays is the inflatable raft or runabout. Only on the larger yachts is it practical to carry a rigid tender (and there are

201

some superb types available if you have room). But even the small-est yacht—including those stunters of twenty feet or less overall —can carry an inflatable, which can also serve as a lifeboat in emergency. As for towing a dinghy, if it is too big and heavy to carry on deck, it is too big for the yacht. No bluewater sailor ever towed a dinghy on ocean passages, and in my opinion it is lubberly to tow one even on inside passages except for short hops from one anchor-age to another. Just for experimentation, we towed our Avon Red-crest through San Juan Channel in a thirty-knot blow one day. First it leaped up and came down overturned, and then it began to corkscrew over the waves. Enough said.

Inflatable dinghies are simple to inflate and deflate, and can be brought aboard and carried to a convenient location partially or fully inflated. Most of them will support a full load when only half-inflated, and this further enhances their use as emergency craft. The inflatables come in many configurations, among them raft or outboard-powered runabout styles, and some can even be sailed. They are also offered as strictly emergency life-saving rafts, com-plete with survival rations and equipment, packed either in small automatically ejecting cannisters on deck or in valises which can be stowed below. I once made a tabulation of reported yacht sinkings in recent years, and found that almost all of them went down in less than five minutes, and one in less than a minute. With an inflatable on deck, you can get off safely even if you have only a few seconds. A more likely thing to worry about is losing your dinghy to the harpies of the shore who will steal anything not cast in concrete; what they can't steal, they vandalize. An inflatable can easily be hidden or taken along on a shore jaunt.

After much thought, we finally ended up with the Avon Redcrest—which is only one of many good-quality brands these days, and which we had purchased back in the days when prices were more reasonable—and an inflatable runabout with outboard motor power for fishing and general utility. I also purchased two "survival suits"—a new wrinkle in sea survival which has been described earlier. This type of survival suit can be stuffed into a small bag or valise and stowed within reach, or hung from the rigging or guard rails ready for instant use. You can even put one on in the water. Once you are zipped up, your body heat will warm you even in water as cold as 35 degrees F.

We carry only two of these aboard—one for the captain and one for the mate. Any guests or passengers are on their own.

Should we go offshore on long passages, we would surely invest in one of the automatic-inflating survival rafts of the new self-righting, fully-covered types. There are too many things that can go wrong on an auxiliary sailing yacht: a broken seacock, whale strike, collision at night or in fog with another vessel or floating obstacle, and probably many other hazards that no one has survived to describe, particularly with a ballasted vessel. An acquaintance who completed a Cascade 36—the smaller version of *Wild Rose*—was cruising off the Oregon coast on a trial run when most of the cast-iron fin keel broke off suddenly without warning, leaving only about a foot of casting bolted to the bottom. Fortunately the sea was calm and the wind light, so he was able to drop the sails and tenderly nurse the yacht back to harbor. Had the keel bolts come loose, or had the North Pacific been in a brisk mood, he would have capsized and sunk in perhaps minutes. A more common accident, no doubt, is stuffing-box failure, which can let in a torrent without one knowing it until the engine room is swamped. This happened to me on the first trial run of *Wild Rose*, and only a temporarily installed automatic bilge pump saved the day.

All emergency survival equipment must be stowed properly and checked frequently—even new purchases. I attended a Sea Grant seminar recently in which a Coast Guardsman tested a cannister raft. Pulling the ripcord did not release or inflate the raft, due mainly to a sticking valve. And once open, this new unit, to everyone's horror, failed to contain the flashlight, batteries, drinking water, flares, and other survival gear it was supposed to have. In this age of incompetence and boobery, one should never rely on anyone else, not even on those with the best reputation.

Hunting and Fishing

Most cruising folk, except in the Pacific Northwest, seem to be strangers to the ancient and honorable sports of angling and hunting. Yet these are natural and enjoyable activities, which also have the practical value of providing fresh, vitamin-packed food for the table. Most of the old-timers like Slocum, Bardiaux, Robinson, Moitessier, Long, and O'Brien, who circumnavigated on shoestrings, supplemented their food supplies this way. Robinson, for example, with Etera, his native crewman, spent months in the southwestern Pacific islands, hundreds of miles from stores and fuel supplies, living on fish they caught and animals (usually feral goats) they shot.

Today, unfortunately, politics makes it difficult to carry even sporting firearms without harassment or at least embarrassment by arrogant and usually ignorant officialdom. Even owning a simple, single-shot, survival-type firearm, to say nothing of a flare gun, can involve you in aggravating red tape in some countries.

But hunting is further discouraged by the requirement for a non-resident or an alien hunting license almost everywhere sport hunting is available. Often the fees are outrageous, and in most cases these fees are not worth it even if they were not excessive. Any attempt to hunt without a license, though, could bag you a big mess of trouble, including some time in the local slammer or confiscation of your yacht. Finally, for the bluewater sailor there are few places to hunt. Even the remote islands are restricted or privately owned, and except in cases of dire emergency, trespassers are not welcome.

Angling for food and pleasure, however, can be done aboard, even underway. It requires no politically undesirable arms and, if outside territorial waters, does not require a permit or license. There are few places on the oceans where one cannot find fish. Indeed, many bluewater voyagers reported being accompanied for thousands of miles by fish, frequently the dolphin or *mahi-mahi*, as well as mackerel and other edible species which found the hull of the vessel either a shelter from predators or a source of prey itself. Slocum commented wryly on this, noting how little fish would bunch up when a predator approached, as if to make as little trouble as possible while being devoured—which also seems at times to be a human trait when faced by oppressors. Harry Pidgeon, on his long passage to Los Angeles from Panama, reported at times being surrounded by tuna as far as he could see in all directions. (Modern sophisticated tuna clippers, however, are rapidly taking care of this situation.)

Many voyagers have complained in the same breath that they tend to lose log rotators to sharks and large fish, and that their trolling lines never seem to hook a fish. Trolled lures must be moving at the precise speed for which the lure is designed. Moreover, color and design of the lure under different circumstances is important. I suspect that most of these complaints are motivated by inexperience or indifference. To perform in a lifelike manner, lures trolled for albacore and other tuna must be moving about six knots. For Pacific salmon, two or three knots is plenty. A great many species of midwater or ground fish cannot be caught trolling. You must jig for them, and this means in continental waters of two hundred feet or less. Pelagic species, such as the tunas, mackerel, herring, and bill fishes, are found almost everywhere in temperate or tropical waters.

Almost every fish that swims in the open ocean is good to eat, poisonous species being more often found in bays and in coral lagoons. There are a number of books available on dangerous marine animals and fishes, and good technical sources of information for the layman are supplied by the International Oceanographic Society at Miami, Florida. Membership is nominal in cost, and the bulletins and publications one gets are more than worth the dues. Another good source of information about freshwater and saltwater fishes, along with an enormous amount of related reading, is *McClane's New Standard Fishing Encyclopedia and International Angling Guide* (see Bibliography). Most countries and states with developed tourist angling publish angling guides describing freshwater and marine fishing in their region.

One can seldom rely on appearances in choosing which species to devour. Some of the most loathsome-looking critters, such as the lingcod, are the most toothsome. In general, however, you should never eat the skin, liver, and other parts of any fish unless you are sure of what you are doing. A fillet, cut from the side of a fish, with the skin removed, is almost always safe and is the proper way to handle most of the midwater and bottom species. Tuna and albacore are almost solid flesh, with only a few big bones. The meat is somewhat stringy, without grain, and frankly is not as good fresh as it is properly processed and canned. Such species as wahoo and dorado are delicious fresh-fried or broiled. Marlin and sailfish are also good eating, tasting somewhat like tuna; and, of course, in the tropics and subtropics there are the delectable little flying fish which often come aboard at night. Fried in butter, they are delicious, with a taste somewhat like smelt or sardines. In the North Pacific, and to a lesser extent in the North Atlantic, you will also find roving schools of salmon, which are regarded as the finest and most valuable species of all. And let us not forget the shellfish, which are found in a variety of species in every ocean of the world.

Fishing tackle takes up little room on a yacht. In addition to the small emergency packet of hooks, line, and lures for life-raft use, here is what we carry on *Wild Rose*:

Crab ring	2 fiberglass trolling rods
Shrimp trap	2 Penn #60 Long Beach model reels
Clam "gun" and rake	loaded with 275 yards of nylon
Rock salt	monofilament 20-pound test
Pickling spices	Assorted nylon leaders (optional)
"Little Chief" smoker	Long-handled gaff hook
Assorted hooks for bait	Large landing net
Assorted trolling plugs	Assorted swivels and split rings
Large attractor blades	Assorted sinkers up to 5 pounds

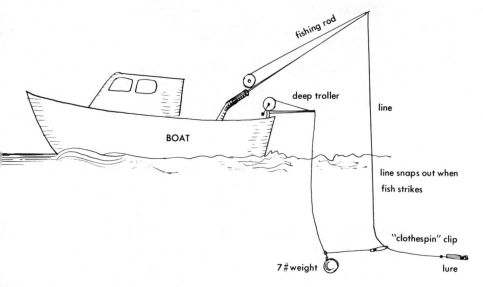

fishing rod

deep troller

line

BOAT

line snaps out when
fish strikes

"clothespin" clip

7 # weight

lure

TROLLING GEAR—Most cruising sailors overlook the marvelous opportunities to catch fish for the table almost effortlessly. The sketch shows a basic and universal arrangement for trolling anywhere in the world for almost any species of food or game fish. The only variables are the speed of the boat; which should be adjusted depending on the species of the fish; the lure or bait, which varies depending on species and local feeding habits; and the strength and type of line and leader used.

Assorted wobbler lures	Hook extractor
Jigs and spinners	Hook sharpener
Rod holders	Fillet knife

Trolling is simple. Put a lure on the end of the line and pull it through the water at the proper speed. For small fish, use a light leader between lure and line; for big fish, attach the lure directly to line. In some cases an attractor blade attached directly to the line, with a thirty-inch leader to the lure, will work where nothing else will. Diving planes of colored plastic are deadly on species that require a slow troll such as salmon. Most fish will be caught right in the tail of the wake. Tuna are caught near the surface on lures, but occasionally at depths up to a hundred feet. Marlin, sailfish, wahoo, dorado, and other large predators will be attracted by a lure skipping in the wake. A depth sounder can be used to find schools of fish. Porpoises are usually a sign of tuna, as they often travel together. The presence of a shark will drive away most fish.

In a calm, or anchored for the night, you can attract fish with a light over the side. In a few minutes the water will be boiling with them, and all you have to do is drop a hook over the side. Even bare hooks will work jigging in this manner.

One night, anchored behind Cabo San Lucas, we fished this way with multihooked herring jigs, catching over a hundred of the rare type of mackerel known locally as cobbies or *cabelitos*. Not only were they good to eat, but they proved to be perfect for billfish bait.

A most effective lure in subtropical waters is the weighted metal jig, such as the "yo-yo." The technique is to cast this lure out from the boat as far as you can, then let it sink naturally to the bottom, if possible, and retrieve it in jerks, holding the rod handle under one armpit and cranking the reel with the other.

In coastal waters, with inlets and mangrove swamps, the enthusiastic angler will find much use for light spinning and fly-fishing equipment. The conventional trout fishing equipment is ideal for this. A longer and heavier fly-fishing rod should be used, however, with number 9 or 10 sinking tip or weight forward lines, short leaders, and large saltwater flies or streamers. Fly tying, incidentally, is a fine hobby to take along on any trip.

Many cruisers take along scuba gear for underwater exploration and photography. Divers can take many fish with spear guns, and also harvest abalone and other shellfish. In coastal waters, though, there are often local regulations prohibiting this.

Shellfish are easy to catch with traps hung over the side at night, or attached to buoys. Crab traps should be attended frequently. If you have hung one from the rail, be sure that you are swinging with the wind and current. You can place shrimp traps in deep holes and bait them the same as you would crab traps—with fish heads or perforated catfood tins. Oysters, clams, and mussels are easily picked at low tide on the flats in regions where they exist—but first be sure the flats are not private property.

Cabin Heating and Cooling

Yachts seem rarely to be designed to enhance comfort; the emphasis is always on ship performance (which is not always achieved anyway). And few yachts built for the consumer market have adequate provision for heating and cooling; in this case, the emphasis is on appearance, to influence the ladies. Yet, for cruisers at any time of the year, and certainly for live-aboards, cabin temperature is a major consideration.

During the year or so *Wild Rose* lay in the water at the moorage being completed, I had an opportunity to experience the problem and do something about it. During this period temperatures ranged from zero, with much ice and snow, to weeks of heat ranging over 100 degrees. At one extreme the water pipes, freshwater tank, engine cooling system, and even canned goods aboard had to be protected against freezing; at the other, the decks got too hot to work on, bedding compound set up too rapidly, and the fridge ran almost constantly keeping the beer cool.

Mildew got started from the droppings of swallow nests falling on deck, and at one time permeated most of the hull. Winter dampness was another problem. To fight this, I first used heat lamps, but because of the fire hazard bought several low-wattage Dampp Chasers and installed them at strategic points.

Sweating is a problem with all boats, particularly those made of fiberglass. We lined the inside exposed hull with carpeting to match the seat cushions. In addition, the floorboards were carpeted with an indoor-outdoor type of material. The overhead was left for last to make sure all leaks were discovered and all top-deck fittings installed. The forward cabin was not so finished because it became a stowage area for sails and supplies.

As pointed out by Robinson in *To the Great Southern Sea*, the normal air circulation on a yacht is clockwise from forward to aft, and all his hatches were designed and hinged to raise aft instead of forward as is common on most vessels. My forward cabin hatch was installed by a workman with the hinges aft, so that it opened forward, before I could have it the other way. Some day I will reverse this myself.

With the aft cabin configuration, *Wild Rose* has an interior divided by the engine room, which I have not found necessary to insulate or otherwise soundproof. The after cabin is surprisingly comfortable under most conditions, with only the companionway and opening ports for ventilation, and a small Cole stove for heat. The main cabin, or saloon, is fairly comfortable on the hottest days (due in large measure to the white reflecting decks), especially with the forward deck hatch and the cockpit doors open. The cockpit vinyl cover aids in this as well, providing shade from the hot sun and shelter from rain. In the winter and on cold days the main cabin is heated with a king-size Cole stove, which doubles as a fireplace and burns any kind of solid fuel, including trash that otherwise would have to be disposed of. The stove is vented through a chimney that passes through the bulkhead and then rises to the deck in the toilet room, thus heating this compartment as well. The chimney's deck plate has so far never leaked, but the stove does produce a black soot that blankets the immediate area.

Slocum, on *Spray*, used an enormous stove built from an oil drum, which would hold even large pieces of logs. Hal Roth, on *Whisper*, finally settled on an oil range of the kind used by Northwest fishermen. Most of the Europeans use those small efficient

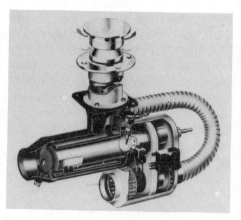

GAS HEAT—The marvelous heating and cooking properties of propane gas are gradually being accepted by yachtsmen and cruising folks after decades of safe, economical, and practical service on millions of road-trailer homes, campers, and motor homes. This efficient little hot-air furnace is the Swedish-built Remotron. It is automatically fired with thermostatic control and hot air is piped to all cabins through flexible hose. It tucks neatly under the deck on the starboard side of the engine room. As shown the combustion chamber is vented through the stack which can be collapsed flush with the deck when the furnace is not in use.

CABIN HEAT—For quick portable heat during the winter season aboard Wild Rose, we discovered that the new efficient kerosene heaters are inexpensive and easy to use. They are ignited by a switch using a single flashlight battery, and will burn all day on one tank filling. They require adequate ventilation, however, and should not be used in closed compartments.

kerosene types, such as the Tilley, which can be tucked in almost anywhere.

We considered every type of heating device before deciding on the solid fuel combination stove and fireplace. Having grown up on North Dakota farms, neither of us like the odor of kerosene stoves. We preferred solid fuel because we could then burn almost anything, including disposable combustibles. When nothing else is available we fall back on our supplies of Presto-Logs, briquets, and cut kindling. Using two of these heaters, one in each cabin, provides enough heat for our immediate comfort and makes it unnecessary to heat the entire boat. Finally, a solid fuel stove vented outside does not create condensation on the inside of the cabin, as do alcohol, propane, and kerosene units.

During mealtimes, and for quick heat, our Shipmate propane stove also provides warmth. It is vented by means of an overhead galley hood and blower. For making a quick snack we use a Sea Swing stove and a can of Sterno.

With the center cockpit configuration, the heat rises rapidly from the cabin up through the cockpit doors to the cockpit. In winter, with the cockpit shelter buttoned up, the cockpit heats up first when the stove is lighted. For this reason we installed the Cole stoves as low down as possible.

Even in warm climates it is necessary to have some means of cabin heat to take off the night or morning chill of winter or the rainy season. In the North Pacific and North Atlantic waters this need is even more urgent. In higher latitudes, cabin heat is a major problem. Keith Lorence, a crew member on the Mexican yacht *Sayula*, which won the Wheatbread's Round The World Race, told in an interview how the crew encountered heavy snow in the Indian Ocean, and incredibly cold weather in the vicinity of Cape Horn, going for weeks without changing the many layers of clothes they had to wear.

Bob Griffith, on his epic circumnavigation of the Antarctic continent, prepared *Awahnee* for the extreme cold by running the engine exhaust pipe completely around the interior of the hull, to provide cabin heat. As we have learned, even a small diesel engine provides an enormous amount of heat that is wasted in most craft. We use part of it to heat water, but still awaiting development by someone is a compact efficient space heater utilizing this source.

We are now installing a small propane-fired forced-air heater for quickly taking off the morning chill in northern waters, and for alternate winter heat. This unit, only about five inches in diameter and nineteen inches long, is automatic and remote controlled. Installed in the engine room, it sends out hot air through ducts to each cabin. The combustion section of the unit is piped overboard through hull fittings. Although expensive, it is compact, efficient, and clean.

A yacht cabin can become unbearable in the tropics under a high sun, although a reflecting white deck will help some. The only ways to minimize this kind of suffering are to put up awnings and take frequent dips over the side. On large yachts it is possible to provide air conditioning (and even small ones can use one of the conventional travel-trailer types), but it is expensive and requires a lot of electrical power. New construction techniques, such as foam-core hulls and decks, provide good insulation. For all yachts, deck insulation with foam and vinyl is easy and practical. On *Wild Rose* it makes a difference of as much as twenty degrees between cabin and outside temperature.

Fuel for Cooking

I am often amused by the continuing disagreement over which fuel is best or safest for the galley. Having had experience with all types, I find that there is only one, and this is propane or "LP" gas. Solid fuel ranges are messy to light and stay hot long after the cooking is done. Diesel oil and kerosene smoke and smell. Diesel ranges usually must have an electrical blower; kerosene types need another fuel—alcohol—for lighting. Alcohol stoves are hard to light and clog up fast—and anyway, in some parts of the world, you can buy bonded rum for less.

On a large boat with lots of electrical power, electric ranges are efficient, but they are not practical on a yacht less than fifty feet in length.

This leaves propane (LP, butane, bottled gas, under various brand names), which is not the same as the "natural gas" available in bottles in some areas such as California. Propane is a by-product of natural gas and of the refining processes used for crude petroleum. It is colorless, odorless, and nontoxic. It has the property of being compressible into a liquid, in which form it is distributed in metal containers or "bottles." It is clean-burning and provides a very hot flame, without odor or fumes or residual deposits. Moreover, it is relatively inexpensive, and available worldwide.

The Coast Guard at this writing does not approve LP for use on vessels carrying passengers for hire, although there is no objection to its use on private vessels. Perhaps this is merely because the agency does not want the extra chore of having to inspect for proper installation. But even the presidential yachts have been equipped with LP stoves for years.

I am more appalled by frequent, irresponsible statements

made by otherwise qualified naval architects to the effect that they wouldn't have LP gas on any boat of theirs. This displays nothing but ignorance of the subject and, worse yet, a closing of the mind to the facts.

LP or propane is one of the safest and most efficient of all fuels. Like any fuel, of course, it must be installed and handled properly. Compared with gasoline, which is used aboard hundreds of thousands of boats for engine fuel, propane is ten times safer, being nowhere near as explosive. Propane gas from a leak, however, will sink into the bilges and become a hazard. But even diesel, kerosene, and alcohol are dangerous under certain conditions.

If any other assurance is needed, keep in mind that millions of recreational vehicles (to say nothing of private homes and farmhouses) use nothing but LP for cooking and heating, and frequently for refrigeration. If it was as dangerous as critics say, I doubt if it would be as widely used.

On *Wild Rose* we installed a standard Shipmate range with propane burners and oven. Originally the gas bottles were installed in a ventilated section of the lazaret, with an overboard discharge. But this required more than twenty feet of hose piping to the galley, an arrangement I didn't like, so I traded the two small bottles in for a twenty-gallon unit, which I mounted on deck with a direct hose line to the galley below. I used high-pressure neoprene hoses instead of the usual copper tubing. At the tank I installed a leak detector which, at the press of a valve, shows any passage of gas with the outlets closed. I regularly test the fittings with a soap and water solution.

I filled the deck tank before I installed it, and though we have used the range for two years, we still have plenty of propane left. Bill and Phyllis Crowe, who took their *Lang Syne* around the world in the 1950s, told me they used nothing but propane for cooking, and the two bottles they carried along lasted the entire circumnavigation.

Installation is simple. All the parts and tanks can be obtained from trailer-parts supply stores and mail-order catalogues. Most tanks are of steel, but aluminum versions are also available. A regulator is needed at the tank, and perhaps a gauge and a leak detector. You can use the gauge itself as a leak detector if you watch it for ten minutes or so for a drop in pressure with the outlets closed. The tanks come with a shut-off valve. Some experts recommend another shut-off valve at a manifold controlling all the burners. I find it a simple matter to turn the gas on at the tank when we want to use the range, and to turn it off again when we are finished, burning off what gas remains in the line.

LP gas can also be used for cabin lighting, for flameless catalytic heaters, and even for propane-powered electrical generators. It is much more efficient than either gasoline or diesel.

For more information on propane installations, write the LP Gas Association, 79 West Monroe St., Chicago 60603; the National Fire Protection Association, 60 Batterymarch St., Boston 02110; and the U.S. Coast Guard.

Ground Tackle
and Anchoring

Anchoring and ground tackle are usually afterthoughts in the process of building or acquiring a dream ship, as if this is a problem which will solve itself in some far-off romantic lagoon. Our first summer cruising Northwest Coast waters convinced me that anchoring is a major part of the ship's routine, and will become more important in the future because of the worldwide shortage of moorage facilities. Because of this problem nine out of ten stops during our first cruising season were spent swinging on the hook, and about half these stops were of an emergency nature because of weather or breakdowns. Even with the electric windlass and a variety of anchors, I became the leading candidate aboard for a cardiac that first month, but from that experience I learned a completely new way of anchoring to be described shortly.

Wild Rose was originally equipped with an electric wildcat-type windlass and five anchors, including a light Danforth left over from a previous boat; a war-surplus heavy Danforth, used on World War II landing craft; an imitation Danforth, which I welded up myself from scraps and had galvanized, a Squid four-pronged folding anchor for rocky bottoms, and a large Benson nonfouling type. Ironically, the first time I used the Benson it became fouled on a heavy logging cable. In addition, there were sixty feet of 3/8-inch chain, some short lengths of vinyl-covered chain, suitable shackles and connecting links, and several rodes of 5/8-inch nylon.

This lash-up seemed completely adequate for normal use —until we got into the Puget Sound and Vancouver Island waters. There we found conditions entirely different. In some places the water would be six feet deep just off shore, and twenty yards out would drop to five hundred feet. With an average eight- to ten-foot tidal range, this made anchoring the conventional way impossible. I soon learned how the local experts do it. You drop a kedge as close to shore as you can get, then ease out to the edge of the drop-off and let go the heavy anchor on enough chain to carry it down over the ledges, backing off again to take up slack. This will usually hold over the change of the tides.

These waters usually have rocky or sandy bottoms, frequently with lots of weed, in some cases the bottom is solid rock covered with weed. Typical of this type was Blind Bay on Lopez Island in the San Juan group. We were chased into this shelter one evening in a forty-five-knot August blow that had hundreds of yachts scurrying for any kind of cover. I anchored with a group at the upper end in twenty feet with two anchors out. Within half an hour we had dragged out into the middle of the bay, where I put down a third anchor and let out more scope. Before we were secure for the night I also had to rig up the Wind Wand vane to stop *Wild Rose* from sailing around the anchors.

Most of the month of August was spent trying to cope with similar situations. We just were not prepared for the lack of good anchorages, the strong tidal streams, and bottom conditions. Days were filled with running for shelter and trying to anchor, sometimes dropping and hauling the hooks three or four times before they held. From the first, I discovered that my pet installation, the homemade anchor windlass, was inadequate for this size vessel under these conditions. First on the list of changes in the work book went a notation to purchase the heavy-duty, fast-retrieve type more commonly used in these waters, and with a remote switch for one-man operation. This would be equipped with rodes as per a formula given me by a local expert in Anacortes:

Use six fathoms of 3/8-inch chain for every situation, plus two fathoms of chain for every fathom of depth, plus a 5/8-inch nylon rode to fill out the necessary scope. The chain adds weight to the anchor, and the nylon provides elasticity to take up shock. To all this attach a suitable anchor. In common use are CQR, heavy-duty Danforths, Northill types. Unfortunately, those clean-cut tactical solutions to anchoring, as depicted in the numerous articles in the boating press, may not work in Northwest Coast waters. For one thing, you seldom have room to let out proper scope. Anchorages are usually crowded, and anchors are dropped straight down to get minimum swing. For another thing, the Puget Sound and San Juan waters in summer are filled with amateurs who have little experience, and with bare-boat charter parties who have no experience and don't care. These people rush in and mob the moorages, or drop their hooks right on top of yours, and make no allowances for swinging. Moreover, they are people who would stand by and watch you drift up on the rocks without lifting a hand to help. You are on your own, and you should be prepared to be completely self-sufficient.

Expect to be anchoring frequently under the worst conditions of weather, tide, and yacht congestion. Have a heavy-duty windlass that can be controlled from the helm, so that you can slip into an anchorage watching the depth sounder and, at the proper moment, letting go the anchor and chain. The same goes for weighing anchor when it comes time to leave. Use a heavy anchor with at least 3/8-inch chain, and even 1/2-inch chain for the primary scope, so that you can anchor on a vertical scope if there is no swinging room. Have suitable stern or stream and kedge anchors available for instant use.

An additional luxury, if you have the space, is a private mooring buoy for use when you find an especially beautiful anchorage where you wish to stay for a few days or weeks. It can be used with your heaviest ground tackle. Be sure you identify it as yours in prominent letters, or you will find someone else swinging on it when you come back from a day of exploring. Even with proper identification, you may find someone using it, in which case you will have to take persuasive action to get rid of the chiseler.

Electrical Systems

Wild Rose has what seems like a complicated electrical system, but it is really quite simple and efficient. The basic system is the standard 12-volt D.C. circuit, with a double bank of batteries for power source. The battery banks are separate and charged with separate engine-driven alternators. The "engine only" bank supplies current only for starting the engine, plus direct lines to radar and depth finders, all of which are used intermittently. The other bank supplies current to the ship's electrical accessories such as cabin lights, running lights, water pump, toilet, blowers, and radios. It is also capable of starting the engine alone. A master switch which can select either bank of batteries or both is used for engine starting.

At present, two batteries are used in parallel for each bank. At dockside each bank is kept charged up by separate automatic solid-state power packs, which operate only when needed to keep the batteries at full charge. The so-called 12-volt storage battery is actually more like 13 volts when fully charged. When the voltage drops to 12 volts the battery is in trouble, and if it drops below this, it is probably ruined and needs replacement. It is very important to keep the battery at full charge, and every yacht should have a hydrometer to keep tabs on battery condition. Obviously, the water level should also be kept up scrupulously. I have installed separate plastic pint-size water containers above each battery bank, so that pure fresh water is available through a tube each time I check the batteries. I made these from the type of canteens carried by bicyclists. In addition, I monitor the battery voltage through simple panel-mounted meters. I have observed that when my batteries register 13.5 volts they are fully charged. When the meter readings drop below 12.5 volts, I know the batteries need attention.

Of course only marine batteries should be used, and in the highest capacity you can afford or make fit. On long cruises it may be well to carry an extra dry-charged battery, to be activated whenever needed in emergency. A diesel engine especially takes a tremendous amount of current for starting. If the engine is the least bit balky, it is easy to run down a battery just when you need it most. For a small diesel such as our Westerbeke 4-107, a battery capacity of about 90 to 100 amps is correct for normal starting, but I would recommend battery banks capable of producing 150 amps or more.

To digress a moment, it is unfortunate that the marine industry has standardized on the 12-volt system for yachts and small craft. They have done so, apparently, to follow the worldwide trend in automotive vehicles. The 12-volt system is not as efficient as either the 24- or 32-volt systems, which are more often used in large vessels and aircraft for obvious reasons. To power a 48-watt small-craft radar, for instance, it takes 4 amps at 12 volts, and only 2 amps at 24 volts. There is much less line loss in 24- and 32-volt systems. A loss of one volt in a 12-volt system is about 8 percent, while in a 24-volt system is only 4 percent. On a 42-foot boat, the distance the current must travel (round trip) often exceeds the recommended distance for standard-size wire.

It is still possible to install 24- or 32-volt systems, but the cost is outrageous and the availability of equipment for this voltage is poor.

Referring to the block diagram of *Wild Rose*'s electrical system, the reader will observe what seem to be three systems. The primary A.C. shore power system has its own circuit and powers the battery

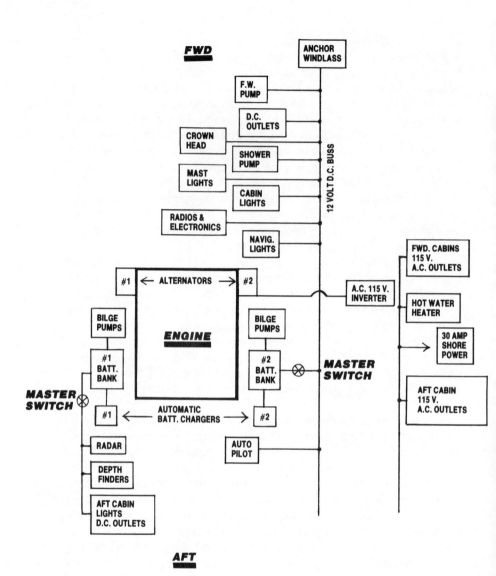

FWD

ANCHOR WINDLASS

F.W. PUMP

D.C. OUTLETS

CROWN HEAD

SHOWER PUMP

MAST LIGHTS

CABIN LIGHTS

RADIOS & ELECTRONICS

NAVIG. LIGHTS

12 VOLT D.C. BUSS

#1 ← ALTERNATORS → #2

FWD. CABINS 115 V. A.C. OUTLETS

A.C. 115 V. INVERTER

BILGE PUMPS

ENGINE

BILGE PUMPS

HOT WATER HEATER

30 AMP SHORE POWER

#1 BATT. BANK

#2 BATT. BANK

MASTER SWITCH

MASTER SWITCH

AFT CABIN 115 V. A.C. OUTLETS

#1 ← AUTOMATIC BATT. CHARGERS → #2

RADAR

AUTO PILOT

DEPTH FINDERS

AFT CABIN LIGHTS D.C. OUTLETS

AFT

ELECTRICAL SYSTEM—Most small craft, and especially sailing yachts produced today, have inadequate or poorly designed electrical systems, or both. If one intends to have electrical power aboard, it pays to provide the best possible for present needs and future potential. This block diagram shows the arrangement of Wild Rose's 12-volt DC and her 115-volt AC shore power. Note that the ship's service is completely separated from the basic engine supply, but that for starting, both banks of batteries can be switched together. Each battery bank has its own automatic battery charger. There is also provision for AC while underway, with a power inverter fed by the auxiliary alternator. It is better not to have any permanent electrical system than to have a poor one. There is, unfortunately, little information available for amateur installations today; but this arrangement used on Wild Rose may suggest ideas to other builders.

charges and A.C. outlets, and of course is not used at sea. In addition to this, I installed a 3,000-watt, 115-volt A.C. inverter system, which is powered by an 85-amp alternator on the engine. This particular model is called the Power Mote. I selected it because, unlike so many inverters, it produces a sine wave instead of the square wave output. The square-wave output is unsuitable for operating many electrical accessories one might want to use at some time, such as a portable television or stereo set.

Theoretically, this unit will provide 3,000 watts of A.C. power at sea and away from shore sources. I must admit that so far I have had little or no need for it; and, in fact, it does not work most of the time, anyway. The concept is a good one, however, and something to consider. At the present time we have found that dry-cell battery packs are quite practical for powering stereo sets and tape recorders, and as yet have found little use for A.C. power at sea.

Although we have provision for 115-volt shore power, we can still use the 12-volt system for everything, as the shore power keeps the batteries up no matter how many accessories are on the line. Away from shore power we watch this carefully and never use more than one accessory at a time. In the case of the Crown Head, I make it a practice to start the engine before flushing, which may not be necessary but eases my worries. The engine is almost always running when it is necessary to use the radar and the radios, of course, to say nothing of the automatic pilot. Under sail, everything not needed is turned off. Usually I just flip the master switch off and rig for silent running, as they say in the movies. To be honest about it, this is the part I enjoy the most. Nothing can equal the feel of a ship coming alive under wind power alone. It is easy to get carried away, though, and thus on long trips fail to give proper maintenance to the electrical system and engine.

There are few reference sources available to guide one in designing and installing an electrical system in a boat. Indeed, some designers act as if they never heard of Benjamin Franklin and his kite. At best, they include somewhere in the plans a "typical" or stylized circuit. Marine electricians can be found at large boating centers, but of course they are expensive. Anyone with a little mechanical experience and some familiarity with electricity, however, can install his own, just as I did. Two good reference sources are: *Your Boat's Electrical System* by Conrad Miller (Motor Boating & Sailing Books); and the Boating Industry Association's *Engineering Manual*. For installing A.C. shore power, see *Wiring Simplified* by H. P. Richter, available in any electrical supply store.

My method was first to install the fixtures in the most convenient place, and then figure out how to route the wires. There is no use having a cabin light where its illumination won't do you any good; nor should some large fixture, such as a fridge or battery charger, be allowed to dominate the space. A lot of compromises are needed.

One major problem was how to provide the heavy amperage needed by the anchor windlass, which is over thirty feet from the batteries. I solved this by using a length of number 2 aluminum house entry cable, which has two large insulated wires and stranded shield for grounding, all encased in a tough outer jacket. This cable runs directly from the ship's supply battery pack to the anchor wind-lass, which is controlled by a foot switch and solenoid. After I had routed this, it occurred to me that it could also be used as a primary bus for all the electrical system forward of the engine room bulk-head, merely by tapping into it, which eliminated a lot of line loss. A sixty-foot round-trip run has a 10 percent drop in voltage for a draw of 25 amps in number 4 wire, for example.

All wire used was stranded AWG (American Wire Gauge), not less than 16-gauge, and mostly 12-gauge. I tried to use color-coded wire with heat and acid-resistant insulation. When the proper colors were not possible to find, I would use a common color and, at the terminal, label it with plastic tape. Whenever possible I soldered joints, except at terminal blocks and fuse panels. In all such connections I used solderless pinch-on terminals, which are expensive but worth it. I didn't use circuit breakers, mainly because of the high cost; I find fuse panels adequate and only a fraction as expensive. In the D.C. systems, I never used a red wire for anything but 12-volts "positive" (+). For the other wires, I used black for all ground or "earth" connections, and whatever I had handy for accessory leads. Most lighting fixtures (except those with cigarette-type plug-in outlets) have no polarity; but practically everything else does, and some can easily be ruined. It is not a good idea to use the old smoke test with D.C. appliances to check polarity.

I hooked up everything temporarily at first and then lived with it for a while to see how it worked. If I didn't like it, I tore it out and started over. I installed some appliances as many as five times before I was satisfied. The permanent wiring should be routed in neat bundles, collected with plastic ties or clips. It is better first to staple the wires and then go back over them with permanent fastenings. It is okay to run wires in exposed places—in fact, it is better, because then they are easy to get at for repairs. There is nothing unsightly about neat runs of wires or pipes, and nothing has to be hidden as in a house.

I finally discovered that, unlike in those pretty magazine ads, all the circuits do not have to terminate in a fancy pilothouse circuit-breaker panel. I found it more practical and easier to install several small fuse panels close to the accessories they protect, with the hot line tapped off the heavy bus. All the lighting fixtures (obtained mostly from trailer-supply houses) were also equipped with on-off switches.

I used heavy, flexible welding cable for all heavy-equipment leads and battery cables. I could cut this wire to the length needed and attach screw-on terminal clamps of the proper size. When I built the mast, I installed heavy duty multiwire cable for the deck, range, and anchor lights, and the topmast strobe light. The radio antenna transmission lines were also installed in the mast at this time.

The shore-power system was designed for maximum load, using the standard three-wire connections and cable (the green wire being the ground). It comes into the hull on the starboard side of the cockpit through a Hubbell fixed waterproof receptacle to fit the Hubbell heavy-duty 30-amp extension cable. Adapters are used at the shore end to fit the wide variety of marina connections you find these days. Most are 15 amp, some are oddball 20 amp, and occasionally you run into a 30-amp shore connection which does not require an adapter.

The shore power comes into a standard 20-amp circuit-breaker panel, from which A.C. is supplied to the automatic water heater and to various outlets for household appliances such as toaster, frying pan, electric heater, and the A.C.-D.C. appliances. The panel also supplies power for the battery chargers.

One popular item I long considered and then decided against getting is the A.C. generator set. So far we have had no need for one, and because of space and noise considerations, I doubt that we ever will. They are efficient, however, and on a large power cruiser I would think they would be almost necessary.

The tools needed to install your own system are inexpensive and readily obtainable at discount stores. They will also come in handy for maintenance work later. Here is a basic list:

Soldering gun	Multimeter (500,000 ohm)
Terminal lug tool	Wire cutters
Screwdrivers	Socket wrench set
Punch for starting screws	Hammer
Pocketknife	Test clips
Cable stripper	Vinyl tape
Rosin core solder	Test light
Battery hydrometer	Plastic toolbox
Pointed nose pliers	

Plus bronze staples, cable clamps, cable ties, reels of wire, fuse and terminal blocks, lug terminals in all sizes, WD-40, and silicone sealer.

In late 1975 the American Boat and Yacht Council published new guidelines for D.C. electrical systems of under 50 volts, which should be useful to anyone doing his own wiring. The publication is E-9, costs three dollars, and is available from the American Boat and Yacht Council, Inc., 15 E. 26th St., New York, N.Y. 10010.

Electronics and How to Become a Ham

When it comes to radio communications on a yacht, few skippers can afford the standard marine line of SSB long-range, medium- and high-frequency rigs, along with the multichannel VHF/FM transceivers and the antenna systems needed for proper operation—to say nothing of the space and battery requirements. While the VHF system is almost mandatory these days for coastal use, the range of these little units is usually less than twenty-five miles, and at present there are not enough coastal stations, run either by the Coast Guard or the telephone company, to make them entirely reliable everywhere and under all conditions.

As for the new SSB, or "Single Sideband," mode, this uses the same marine frequencies as the old AM, or "Amplitude Modulation," as well as the same antenna systems. The only difference is in the more efficient signal produced in the transmitter (five times as

227

powerful, with only a third of the band width). Marine SSB, like AM, is primarily for commercial and military vessels on the high seas, and while it has long-range capability, it is still limited and involves going through commercial communication circuits.

The Amateur Service

Only in recent years have yachtsmen discovered ham radio, that worldwide network of amateur radio enthusiasts who routinely communicate among themselves and within the bands of frequencies allotted to them by international agreement. The Radio Amateur Callbooks (directories of hams listed by call letters and addresses, published by the Radio Amateur Callbook, Inc., 925 Sherwood Drive, Lake Bluff, Ill. 60044), currently list about 300,000 licensed radio amateurs in the United States, and 250,000 abroad. This is certainly an underestimation, for in Japan alone there are at least 500,000 hams—possibly even one million.

A yacht equipped with amateur gear and suitable antennas can communicate with someone else, somewhere, at any time, day or night, from literally any place on earth that you can take a yacht. Frequently you can raise an amateur within telephone distance of your home and "run a patch" through to your family or friends. You have a choice of using "CW," or Morse code, conventional voice telephony (with or without "Vox," or voice-operated microphones), radio teletype machines, and even long-range, two-way television, or "ATV."

About the only major requirements are that the communications be noncommercial, that the operating regulations of the license-issuing nation be observed and, of course, that the station and operator have a valid license.

I have been a ham since high school days, renewing my license every five years. I have found it a most absorbing and fascinating hobby, a relaxing and, in times of illness, most therapeutic diversion. I have always had a well-equipped home station and, most of the time, a mobile rig in the car. Even from the latter I have worked other hams in many parts of the world. So when I acquired a boat large enough for the battery power needed, the very first piece of electronic gear that I put into it was an amateur mobile unit.

In my limited cruising experience I have found that ham radio is the *only* really dependable and efficient means of communication on the coastal waters of the Pacific Northwest and Mexico. In fact, amateur radio is the only communication that yachtsmen in Mexican waters have with the States and with each other, and they conduct a regular daily network.

From my experience, I would recommend that a yacht first be

PORTABLE COMMUNICATIONS—On board Wild Rose, we use two auxiliary walkie-talkie-type VHF/FM transceivers, both powered by penlite batteries, with an output of about 1 watt. These are the Drake model 22C 12-channel ham rig and the Model 22M 6-channel Marine Band VHF rig. They have built-in antennas, but also can be connected to the permanent shipboard VHF whips.

HAM STATION—A typical on-board ham radio station would consist of these three units: the five-band transceiver on the bottom (in this case a Swan solid-state 200-watt model); over this, the Dentron transmatch; and in the transmission line, the combination power-output and VSWR meters.

equipped with the standard marine VHF/FM transceiver, but that anything beyond that be Amateur Band and "CB" (Citizens Band) gear. (Even many merchant and military ships and stations have ham operators among their radio shack crew, so you're never without an audience!)

The Amateur Radio License
Many folks confuse or intermingle CB radio with Amateur Band or ham radio, which hams consider an insult. The CBers, who are also called Chicken Banders or Cry Babies, and a number of other, unprintable epithets, have earned their unsavory reputation through illegal operations over the years. This disgusts most hams, who earned their license privileges the hard way and jealously monitor and police themselves to maintain their good image.

To get a CB license, all you have to do is fill out an FCC form, submit it with the fee ($4 at this writing), and in due time you are issued a license and call sign. It is estimated that about 90 percent of the CB operation in the States is now conducted illegally—the operators having no license, using excessive power, and broadcasting beyond the maximum permitted limit of 150 miles. At the same time, there are perhaps ten times as many CB units in operation as there are ham units—which means that the electronics manufacturers themselves are the main reason for the widespread CB violations. The CB market is much more profitable than the Amateur Service.

At this writing, the Federal Communications Commission has plans for restructuring the Amateur Service, but the process will take years to complete. At present the various classes of amateur licensing are in ascending grade: Novice, Technician, General, Advanced, and Amateur Extra Class. The frequencies on which you may operate are determined by the class of license you hold. All of the classes require the ability to send and receive Morse code, from five words a minute for Novice and Technician to twenty words per minute for Amateur Extra. In addition, you must get a passing grade in a written examination that includes elements of radio theory, rules and regulations, and operating procedures. Almost anyone who can read can pass the exams for the Novice and Technician classes, after studying the manuals available. Most people have no problem with the General, which gives you most of the frequencies and power privileges. The exam for Advanced class is fairly easy, too, once you pass the General and have some experience. The exam for Amateur Extra class is tough, though, in the theory and in the code efficiency, and in addition has a two-years'-experience requirement. The latest edition of the ARRL Radio Amateur License

Manual (see Bibliography) is a condensed source of FCC license requirements and sample test questions.

Other countries have different license requirements, and in some cases do not require written examinations or proficiency tests. Amateurs of one country can usually obtain a permit to operate within the territorial limits of reciprocating countries. There are currently some restrictions on operating in or out of a few nations in Asia and Africa, but not the U.S.S.R., as one might think. There are many Soviet hams, and amateur communications behind the Iron Curtain are common. The "hams" may or may not be intelligence agents, but so far their operations appear to be nonpolitical.

Happily for yachtsmen, those countries most often on the circumnavigator's itinerary are filled with radio amateurs and, armed with a Callbook, you can make a lot of friends and find a lot of doors open through this wonderful hobby.

Amateur Radio Frequencies
Amateurs have by far the greatest number of operating frequencies of any other single service. They range from 1800 to 2000 kHz (or kilocycles), called the 160-meter band up through the 75-meter or 80-meter band, from 3500 to 4000 kHz; the 40-meter band from 7000 to 7300 kHz; 20-meter band from 14,000 to 14,350 kHz 15-meter band from 21,000 to 21,450; 10-meter band from 28,000 to 29,700 kHz; the 6-meter band from 50 to 54 mHz; the 2-meter band from 144 to 148 mHz (or megacycles); the 220 band from 220 to 225 mHz; and the 450 band from 420 to 450 mHz. These generally operate worldwide, although in New Zealand and Australia hams are also allowed from 26,960 to 27,230 kHz, which cover part of the American CB band.

The bands which most amateurs use currently, and which are most useful to the yachtsman are:

75-meter   Requires the longest antenna, up to about 120 feet; is the best for local (within 500 miles) communications, "ragchews," and networks during the day; and for "DX" up to several thousand miles after dark.
40-meter   A good all-purpose band day or night, but after dark is crowded with foreign broadcast stations and lots of "heterodynes." An excellent "mobile" band. The antenna required is about half the length of "75" and about twice that needed for "20."
20-meter   This is the DX band most often used, and is excellent but crowded at any time of day or night. This is the one you would normally use for long-distance, worldwide, serious communications with the States.

15-meter   The results you get on this band of frequencies will, at times, astonish you. Sometimes a station on the other side of the world comes in as loud as one in the next block. It is not "open" all the time, however, so you have to play it literally by ear.

10-meter   A super band for worldwide communications, but it is affected by an 11-year sunspot cycle, so it is either at its lowest, rising to its highest, or descending again in efficiency. It is a good ragchew band for local operating on the ground-plane propagation.

6-meter   A good band, but not as much used, it can be used in the AM, FM, or SSB modes. Excellent for local and regional communications, and when the skip is in, for national and even overseas contacts.

2-meter   This is available in AM or SSB voice communications, but is most used in the VHF/FM mode quite similar to the marine VHF band. The equipment is available in amazingly compact and sophisticated units, all under 5 watts output. In the United States and Canada, amateurs maintain a vast network of repeater stations, which form an almost unbroken linkage useful to the coastal navigator as well. My 1-watt handy-talky has on numerous occasions outperformed my 25-watt marine transceiver. I consider it essential for shipboard use.

Amateur Equipment
In the olden days we all built our own receivers and transmitters, and often even designed them from scratch. They were big, heavy, and clumsy, with limited versatility and over-sensitive to adjustments. With their great panels of meters and switches and levers, and banks of glowing tubes, they filled even the builder with awe and self-satisfaction. Today's "appliance operators" never build from scratch, although some of them buy kits and put them together, which does not save any money but does give one the feeling that he is "building."

Practically all ham gear today is factory-built, and most of it now is solid-state with integrated circuits and modules, and printed chipboards for easy replacement. The gear is a product of the worldwide solid-state technology, which gets more sophisticated and expensive each year. In truth, it is cheaper to buy a factory-built set than it is to buy the components and build one yourself. If you buy your gear and therefore become an appliance operator, you will find that you have too much invested in it even to try to service it yourself, which will void the warranty and lower its resale value. These are facts of life, and I'm not arguing for or agin 'em, but a lot of hams are still conscience-stricken on the subject.

Most ham rigs are now SSB transceivers, with the receiver

and transmitter built together and using some of each other's circuits. Most of them are "all-band," meaning that they include the 75-40-20-15- and sometimes 10-meter bands. The main difference from, and advantage over marine units is, incidentally, that you can tune across the entire band in the Amateur Service with the "VFO" (Variable Frequency Oscillator), instead of being "rock-bound" on specially assigned channels. It is possible to get amateur rigs which have the 160-75-40-20-15-10 or any combination of these, and it is also possible to obtain single-band rigs for the 75- or 40- or 20-meter bands; but the most common and most useful to the yachtsman is the 75-40-20-15 combination.

Separate rigs are needed for the 6-meter and the 2-meter bands. The latter is the most important and useful, and should be obtained in the VHF/FM mode, either in the hand-held or fixed unit. Most of these are direct crystal controlled, with a separate crystal for transmitting and receiving. This is costly, but a 12-channel rig is generally sufficient for use in any region. I once drove from Portland, Oregon, to Halifax, Nova Scotia, and back, using only one channel—the popular repeater channel, 34-94. Coming into favor at this writing are the rigs with frequency synthesizer, which eliminates crystals. This is more important with the marine-type VHF rigs, where you have a choice and often a need of 55 channels worldwide.

The difference between the ham and the Marine VHF/FM service was made clear to me on a cruise to the San Juan Islands. With the Amateur Band 1-watt handheld unit I could work anywhere in Western Washington and British Columbia, through the repeater atop Mount Constitution. With the Marine 25-watt rig, I often could not raise even the marine telephone operator, which had its antenna in the same location.

On *Wild Rose*, my ham station is equipped with an Atlas 210X transceiver, slightly larger than a shoebox, but with 200 watts input capacity; and a hand-held 1-watt Drake TR-22 VHF/FM. The Atlas covers the 75-40-20-15-10 bands. The Drake has crystals for twelve channels. The Atlas draws only 16 amps at full power, and about half an amp in receive only.

Operation

The FCC has some special regulations for amateur or "mobile" stations aboard ships or aircraft:

In addition to complying with all other applicable rules, an Amateur mobile station operated on board a ship or aircraft must comply with the following conditions: (a) The installation and operation . . . shall be approved by the

233

master or captain; (b) The amateur mobile station shall be separate from and independent of all other radio equipment . . . ; (c) The electrical installation . . . shall be in accord with rules applicable to ships . . . ; (d) The operation of the amateur mobile station and its associated equipment, either in itself or in its method of operation, shall not constitute a hazard to the safety of life or property.

The key to that clause is the word "mobile." The station is "mobile" only when detached from any dock or permanent mooring. If the vessel can be got into motion immediately, such as when at anchor, it is regarded as mobile. Otherwise it is "fixed," as with a home station, or "portable," as when operating from a temporary fixed location.

If operating in international waters, usually twelve miles or more offshore, the station is considered "marine mobile" but is usually signed just plain "mobile" followed by the ITU Region designator. All of the Americas are in Region 2. Operation in the coastal waters of a foreign country requires a permit from that country. If outside the boundary of Inland Rules of the Road, I would sign simply as "W7PFL mobile, Region 2," no matter in what part of the Pacific I was. In actual practice, I give it as "Region 2, marine mobile," followed by the location, such as "200 miles off Cape Blanco," or the approximate latitude and longitude. At the dock or anchorage, I sign my location as "mobile, Sausalito, California," or, if in Mexican waters with a valid permit, as "mobile, Cabo San Lucas," with the further intelligence that we are aboard the yacht *Wild Rose.*

In international waters you can operate only on 7 mHz or higher.

Antennas and Other Gear
A yacht under sixty or seventy feet has a problem with any medium- or high-frequency antenna. VHF/FM and CB antennas are simple, usually base-loaded, and do not require a ground. But it is essential with Marine Band and Amateur Band antennas that there be a proper grounding system to beat against for proper loading of the transmitter. Receiving antennas are not critical, and even a clamp to a stay or shroud is adequate. But modern transceivers use the same antenna, with relay switching from one to the other automatically as the mike button is depressed or released.

In the case of Marine Band antennas, most transceivers are tuned to a particular frequency, such as the international calling frequencies, and locked in by crystals. Amateur Band rigs can be tuned all the way across a band, and then switched to a different

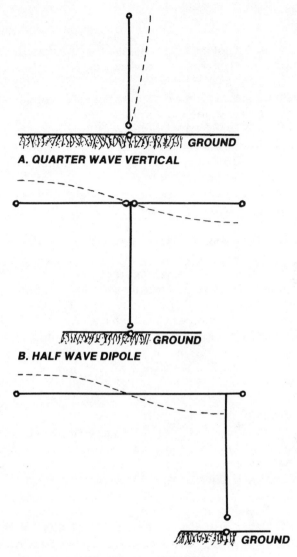

A. QUARTER WAVE VERTICAL

B. HALF WAVE DIPOLE

C. END FED RANDOM LENGTH WIRE

RADIO SIGNALS—The three basic forms taken by radio waves transmitted through different types of antennas are shown in these sketches. The solid line represents the actual electrical length and form of the antenna wire. The dotted line is a greatly simplified pattern of the sine wave sent out into space. The principal difference between the three is that the vertical pattern is half below ground ("ground" meaning earth or sea), and thus has the lowest angle of radiation. Each type of antenna has its advantages and disadvantages, depending upon the actual frequency transmitted. The drawing also illustrates why a good ground is essential to radio-wave propagation.

band as well. An antenna is resonant—that is, properly tuned to the frequency being generated by the transmitter—only at one specific frequency. If crystals for other frequencies are switched in, or a VFO setting is changed, the fixed antenna goes off resonance in proportion to the change in the dial setting or crystal frequency. Since it is not practical to change the length—and thus the frequency—of an antenna, other means are used to maintain a resonant signal. One way is by the use of the broad-banded antenna, which sacrifices some efficiency and power output in order to remain tuned within acceptable ranges as the frequency is changed in the transmitter. This is the typical medium- and high-frequency vertical antenna used on merchant and military vessels.

The other common antenna used is the dipole which is a horizontal wire, fed in the center with two equal legs which radiate a figure-S pattern of half a wavelength. The common vertical antenna radiates a quarter-wave pattern, which relies upon beating against ground to supply the other quarter-wave. The vertical also has a high angle of radiation, which is often advantageous. In general, however, the half-wave dipole is the most simple and efficient antenna for all-around use. Its length is usually cut to the frequency in the center of the band or between the most commonly used frequencies or channels.

The end-fed long wire antenna is often seen on the masts of large ships, but the length required exceeds that possible on a yacht. One exception I know of is the 70-foot yacht owned by John Cecil (W7BQQ) of Fallon, Nevada, who uses a random length of wire from the masthead down to an antenna tuner, with the vessel's deck safety wires and stanchions used as a counterpoise, without an earth ground.

Earl Schenck, Jr., of Seattle, who has cruised extensively in the North and South Pacific aboard his 48-foot ketch *Eleuthera*, maintained regular schedules on the 20-meter ham band with an insulated triatic stay for an antenna, fed with a 35-foot transmission line to a Johnson Matchbox antenna tuner.

Dipoles are most frequently used when a ship is anchored or tied up, since they have to be raised among the rigging, and they are usually (especially on single-mast vessels) employed in the "inverted V" or "droopy dipole" configuration—that is, with the center raised to the topmost point of the mast, and the ends coming down to suitable tie points on the bow and stern. The transmission line comes down from the center along the mast to the transceiver.

Beams, or "yagis," are seldom if ever used on a yacht. These are similar to the television rooftop antenna, but would have to be five or ten times larger to match the Amateur and Marine frequencies. Moreover, they are too directional for use aboard a vessel. I know of one instance in which two Amateur Band automobile whip antennas were attached together base to base, then mounted as a horizontal dipole sixteen feet across, which did not need a ground.

Auto-type antennas cannot be used as Marine antennas without adaptation, because they are designed to use the metal car body as a counterpoise or the ground side of the radiation pattern. On some vessels, an Amateur Band whip such as the Hustler or Webster Band-Spanner can be used, mounted at a convenient point on the rail. The mobile whip or loaded-whip quarter-wave antenna can be adapted by using a longer transmission line to the transceiver, the length arrived at by experimentation. I had some success with the Webster and about eight feet of coaxial cable transmission line. Another solution is to use the next-highest frequency loading coil.

On two-masted vessels, various dipoles and flattops can be strung between the sticks. Metal masts can be fed directly as verticals. An insulated wire can be tacked to a wooden mast, cut to the proper length, and fed at the bottom.

Usually a great deal of experimentation is needed to adapt any of these antennas for Amateur Service on a boat. The tall Marine Band vertical antenna, which has a range of from 2000 to 4000 kHz, can be adapted for use in the 75 and 40 meter band.

On *Wild Rose* I finally wound up with the following: a vertical deck-mounted CB, which folds down; a spare vertical VHF/FM, which also folds down on the deck; a Marine Band VHF/FM vertical on top of the mast; an Amateur Band VHF/FM whip also atop the mast; a 2000 to 4000 kHz vertical attached at deck level, which can be laid down flat; and a coaxial dipole inverted-Vee-type horizontal antenna for each Amateur Band, cut for the center frequency in each band. These are raised only when in port or at anchor because of the interference with rigging and sails. Later I discovered that an automotive type loaded whip clamped to the pulpit rail, with the lifelines performing as a counterpoise, worked best of all.

This is far more elaborate than the average yachtsman would consider, unless he were a ham. But, as indicated by the letters I have seen from the "Cruising Commodores" of the Seven Seas Cruising Association, most serious bluewater people are now taking the exams and getting their Amateur Band "tickets."

Matching and Grounding
The connection between the antenna and the transmitter is the "feed line" or "transmission line." This is usually coaxial cable with an impedance of 50 to 53 ohms to match the final tank circuit of the

transmitter. When the impedance is "matched," it is like the adjustment of the nozzle of a garden hose for maximum pressure and distance. When there is a mismatch, there is an enormous waste of power, a greatly reduced signal radiating from the antenna, and often the odor of burned-out tubes and transistors inside the transmitter.

In some types of antenna the length of the transmission line is critical, but in most cases it is not. In practice, however, if coaxial cable is used, the larger type—commonly RG-8U—should be used for any run over ten feet because of its lower line losses. Most Marine Band-type transceivers come with the smaller cable—RG-58. If the run to the antenna is ten feet or over, this should be replaced with RG-8. The same is true of Amateur Band gear. Open wire transmission lines are almost never used on a yacht, but are common on ships.

Even with a transmission line which has the same impedance as the final tank, it may not match the antenna impedance. If not, the standing wave ratio and reflected power will be proportionately out of balance. The symbol for this component of matching is SWR or VSWR. There is a simple and inexpensive unit called the Standing Wave Ratio and Power Meter available which, inserted between the transmission line and transmitter, will indicate how much of a mismatch there is on the line.

There is not much that can be done to remedy this mismatch without changing the length of the antenna legs, "pruning" them to the operating frequency. Another device, called the matchbox or matching antenna tuner, however, is a good substitute. One design called the "transmatch" is found in the ARRL Handbook and is capable of matching any impedance over the range from 3 to 30 mHz, which covers all the common Amateur Band and Marine Band frequencies used. No radio transmitter aboard any vessel should be without an antenna tuner or at least an antenna matching transformer, which is a similar device that works on a different principle. I use both the matching transformer and the matchbox for my Amateur Band gear on *Wild Rose*.

For all radio transmitting antennas aboard ship, except the VHF and the CB, an earth ground is essential to good radiation. A salty ocean makes a good "earth" ground, but there are some problems. The boat's grounding system has three functions: lightning protection, corrosion prevention, and "rf," or radio frequency ground path. In the latter case, the larger the area exposed to salt water, the better the rf ground and antenna efficiency. (Lightning protection and corrosion-proofing are outside this discussion, but are dealt with in the reference sources in the Bibliography.)

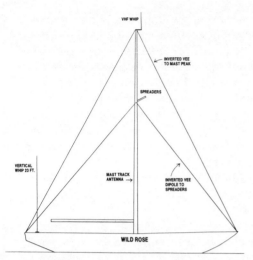

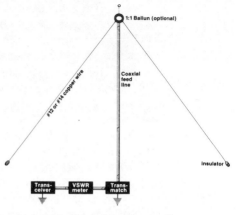

ANTENNAS—Sketch shows four different types of ham radio antennas tried aboard Wild Rose. They are the VHF mast top whips, the two different inverted-Vee dipoles, the stern-mounted vertical, and the mast track vertical. Best results have been with the VHF mast top whip and the stern-mounted high-frequency vertical, including the pulpit whip, not shown.

HAM ANTENNA—Block diagram shows arrangement of a typical inverted-Vee antenna, using the main mast as center support and the two legs of the dipole at about 90 degrees from horizontal. The balun is optional and can be an insulated center connector of use suitable for marine environment. The VSWR meter is also optional, but the transmatch is a necessity. The center feedline can be any length of coaxial cable, preferably RG8 or the large-diameter-type for low loss. This type of antenna can be cut for any frequency from 1800 kHz to 60 mHz, limited only by the mast height and length of the vessel. Antennas in the VHF spectrum are almost always verticals or vertically polarized.

One type of ground is the hollow copper tubing attached along the keel. Another is the copper screening imbedded in fiberglass hulls or screwed to wooden hulls. In any case, a ground plate such as this should be at least ten square feet or one square meter in expanse. The plate does not actually have to have contact with water, although this is preferable. The noncontact-type ground is called the "capacitance ground" and works fairly well. On *Wild Rose* I use the six-thousand-pound cast-iron outside keel as a capacitance ground, which works efficiently because of its mass. The ground connection is made by web cable from the keel bolts in the bilge.

Those patented sintered plates which are bolted onto the outside hull surface are only as efficient as their actual size allows. They have no magical electrical properties.

In one instance I know of, a fairly efficient ground system is comprised of all the shroud chainplates connected by number 8 aluminum wire, which is in turn connected to zinc teardrops on the outside of the hull. This also gives good lightning protection.

Some sailboats carry all their ballast inside. This is not only a hazardous installation if the vessel is not otherwise protected from lightning, but also is bad for the hull in a grounding. This type of ballast can, however, be used as a capacitance noncontact ground.

In all cases, the ground connection to the transmitter should be as short as possible, to avoid spurious emissions and a cabin full of rf currents.

Citizens Band Service
In 1958 the FCC set aside twenty-three channels in the old Amateur 11-meter band to provide low-cost communication for small businesses such as construction firms and delivery services, and anyone else who needed it. As this is being printed, the FCC has announced that the CB band would be expanded and other modifications made in the regulations. The power input was limited to 5 watts and the distance or range to the local area. No qualifications are needed, other than need and payment of the license fee. As the service grew, it became more of a hobby service for those who could not or did not want to study and take the regular ham examinations. As the use spread, the band became overloaded, filled with obscene language and over-the-air threats to others, and souped-up signals that interfered with others clean across the country. Most of these outlaws did not even bother to obtain a license, but used such handles as "Midnight Raider," "Sundown Kid," "Beer Gut," and "Pussycat," instead of call signs.

In 1975 there were more than six million sets in use, priced between $150 and $500 and used by everyone from housewives to farmers to truck drivers to doctors—and boaters. The number of users doubles every year. CB is here to stay, unless it kills itself.

The CB channels are much used in coastal areas by charter boat operators, private yachts, and shore stations. These channels are *not* monitored by the Coast Guard, but in emergency a message can be relayed from a CB source to the CG via another means such as a Marine Band channel.

Although there is no real policing or official monitoring, Channel 9 is regarded as an emergency frequency, Channel 13 as an unofficial marine emergency frequency, and Channel 11 is used for establishing contacts. Truckers, who are all wired for CB and use the units for passing on information about the location of "Smokey Bears," weigh stations, and good places to eat, all use Channel 10.

CB can be generally described as organized chaos, but it does come in handy on a yacht, and it is the cheapest two-way communications you can have.

Other Electronics

In addition to communications equipment, most yachts today are equipped with one or more pieces of additional electronic gear. In my opinion, the most important of these is the depth sounder. I would, in fact, rather have a depth sounder than anything else, including communications gear, if I had to choose. It is almost indispensable for navigation, with or without charts. It will help find your position by means of soundings when nothing else is available. It will keep you off shoals and rocks. And, of course, you can use it for fish finding.

On *Wild Rose* we have two depth sounders—one operating on the ship's electrical system, and the other on a separate battery. The transducer is mounted on the inside of the hull, forward of the keel in a box filled with mineral oil, instead of through the hull. Nothing protrudes from the bottom, and there is no problem of fouling the transducer face. With this arrangement, I find it necessary to hook the unit up directly to a power source, and even so there is a slight loss of sensitivity. But the compromise is worth it.

Both of these units are inexpensive models designed and built for pleasure and fishing boats, but both of them work amazingly well and are extremely accurate.

One of them, the portable battery model, registers up to sixty feet. The other is supposed to register up to seventy feet or seventy fathoms, but doesn't; its maximum range is about forty fathoms. Both of them use the conventional neon light and circular dial system. Other models are available which use the needle-meter or paper recording systems.

If I have to replace either of my depth sounders, I will buy a first-class commercial model which will register up to 100 fathoms. With this, it is possible to follow the 100-fathom curve in coastwise navigation with ease and, in conjunction with the compass and perhaps an RDF, run very accurate courses.

For anchoring and running inside passages I use the depth sounder constantly, but in the feet not the fathom position, for more accuracy. It is an essential piece of gear in these instances, and in some of the places we took *Wild Rose* that first summer we kept both units on constantly. The old sounding lead and handline are all right—if you have a crew. With a yacht as big as *Wild Rose*, and only the two of us, we are too busy doing other things.

The next most useful piece of gear is probably the RDF. On a sailboat, the fixed models are awkward and often inaccurate. I prefer the hand-held models, which you aim like a gun. With this type you can find an interference-free spot aboard and get a more accurate radio-beacon fix. The unit can also be used as a bearing compass. The main problem, I have found, is the lack of radio beacons and the low power of the existing ones. For coastwise cruising there should be more of them, and the range should be extended to 100 miles.

The obvious next purchase, if funds are available, is either the small-craft radar or the loran, or both. (Both were subsequently installed.)

I have had considerable experience with loran on offshore fishing vessels and find this system extremely accurate and useful. Often we would set the unit on the known coordinates of the harbor and leave it on automatic tracking all day. This way we could pinpoint the good fishing and guide ourselves back even in heavy weather and fog. Used along with compass and depth sounder, it is simple and highly effective.

Loran now includes two systems—A and C. The latter is more accurate and is being phased in for commercial and merchant use. It is also more costly, and in many places too sophisticated for the need. The modern A system units are so inexpensive and efficient that no respectable offshore yacht should be without one. Loran A will also be with us in the foreseeable future, and can always be converted to C mode when necessary.

Loran, however, is of no use on inland and inside waters, where I had intended to do the first year's cruising. Therefore, when it came to making a decision I sprang for radar. I settled upon a British-made small-craft radar with a maximum range of sixteen miles. I could only get a maximum of about four miles, however, because it was mounted on the cabin trunk deck just behind the mast. Actually, this proved to be all the range we needed for coastal and inside passage work. The unit draws only 4 amps for a power consumption of 45 watts, or about the least of any piece of gear aboard. Even though I had had no experience with radar, I found it easy to learn to use, and with a little practice I could quickly identify blips. On its very first real trial, we rounded treacherous Cape Flattery and entered the Strait of Juan de Fuca in a dense fog, using the large-scale chart and the radar screen. During the next month, the radar helped us on two different occasions in fog and unknown waters. I consider that it paid for itself that first summer of cruising.

The argument can be made that one can get along all right without all this junk, and of course this is true—provided you have unlimited time, a predilection toward haphazard adventures, and can afford to lose a sixty-thousand-dollar investment on some rocky lee shore in a fog. At the same time, one should never depend completely on electronic aids, as sooner or later they are certain to fail or get out of adjustment. Always have a backup system, but if you can afford to have extra electronic gear, by all means use it.

The last piece of electronic gear I invested in was an autopilot. Although I installed it carefully, and rechecked all connections, I have never been able to get this unit to work properly and dependably. I have therefore put it way down on the priority list. After all, I found a more reliable and efficient "automatic pilot" the first time my bride sailed with me on Wild Rose and found out how easy it was to drive, even in boisterous weather.

For general radio listening, we have installed, semipermanently, a Zenith Transoceanic "all-band" portable, which operates off AC shoreside or a set of D batteries. The coverage includes a VHF weather band, FM and AM broadcast stations, mediumwave and shortwave bands, foreign broadcasts, ships and aircraft, as well as the WWV and WWVH time signals. It is a high-quality piece of machinery, but it has two drawbacks—no bandspread for the Amateur Band frequencies, and no SSB mode. You have to use the BFO or Beat Frequency Oscillator to tune in Single Sideband, as well as CW code.

101 Notes
From Wild Rose's
Commonplace Book

1. One of the nicer things modern technology has produced is synthetic waterproof carpeting. We found it ideal not only for floor covering, but also for padding ladders, sound- and sweat-proofing the inside of the hull, and even for soft, nonskid deck and cockpit treads.

2. Never use the electrical fridge for food storage. Use it only to cool or chill food that is going to be consumed soon—except for perishables, of course.

3. A sailboat cockpit is often the most miserable and uncomfortable operating station ever devised on land or sea. Smart yachtsmen have long since discovered that a simple dodger or canopy can be the helmsman's best friend, and in port can add an extra "room" to the vessel. It is adaptable to all climates, and practically a necessity in the higher latitudes. It generally must be tailored

for each individual boat, and ideally should be designed for easy removal. Vinyl is the best material at present.

4. Anyone who has an engine aboard and does not run it under a load at least an hour a day might as well use it for an anchor. Lack of such use is the principal reason for the problems sailing skippers agonize over and complain of.

5. We carry powdered drinks instead of cases and cases of bottles. Some kind of water filter will greatly improve the quality and taste of such reconstituted drinks, which come either sweetened or unsweetened. We do carry a few bottles of carbonated drinks and, of course, a small supply of beer and wine. Carbonated drinks will sometimes quench a thirst when nothing else will. As yet there is no dehydrated form of beer and wine, fortunately.

6. A spare depth sounder powered by separate dry cell batteries is the best backup piece of electronic gear available.

7. Fishing to provide food and sport is a natural extension of cruising and should not be overlooked.

8. Tapered wooden plugs, made from a length of doweling, should be stored convenient to all through-hulls, along with rags and a hammer for quick emergency use.

9. Wells filled with mineral oil holding the submerged transducer for the depth sounders proved more desirable in our case than a through-hull installation.

10. Do all the big jobs first, and the little ones will take care of themselves.

11. Acetone, WD-40, Tupperware, and Vaseline are the boat owner's best friends.

12. PVC pipe has many uses aboard, such as for turnbuckle boots, cable covers, rod and flag holders, anchor chocks, and conduit.

13. No galley sink should be without a direct saltwater pump.

14. We discovered that bins are more practical than drawers in the cabins, but if drawers are used, cut out handholds instead of using metal pulls. These not only make it easy to pull out drawers, but also provide air circulation.

15. A Swing Stove or equivalent, with Sterno canned heat, will provide a quick and easy heating and cooking source for snacks and small meals underway, so you don't have to bother with the big range.

16. Plastic bags and ties of all sizes have endless uses aboard. We also find the plastic waterproof 35 mm film containers excellent for storing small parts.

17. Diesel engines should have at least three stages of fuel filtering, and a duel system would not be excessive. There should be a *complete* kit of spare parts including extra injectors, gaskets, water pump, oil filters, high-pressure fuel lines, fan belts, extra piston or two, raw water pump and filter, spare hoses, stainless hose clamps of all sizes, fuses, spare alternator, and of course extra lubricating oil.

18. Auto tires in the compact-car sizes make almost indestructible fenders, and are free for the asking at any service station. They should have large drain holes cut in them, and for a tidy job, covers of canvas or vinyl can be made.

19. One of my greatest inspirations I call the Handy Donald. This is a wooden stand which will hold reels of various sizes. I used it for storing reels of electrical wire, rope and lines, anchor chain, and water hose. It is easily portable and stowable.

20. Duplicate spare parts, light bulbs, and fuses should be carried for every fixture and accessory aboard.

21. Ice chests carried on deck greatly supplement refrigeration devices aboard, and can provide storage for bulk perishables, bottles, and any fish caught.

22. Heavy chain makes the best anchor rode in Northwest Coast waters. For the deep anchoring that is sometimes necessary, one should consider cable. About six hundred feet of 3/8-inch flexible cable can be easily stowed on a small drum provided on some makes of anchor windlasses.

23. Never send in a warranty card until the device or unit has been installed and tested. Legally, however, lack of a warranty card does not relieve the manufacturer of responsibility for defective merchandise.

24. We use plastic dishes and glasses as our permanent utensils, since they are safe and unbreakable. For ordinary snacks we use paper plates and cups, which can be disposed of in the fireplace.

25. Portable appliances such as tape recorders and record players are best operated off dry-cell batteries to save the ship's 12-volt system from excessive drain.

26. A wet suit will provide the helmsman with a warm and comfortable body protection in the worst weather, to say nothing of better survival chances if he is accidentally washed overboard. A wet suit will also save your dry clothes for use below. A new innovation is the "Survival Suit," which can be pulled on over all your clothes, including sea boots, in a matter of seconds. It is made by the Imperial Mfg. Co., Bremerton, Washington.

27. Any well-founded yacht should have several up-to-date logbooks. *Wild Rose* has a conventional ship's log for a permanent

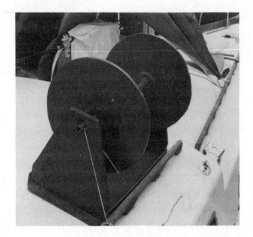

HANDY DONALD—I designed and built this multipurpose tool of plywood scraps. It has been used as a wire dispenser during the electrical wiring of the vessel, and for rope, line, and anchor chain stowage.

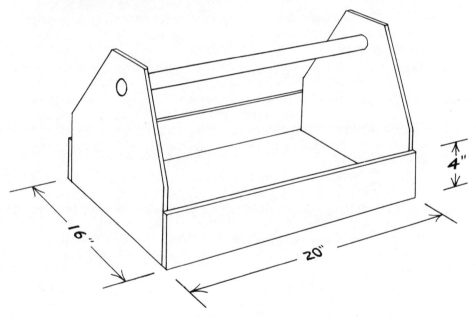

HANDY DONALD—Details and dimensions of a simple maintenance tool used aboard Wild Rose. It can be used as a carryall, a rack for holding reels of wire for dispensing, a reel of anchor line for storage, and for many other purposes.

record of operation and navigation away from the dock. She also has a construction and maintenance log for keeping track of all work, modifications, and maintenance aboard. There is also a separate log of stores, spare parts, and sail inventory, along with a list of bulbs, fuses, blocks, and charts.

28. The most distressing and frustrating thing about cruising is the way things seem to get lost or misplaced. Even a small boat is capable of carrying an astonishing variety of supplies and stores. I found that by dividing the ship up into compartments and numbering them, I could keep a fairly up-to-date catalogue of parts and their location.

29. If you carry an ice cooler on deck, plastic pails of quick-frozen water will keep longer than store-bought block ice. And when it melts, you have a pail of ice-cold water. Don't use frozen beer.

30. For coastwise cruising, a small ice cream maker is entirely practical and greatly adds to the enjoyment and morale of the crew and passengers.

31. I use a portable tape recorder for recording weather reports and messages. This way I can replay them later to refresh my memory, or to have a permanent record.

32. With a 35 mm camera and black and white film, you can make a permanent record of everything on the boat, topsides and below, that can possibly be stolen or damaged. Nothing convinces an insurance adjuster more.

33. Instead of an aluminum mast, I built my own out of 3/4-inch mahogany-faced waterproof plywood in the form of a box girder, both screwed and glued. I then painted it with eight coats of Pettit epoxy in "Bikini Blue," #4216 Part A and #4027 Part B, over three coats of the recommended white prime. After four years' exposure to a marine environment, there is not the slightest sign of erosion.

34. If possible, design a main cabin table so that it can be folded up out of the way, or removed and stored. This will greatly add to the spaciousness of that room when no one is eating or writing there. Trailer-supply houses handle the hardware for building many variations of the saloon table.

35. For sails under four hundred square feet, a careful analysis can eliminate many expensive deck winches. Small sails can easily be raised and handled without such complicated hardware.

36. The best all-around lubricant on board is Vaseline. It can be used for sail slides, winches, turnbuckles, fairleads, blocks, gooseneck; for electrical panels to prevent corrosion, over window leaks, and also for medical purposes.

37. We soon discovered that the old-fashioned bosun's chair was a most dangerous and inefficient method of getting up the mast. Instead, I installed aluminum mast stirrups which enable one to "walk" up to the very top with the greatest of ease and safety. The total cost of the stirrups was less than a hundred dollars. Of course, one should not go up the mast at all without an adequate safety belt securely attached.

38. It is now practical for even the smallest yachts to carry aboard a solid-state Marine Band VHF/FM transceiver. This is useful for contacting the Coast Guard in emergencies, as well as for ship-to-ship and ship-to-shore communications within a radius of twenty-five miles or so. It can also be used as an extension of your home telephone. Your call letters can be registered with the telephone company marine service and calls charged to your account; or, when making a shore call, you can call collect or charge the call to your home telephone number. Obviously, through your nearby marine operator, you can then make a telephone call to any telephone in the world.

39. If much time is spent dockside, such as during the winter, consider the use of an electric blanket on the bunk.

40. I found that UHF coaxial through-wall connectors, with washers and nuts, make excellent through-bulkhead and deck connections for radio antennas. Such a connection costs only about three dollars, as compared with forty dollars for a regular marine fitting.

41. When shopping for parts, always carry a small magnet to test for ferro traces. It is surprising how much "stainless" and "bronze" has iron in it.

42. Before installing permanent fixtures, put them in temporarily and "live" with them for a while to make sure they are convenient and comfortable.

43. We carry surplus charts, not in use, rolled up in plastic tubes and stowed in the sail locker out of the way.

44. The best place to carry a dinghy while cruising inshore is on davits off the transom.

45. The greatest time wasters during the construction and outfitting of a boat are uninvited visitors and onlookers, and your own tendency to stand back and admire your work. Try to keep visitors away, or ignore them. To keep yourself busy and unslothful, have your work all planned out ahead when you arrive, and then pitch into some easy job first to stimulate your ambition.

46. It is surprising how easy it is to lose valuable parts and tools overboard. Eternal vigilance will save much money, time, and frustration.

47. When boring holes for U-bolt-type deck fittings, make the holes one size larger than the bolt, to avoid having to force the bolt through.

48. When installing turnbuckles, install all of them the same way, so that they can all be adjusted in the same direction. This will save time during tune-ups.

49. We carry bolt cutters with a capacity up to 3/8-inch, but find that these do not cut stainless cable easily. A hacksaw should be carried for this emergency. Stainless cable of this thickness will also frustrate thieves.

50. An item too often neglected on custom and mass-produced yachts is the hand hold. The motion of a small vessel in rough seas is almost impossible to describe, and it is a motion you cannot avoid or escape. For prevention of injury and exhaustion, you must have something convenient to hang on to. I installed mahogany and teak hand holds all the way around the inside cabins, and additional ones wherever I could find a place for a short length. I have not been sorry. These grabs can be obtained unpainted but bored and with stainless bolts, nuts, and washers.

51. We had custom-made mattresses, which also are day cushions, fitted by a local firm in pleasing and enduring patterns. They are filled with a nonabsorbing synthetic foam and are reasonably soft for sleeping. Don't use any foam rubber aboard—it becomes soggy at the first wetting.

52. We use special sleeping bags made for marine use (in our case by the Coleman Company), with removable sheets, and occasionally a blanket on top, for complete comfort under most conditions.

53. We are not television watchers, nor are we card players. We do a lot of reading, but don't like to have a nose in the books all the time. We therefore look forward to the availability, at reasonable cost, of video tape or disc players, with monitor screens. With such outfits you can show movies, opera, ballet, travelogues, or musicals on a rental basis, without commercials, whenever you wish to schedule an evening's entertainment.

54. Dream ship builders exhibit a singular lack of imagination in their choice of names. Overworked are such heavenly bodies as Polaris, Venus, Sirius, Vega, Orion, Corvus; also elements such as Stormy, Sirocco, East Wind, West Wind, Wind Song, geographic points such as Olympus, Finisterre, Cape Ann; and fish such as Dolphin, Marlin, Bonito (although I've never seen one named after the Irish lord). You might also try to avoid girls' and babies' names, secret thoughts, romantic songs, trees, famous men—the egocentric French circumnavigator named his dream ship after himself, Alain

Gerbault. There are also crazy names such as Slo-Mo-Shun, Liki Tiki II, Mar-Don, Banjo Eyes, and so on.

Richard Gordon McCloskey once had a rivalry with *Yachting* editor Bill Taylor to come up with the most unusual boat names. Among them: Question Mark, Picket Fence, Comrade Cherry Loin-fruit, and Machozenozzle's Fondest.

Wild Rose was chosen because it is the official flower of our birth state, North Dakota, because it is a pet name for my bride, and because it fits nicely on the transom, on labels, and on stationery. Our dinghy is called *You-You*, which is French for dinghy. The main consideration, however, is convenient length (for signal flags), and intelligibility over the radio.

55. The well-equipped cruiser should be able to record his adventures on film. We carry a 35 mm single-lens reflex camera for black and white and color stills, and have added recently a Super 8 movie camera and a 35 mm underwater or waterproof still unit for wet weather on deck and for possible use with scuba gear.

56. During our first real winter storm in northern waters, with winds of thirty knots and temperatures in the 30s, we found our Cole stove in the main cabin not only impractical, but downright hazardous. Gusts of wind would periodically blow back down the chimney, put out the fire, and send a cloud of smoke billowing through the cabin. At other times, the stove would roar and become so hot that all the metal, including the chimney, would become red-hot. The bulkhead behind the stove and pipe became so hot that it burned our hands just to touch it.

At the first opportunity, we replaced this with a small cast-iron fo'c'sle stove, using a new routing for the pipe and more efficient deck iron and Charlie Noble. Unlike the sheet-metal Cole stove, this one holds its heat for some time after the fire has burned out, draws well, burns anything, and has a top for cooking if desired. We later found that this stove required tending constantly, and too much space for fuel. We finally settled on the Dickinson diesel-fired automatic range.

57. In our ship's library most of the books are paperbacks, which stow easily and do not become soggy or mildewed. Reference books and hardbounds are stowed in places where they are not likely to become damp. The latter includes volumes on oceanography, natural history, and geography that help make cruising more meaningful.

58. After only a couple of days aboard without a bath or shower, one begins to get ripe. It is not usually convenient to use our shower underway, but it is surprising how easy it is to take a bath with only a quart of hot water in a washbasin or pan. My

method is this: With the water as hot as I can stand, I soap a wet washrag, then rub it over my entire body. Next I soak and rinse the rag, leaving it still dripping with rinse water, and go over the same route again and again until my body is clean and fresh, incidentally standing on a soiled towel to catch the drops.

At first I shaved with the clean hot water before sponging off, but soon I acquired a good battery-powered electric razor which freed me from the sink and water entirely.

59. We keep a complete stock of canned staple foods aboard, in the small sizes that can be consumed in one meal without leftovers. Our supply is normally enough to last for several months if need be. A key to the code numbers stamped on the can is usually available from the processor, for possible use in keeping a record of the age of the cans and the contents in case the labels come off. For daily use on cruises, we shop whenever possible for fresh fruits, vegetables, and other products.

60. We keep a small sourdough starter going on board for baking bread, biscuits, pizza shells, cakes, doughnuts, French bread, cookies, and real old-fashioned sourdough hotcakes. There is nothing better to eat and the pungent aroma while cooking is enough to blow your mind with ecstasy.

61. Although *Wild Rose* has seven bunks, we consider that she "sleeps" only two, with the exception of occasional guests aboard for overnight or short cruises. The forward cabin is used for sail stowage, so that eliminates two bunks. The aft cabin is used as a den and writing office, which takes care of two more. This leaves two in the main cabin, which we occupy, plus a pilot berth above, on the starboard side. This has become a catchall for clothes, gear, charts, cameras, and other junk that might be needed in a hurry. I can think of nothing we would abhor more than our dream ship crowded with seven people—this would have too much of the *Grapes of Wrath* atmosphere. Overcrowding a boat with nonfamily guests can quickly ruin your yen for cruising. As Ernest Gann once wrote, there comes a time when furnishing others with a yacht and plush resort accommodations, including food and liquor, at your expense, becomes unacceptable. Better to avoid this habit at the beginning.

62. Almost a necessity for cruising is a large aluminum or stainless kettle or pot, for use in boiling crabs and shrimp, baking bread, or making soup if you have a lot of relatives dropping in dockside. In between these duties it can be used for storage of miscellaneous items.

63. Those gallon-sized plastic milk containers have a multitude of uses aboard (after you have finished up the milk). They can

CRABBING—The author setting out a crab trap after the storm, while anchored in peaceful Blind Bay. Most cruising boats in Northwest Coast waters carry at least one folding crab pot like this, plus a shrimp trap, as well as fishing gear. Crab bait can be fish heads, spoiled meat, or a can of cat food punched full of holes with a beer-can opener.

be used to store spare emergency water or waste oil from the engine change, for mixing and storing juices, and even for mixing powdered milk. Plastic bleach jugs can be turned into marker buoys for crab traps and anchor, used for stowage of kerosene and alcohol, and cut down into hand scoops for bailing the dinghy.

64. Homemade pillow covers, matching the decor and fitted with zippers, are ideal for stowing blankets and sheets out of sight but handy.

65. For small things, we use hanging shoebags, small swinging hammocks, and stow bags.

66. Instead of glass mirrors, we used those new synthetic types with self-attaching backs, placed where the light is best. These went up the minute my bride came aboard.

67. I originally installed an integral stereo system, but found that the speakers took up too much room and the whole thing was just too complex, so I tore it out. Now we use an inexpensive portable eight-track unit, with built-in speakers, powered by dry-cell batteries. We can stow it away when it is not in use, take it up into the cockpit while underway, or bring it ashore for picnics.

68. For long runs in nasty weather, we keep vacuum bottles of coffee, hot cocoa, or tea in bottle racks convenient to the helm. These can also be used for hot soup in weather too rough to cook.

69. For strapping down gear such as ice coolers, spare poles, small anchors, inflatables, and so on, we keep a stock of deck eye straps in various sizes, which can be screwed or bolted to deck or bulkheads, and used in conjunction with strops and elastic tie-downs. Other useful gadgets are flashlight clips and folding coat hangers, which can also be used for hanging coils of line, extension cords, and other such items.

70. We learned the hard way to buy the best (i.e., the most expensive) foul-weather gear available. Inexpensive gear not only tears easily, but is usually not even water-repellent after a couple of days of hard use. This gear should be tried on to make sure it fits properly and is roomy enough to go over your outer clothing, including sweater and jacket.

71. We found the standard plastic bucket unsuited for bailing or hauling because of the metal handle, which usually pulls out at the wrong time. A folding canvas bucket with roped handles is a more helpful piece of gear.

72. Most yachtsmen think signaling and signal flags are passé, but I believe they are gradually coming back into favor. We could not afford a complete set of international signal flags in the minimum size we needed (at least two feet square). However, since I received a flag code identifier with my documentation, I first

purchased the flags for this: W Y Z 9 3 0 4. This signal is also my Marine Band radio call sign. Hoisted on the spreader, it not only identifies *Wild Rose,* but also gives our call sign. In addition we carry the big yellow Q or quarantine flag, the diver's flag for scuba operations, plus code pennant, NC, D, O, K, W, A, C, N, and P. The radio code, and other standard one- or two-letter signals, such as NC, are kept hanked together and ready for hoisting.

73. Maybe it's because these tired old eyes don't work so well, but we carry four pairs of binoculars: one set of 7 × 35s for spotting buoy numbers and so on when the boat is jumping around, a set of 7 × 50s for night use and for better viewing in general from a relatively steadier platform, one pair of big 10 × 50s for reaching the horizon, and a cheap pair of plastic, waterproof 7 × 35s for backup and dinghy use. Another reason we have so many is that I had collected several of these over the years in my wildlife work.

74. Another handy device in Northwest waters is the viewing chamber, which is merely a boxlike affair with a glass bottom through which you can view things under water.

75. Plastic tape in all sizes and colors is most handy to have around the yacht for use in wiring, wrapping turnbuckles, emergency repairs, sail mending, and a hundred other things. We discovered that heating-duct tape is fine for more rugged uses, including insulating stove pipes, but is expensive.

76. When we are not aboard, and the vessel is closed up, we leave a heating rod in each compartment. These are safe even to the touch, since they are limited to a temperature of about 150 degrees, and have a low shore-power draw.

77. One of the most useful gadgets the mail-order specialty houses offer is the teak or mahogany spice rack. We needed two of them to keep our condiments handy and out of the way.

78. For running cable and fuel lines through a deck or bulkhead, we found the Delrin plastic through-hulls, which come in various sizes, cheap and handy. After the cable or hose is passed through, the hole is then sealed with bedding compound.

79. One of the most helpful accessories you can have is a folding cart for hauling stuff on and off the dock. At most marinas, the cart is either in use all the time or has been stolen.

80. Expensive, but useful away from a good weather information source, is the recording barograph. This leaves a continuous and permanent record of the changing pressure systems, by which you can predict your own weather.

81. *Wild Rose* has a tendency, indeed a joyous desire, to sail around her anchor. We stopped this by lashing the Wind Wand vane in place. But a small sail hoisted on the backstay will also do

the same thing. It will also hold your bow up while tethered to a sea anchor.

82. Most guidebooks are out of date as soon as published, and many are worthless anyway, just taking up shelf space. None of them tell you such critical things as how deep the anchorage is, and whether or not it will accommodate your size yacht. We made our own guidebook as we went along, the hard way, in appendices to the ship's log, and also took photographs where possible.

83. We carry two pressure cookers aboard—a large and a small one. Although we have so far used them very little, we anticipate that we will have use for them in the future, not only for cooking in rough weather, but also for canning. We consider a pressure cooker essential.

84. We also consider a portable water filter essential, even with "safe" shore-water supplies. Many marinas put so much clorine in the water that it is undrinkable and also taints coffee and orange juice. An in-line charcoal-type filter will remove this taint automatically. We also have a small hand-held filter that purifies a quart of water a minute. Most people don't know what really pure, fresh, cold water tastes like. Try it sometime—you'll like it.

85. All critical hose connections in the engine room, hot-water systems, and through-hulls should be double-clamped. The standard worm screw type of clamp has a tendency to loosen by itself. A glob of bedding sealant will usually stop this.

86. Like most modern cruising yachts, *Wild Rose* has large doghouse windows. This is fine for normal cruising, as they brighten the cabins, but I made heavy shutters to be screwed over the glass windows in case of severe weather. I cut them out of half-inch marine plywood, sanded the edges, sealed them with Rez, and then stained them a mahogany color. They can be attached through permanent clips or by long screws, or—in a real emergency—simply nailed to the cabin sides.

87. One-way check valves should be used in the hot-water tank intake line, and in other applications where the pump is higher than the intake.

88. Ordinary sink drains with strainer cups can be used for cockpit drains. We recommend placing several in each corner. Water taken into the cockpit must be removed as quickly as possible.

89. I wired in 12-volt cigar-lighter-type receptacles at strategic places around the cabins and cockpit, to be used for small accessory power sources, such as a portable utility pump.

90. *Wild Rose* lies smoothly and comfortably under bare poles a-hull, or broadsides to the seas, at least up to approximately Force 6 and 7, which is the maximum we have tested so far. But

anticipating that we might sometime have to tail a drogue or run off, I purchased fifty fathoms of bright yellow poly rope of one-inch diameter. This type floats and thus will not foul underwater parts. Moreover, it does not stretch, as nylon does. Around moorages this should be stowed out of sight, as it is too attractive for deck and mooring use. I lost ten fathoms of it before I realized this.

91. I believe in keeping a firearm aboard in case of emergency. Abroad, this is a nuisance and a source of much red tape. For this reason, avoid carrying any kind of weapon of a military type; this includes the popular .30 caliber M-1 carbine of World War II vintage. I carry a single-shot 20-gauge shotshell and .22 caliber rifle combination, sometimes called a "survival gun." This is innocent enough for most customs people, although nowadays even single-flare launchers are suspect in some ports.

92. For storm oil, we found that linseed oil is most practical and does not smell or mess the decks as does fish oil. So far, of course, we have had limited experience with either.

93. We found the engine water-temperature meter unreliable for monitoring engine condition. An exhaust-temperature meter is much more useful and revealing.

94. Our vote goes to unfinished teak trim inside and out. Not only is maintenance easier, but to us teak has the exotic scent of curry powder, spices, and romantic places. And a little teak trim goes a long way.

95. A handy thing to carry aboard is a mooring buoy with the ship's name on it, to be used for extended anchoring in out-of-the-way places. We also carry a 20-foot, 3/8-inch stainless pennant for mooring to the buoy. It doesn't hurt to label the buoy "private"—but this won't keep some dudes from chiseling on you anyway.

96. We carry a large supply of all sizes of cable clamps, toggles, and shackles. You can't have too many. We also carry a spool of stainless 3/16-inch cable with Nico Press fittings and tool.

97. Two much-neglected sailor's aids are the bullhorn and the signal lamp. The amplification of a battery-powered horn is useful for deck-to-deck and deck-to-dock communications. As for the signal lamp, sometimes called the Alden lamp, this is too handy an emergency device not to have. Hal Roth used this to good advantage when *Whisper* went aground on a remote island in Tierra de Fuego.

98. It is essential to maintain ample room around the engine so that you can easily inspect, clean, and get at it in an emergency. Ample air space also aids in cooling. We go over the engine thoroughly with a cleaning rag at least once a week, in this way also

making a detailed inspection. At the same time I tighten all hose clamps and set screws. This whole operation is good for one's peace of mind, too.

99. I consider a proper boom gallows essential for a cruising yacht. We found it useful not only for securing the boom, but also for hanging the ship's bell, an anchor light, and other spur-of-the-moment innovations. I made it from a piece of teak, some aluminum tubing, and tube sockets. It can be raised, lowered, or easily removed altogether.

100. I not only installed the standard red and green running lights on the cabin sides, but also elected to use the optional red and green mast lights under the International Rules. This gets the lights fifty feet above the water, where a ship might see them better. I also installed a white strobe light on the masthead which can be seen for twenty miles in hazy weather.

101. Although it seems basic, few yachts carry a separate mast track for storm trysails. I had some extra track left over, so I ran it up alongside the mainsail track. It proved to be enough to handle the storm sail, which can thus be bent on ready for instant use when it is necessary to reduce sail or heave to.

A dream ship is never really completed. If it were, then there would be nothing to look forward to.

BIBLIOGRAPHY

The following are selected technical publications and interesting related reading for real-life and armchair cruising—some I've quoted from, and others are just nice to have around. Most are available through libraries.

Reading and Reference

Anderson, Bern. *The Life and Voyages of Captain George Vancouver, "Surveyor of the Sea."* Seattle: University of Washington Press, 1960.

Beebe, Robert P. *Voyaging Under Power.* New York: Seven Seas Press, 1975.

Borden, Charles. *Sea Quest.* Philadelphia: Macrae Smith Co., 1967.

Bruce, Erroll. *Deep Sea Sailing.* New York: John de Graff, Inc., 1973.

Chapman, Charles F. *Piloting, Seamanship and Smallboat Handling.* New York: Motor Boating & Sailing Books, 1975.

Childers, Erskine. *The Riddle of the Sands*. London: Rupert Hart-Davis, 1969.

Colvin, Thomas. *Coastwise and Offshore Cruising Wrinkles*. New York: Seven Seas Press, 1972.

Cook, Captain James. *The Explorations of Captain James Cook: As Told By Selections of His Own Journals, 1768–1779*. New York: Dover Publications, Inc., 1970.

Devereux, Frederick L. *Practical Navigation for the Yachtsman*. New York: W.W. Norton and Co., Inc., 1972.

Elan, Patrick and Mudie, Colin. *Sopranino*. New York: John de Graff, Inc., 1958.

Gann, Ernest K. *Song of the Sirens*. New York: Simon and Schuster, 1968.

Gatty, Harold. *The Raft Book.New York: George Grady Press, 1943.

Gibbs, James A., Jr. *Sentinels of the North Pacific*. Portland, Oregon: Binfords and Mort, Publishers, 1955.

Guzzwell, John. *Trekka Around the World*. New York: John de Graff, Inc., 1963.

Herreshoff, L. Francis. *Sensible Cruising Designs*. Camden, Maine: International Marine Publishing Co., 1973.

———. *The Common Sense of Yacht Design*. Jamaica, N.Y.: Caravan-Maritime, 1973.

———. *The Compleat Cruiser*. New York: Sheridan House, 1972

Hiscock, Eric, *Sou'west in Wanderer IV*. New York and London: Oxford University Press, 1973.

Holm, Donald. *The Circumnavigators*. Englewood Cliffs, N.J.: Prentice-Hall, Inc., 1974.

———. *Fishing the Pacific*. New York: Winchester Press, 1972.

———. *Pacific North!* Caldwell, Idaho: The Caxton Printers, Ltd., 1960.

Holm, Don and Myrtle. *The Complete Sourdough Cookbook*. Caldwell, Idaho: The Caxton Printers, Ltd., 1972.

Howay, Frederick W. (ed). *Voyages of the Columbia*. New York: Massachusetts Historical Society, Collections vol. 79.

Johnson, Peter. *Ocean Racing & Offshore Yachts*. New York: Dodd Mead and Company, 1972.

Leighton, Caroline C. *Life At Puget Sound with Sketches of Travel in Washington Territory, British Columbia, Oregon, and California, 1865–1881*. Boston: Lee and Shepard, Publishers, 1882.

Letcher, John S. *Self-Steering for Sailing Craft*. Camden, Maine: International Marine Publishing Co., 1974.

Lipscomb, James. *Cutting Loose*. Boston and Toronto: Little, Brown and Company, 1974.

Luxton, Norman Kenny (ed. by his daughter Eleanor Georgina Luxton). *Luxton's Pacific Crossing.* Sidney, B.C.: Gray's Publishing, Ltd., 1971.

McArthur, Lewis A. *Oregon Geographic Names.* Portland, Oregon: Binfords and Mort, Publishers, 1974.

McClane, A.J. *McClane's New Standard Fishing Encyclopedia, and International Fishing Guide.* New York: Holt, Rinehart, and Winston, 1974.

McDonald, Lucile. *Search for the Northwest Passage.* Portland: Metropolitan Press, 1958.

Maury, Richard. *The Sage of Cimba.* New York: Harcourt, Brace, 1939.

Miller, Conrad. *Your Boat's Electrical System.* New York: Motor Boating and Sailing Books, 1973.

Moitessier, Bernard, *Sailing to the Reefs.* London: Hollis & Carter, 1971.

————. *Cape Horn: The Logical Route.* London: Adlard Coles, Ltd., 1969.

Nicholson, George. *Vancouver Island's West Coast, 1762–1962.* Victoria, B.C.: Morriss Printing Co., Ltd. 1965.

O'Brien, Conor. *Across Three Oceans.* London: Edward Arnold and Co., 1927.

Phillips, James W. *Washington State Place Names.* Seattle: University of Washington Press, 1971.

Pinkerton, Kathrene. *Three's a Crew.* New York: Carrick and Evans, 1940.

Piver, Arthur. *Trans-Atlantic Trimaran.* San Francisco: Underwriters Press, 1961.

————. *Trans-Pacific Trimaran.* Mill Valley: Pi-Craft, 1963.

Robinson, William A. *To the Great Southern Sea.* New York: John de Graff, Inc., 1966.

————. *Return to the Sea.* New York: John de Graff, Inc., 1972.

Roth, Hal. *Two On a Big Ocean.* New York: Macmillan, 1972.

Slocum, Victor. *Capt. Joshua Slocum.* New York: Sheridan House, 1950.

Smeeton, Miles. *The Misty Islands.* Lymington, England: Coles, 1969; New York: John de Graff, 1969.

————. *The Sea was Our Village.* Sidney: Gray's Publishing Ltd., 1973.

Smith, Lynwood. *Common Seashore Life of the Pacific Northwest.* Healdsburg, Calif.: Naturegraph Company, 1962.

Street, Donald M. Jr. *The Ocean Sailing Yacht.* New York: W.W. Norton and Company, Inc., 1973.

Tracy, J.P. *Low Man on a Gill-Netter.* Anchorage: The Alaska Northwest Publishing Co., 1974.

Tyler, David B. (ed.) *The Wilkes Expedition. The First United States*

Exploring Expedition (1838–1841). Philadelphia: The American Philosophical Society, Memoirs, No. 73, 1968.

Voss, John C. *The Venturesome Voyages of Captain Voss*. New York: C.E. Lauriat Co., 1926.

Whelpley, Donald A. *Weather, Water, and Boating*. Cambridge, Md.: Cornell Maritime Press, Inc. 1961.

Wightman, Frank A. *The Wind Is Free*. New York: John de Graff, Inc., 1972.

Zadig, Ernest A. *The Complete Book of Boating, Second Edition*. Englewood Cliffs, N.J.: Prentice-Hall, Inc., 1976.

Guidebooks

Akrigg, G. P. V. and Helen B. *1001 British Columbia Place Names*. Vancouver, B.C.: Discovery Press, 1969.

Calhoun, Bruce. *Cruising the San Juans*. Newport Beach, Calif.: Sea Publications, 1973.

———. *Northwest Passages*, Vol. I & II. Newport Beach, Calif.: Sea Publications, 1972.

Carey, Neil G. *A Guide to the Queen Charlotte Islands*. Anchorage: The Alaska Northwest Publishing Co., 1975.

Morris, Frank, and Heath, W.R. *Marine Atlas Vol. I*. Seattle: P.B.I. Co., 1973.

———, and Burg, Amos. *Marine Atlas Vol. II*. Seattle: P.B.I. Co., 1.73.

Sea. *Boating Almanac, Pacific Northwest Edition* (annual).

West, Carolyn and Jack. *Cruising the Pacific Coast, Acapulco to Skagway*. Newport Beach, Calif.: Sea Publications, 1974.

Government Publications

Canada: Canadian Hydrographic Service, Marine Sciences Directorate, Federal Building, Victoria, B.C. Canada V8W 1Y4.

U.S.: Distribution Division, C44, National Ocean Survey, Riverdale, Maryland 20840.

British Columbia Small Craft Guide, Vol. 1, (1973): Gulf Islands, Sooke to Nanaimo.

Canadian Nautical Charts, Bulletins No. 13 and 14.

Canadian Tide and Current Tables, Vol. 5: Juan de Fuca and Georgia Strait; Vol. 6: Barkley Sound and Discovery Passage to Dixon Entrance.

H.O. Publication No. 102: *International Code of Signals*.

H.O. Publication No. 602: *Wind and Waves at Sea, Breakers, and Surf*.

List of Lights, Buoys, and Fog Signals: Pacific Coast.

Nautical Almanac (annual).

Nautical Chart Catalog, Nos. 2 and 3.
Publications of the American Radio Relay League, Newington,
Conn. 06111:

> *How To Become A Radio Amateur*
> *Learning the Radiotelegraph Code*
> *The Radio Amateur's Handbook*
> *The Radio Amateur's License Manual*
> *The Radio Amateur's Operating Manual*
> *QST Magazine.*

Rules and Regulations, Volumes IV, V, VII, and VIII. Federal Communications Commission, Washington, D.C.: U.S. Government Printing Office.
Sailing Directions, B. C. Coast, Vol. I: South Portion.
Sailing Directions, B.C. Coast, Vol. II: North Portion.

Miscellaneous

BIA Engineering Manual. Chicago: Boating Industry Association (current edition).
Holm, Bill. *Northwest Coast Indian Art.* Seattle: University of Washington Press, 1965.
Radio Amateur Callbook: United States and foreign editions. Available from 925 Sherwood Drive, Lake Bluff, Ill. 60044.
Richter, H.P. *Wiring Simplified.* Minneapolis: Park Publishing Inc., 1975.
S.S.C.A. Commodores' Bulletin. Monthly newsletter of the Seven Seas Cruising Association, North Palm Beach, Florida. Available to nonmembers by subscription.